BRINGING LIGHT TO SHADOW

A Dog Trainer's Diary

by PAMELA S. DENNISON

Dogwise Publishing
Wenatchee, Washington U.S.A.

www.dogwisepublishing.com

Bringing Light to Shadow: A Dog Trainer's Diary
Pamela S. Dennison

Published by Dogwise Publishing
A Division of Direct Book Service, Inc.
PO Box 2778
701B Poplar
Wenatchee Washington 98807
1-509-663-9115, 1-800-776-2665
website: www.dogwisepublishing.com   email: info@dogwisepublshing.com

Graphic Design: Shane Beers — Cincinnati, Ohio

Library of Congress Cataloging-in-Publication Data

Dennison, Pamela.
Bringing light to shadow : a dog trainer's diary / by Pamela S. Dennison.
p. cm.
ISBN 1-929242-17-4 (alk. paper)
1. Dogs--Training. 2. Dennison, Pamela--Diaries. 3. Dog trainers--Diaries. I. Title.
SF431.D445 2004   636.7'0887--dc22   2004018160
ISBN: 1-929242-17-4

Printed in the U.S.A.

Photo Credits
Virginia Wind: Days 23 and 29.
John Palmer: Days 136, 275, and 390 (last two)
Cynthia Palmer: Days 205, 252, 280, 281, 306, 313, 327, 432, 495, 530, 539
Lisa Pattison: Day 471
Lisa Judge: Epilogue (Approaching the Judge)
Steve Surfman: Epilogue (Agility shots)
Patti Merlo: Day 512
Jim Dennison: Day 136, Epilogue (Awards, Easton, Supermarket)
Pam Dennison: Cover photo. Day 278, 390 (first), 481, 516, Epilogue (Visit with Jane)

Table of Contents

Dedication and Acknowledgements————————————iv

How It All Started————————————————————1

1 — Hope is the Denial of Reality————————————3

2 — Close Only Counts in Horseshoes and Hand Grenades———34

3 — The Test of a Vocation is the Love of the Drudgery
it Involves————————————————————————57

4 — Serendipity is the Ability to Make Fortunate Discoveries
By Accident———————————————————————97

5 — Climb High Climb Far, Your Goal the Sky,
Your Aim the Star————————————————————120

6 — There Are Two Ways to Live————————————————146

7 — It's the Constant and Determined Effort That Breaks
Down Resistance————————————————————175

8 — I Think I Have Ended Up Where I Intended To Be————205

Epilogue——————————————————————————219

Appendix, Resources————————————————————225

Author Biography————————————————————231

Dedication:

To Shadow, "Ewe Are Beyond a Shadow of a Doubt, CGC, R1MCL, R2CL"
for changing my life for the better; and to all of the owners and rescue people
that want to help dogs like him, knowing that the process won't be easy, but
worthwhile things rarely are.

Acknowledgements

The list of people who helped me to help Shadow is almost endless. My eternal appreciation goes to Carolyn Wilki, who was the first to show me how incredibly small the approximations have to be when starting out the retraining process and how to actually see progress in those tiny steps. A "price beyond rubies" for having faith in me and Shadow, when I had none.

To Ted Turner, who taught me to use my brain (not an easy feat!) and dedicated countless hours of his precious and valuable time to communicate back and forth, risking carpal tunnel by typing so much. His ever-present humor, endless patience, and prodding have meant the world to me.

To John and Cynthia Palmer, for their constant, steady and faithful help, wonderful friendship, confidence, and for always being there. For having been involved in so many "firsts," such as the first people to get bitten (a dubious distinction, I am sure), to groom, board, hug, and train Shadow; yet through all of that, had no fear of him.

To my endless and continuing list of dog bait friends in no particular order (and please forgive me if I left anyone out—it isn't on purpose): Jane Killion, Jennifer Petersen, Virginia Wind, Stacy and Keith Modica, Gerry Cassidy, Andrea Kelly, Eve Cutter, Janet Seltzer, Carol and Jeff Vitelli, Diane Zdrodowksi, Dr. Karen Dashfield, DVM, Ethel Abelson, Jane Berger, Karen Luzzi, Lori Klimko, Terri Bright and Richard O'Connell, Kathy Riley, Dr. Jon Bertoldo, DVM, Marsha Dominguez, Kris Kelleher, Lisa Dennison, Lisa Pattison, Lisa Judge, Claire Gelok, Laurie Shuren, Irene O'Connor, Jon Katz, Ali Brown, Diane Mayer, Vanessa Clapper, Todd and Fred Gross, Peri Basil, Jennifer Nourse, Richard and Zelda Gross, Alex and Ben Gross. Also to my students and friends who read and gave me feedback on the original version of my diary.

To my friend Jacky Sach, for giving me the idea for the original layout, and for having faith in this book, and me as a writer. Last but certainly not least, to Larry and Charlene Woodward and Barb Steward from Dogwise Publishing for their valuable editing and encouragement in bringing this book to fruition.

It's kind of fun to do the impossible.

—Walt Disney

How It All Started

There is no doubt in my mind that I am crazy. Who else but a crazy person would look at a Border Collie rescue site on the Internet, e-mail the contact person back and forth for weeks, ask all sorts of questions about one of the dogs, while telling herself the whole time she really wasn't interested in the him? Who else but a crazy dog person would make a firm decision not to take the dog, then drive four hours each way just to "go look at him," all the while wondering, "Just what am I doing? I don't want another dog!" So, here I am now, a crazy person with an equally crazy dog. I am Pam Dennison, a dog trainer, and Shadow is my sixth rescue dog. I assumed, with a history of five dogs to my credit—all successfully rescued and rehabilitated—that I could quickly and easily turn this dog into the competitive obedience, agility, and sheep herding dog that I wanted him to be.

Unbeknownst to me, I had a human-aggressive dog on my hands. I did not truly realize or comprehend the magnitude of the work, total dedication and commitment required to help him. I had been humbled by a forty-pound, 12 month old Border Collie.

This journal chronicles our struggles together, from recognition of the aggressive behavior to the painstaking efforts to turn Shadow into my dream dog: confident, calm, focused, and friendly. It is the story of taking him from a human-aggressive dog to passing his AKC Canine Good Citizen (CGC) test. I have included my actual journal entries as well as training concepts and comments on what I learned in hindsight as I went through this experience. You will see that I made quite a few mistakes, especially in the beginning of the retraining process. I could have, quite easily, edited out all of them to make myself look better, but that is not what this book is about. The purpose of this book was not only to show the mistakes, but also to highlight them so that you might learn from my errors. Part of my intent is to demonstrate what does not work as well as what does when retraining an aggressive dog. I understand firsthand the denial, frustration, and anguish that comes with living with an aggressive dog. I want you to know that I feel your pain, but there can be a light at the end of the tunnel.

Working with Shadow quite literally changed my entire life for the better. I started out my dog training career focusing on pet classes and competition obedience. The addition of Shadow has enriched my life, and my work now includes training aggressive dogs. There are days when I get so many calls for help with aggressive behaviors that it scares me; and yet I am grateful that I am now able to help these people. It has made me a better trainer and a better person and I now hold aggressive dog classes and camps based on my work with Shadow.

Every night, I thank him for coming into my life.

If just one person learns from my successes, I will be pleased. If just one person learns from my mistakes, I will be overjoyed. And thus began the greatest adventure of my life. This is Shadow's story...

1

Hope is the denial of reality.

—Margaret Weis

Homecoming

MAY 29 — DAY 1

Packed up my three dogs—Carrie, Cody, and Beau*—and my husband Jim to meet Fitz, Shadow's original name. After about an hour of scuffling and posturing, all of the dogs were playing nicely. Fitz was a bit nervous about me and Jim, and in fact, hid under the deck at first. Once Jim dragged him out (gently of course!), Fitz took some food and I started training him for **eye contact**. I vacillated about bringing him home but couldn't think of a good enough reason to leave him, so home he came.

The four-hour trip home was fine and none of the dogs appeared stressed. Once home, Fitz was nervous and unsure. He went from room to room exploring and urinating all over the house. Normal for a new dog to do this. Of course, it was thrilling to have him urinate in the heat grate... He aggressed

TRAINING CONCEPT

Eye contact: The first thing I like to teach a dog is eye contact. If you don't have your dog's willing eye contact and focus, you can't teach him anything because he won't be paying any attention to you.

Crate training: I always have new dogs sleep in a crate for the first few nights. That way I don't have to worry about what they will do, both in terms of bothering the other dogs or me and Jim. We were lucky that Fitz was already crate trained, so this wasn't a problem for him.

---

*Carrie, a 12-year-old Border Collie mix, Cody a 7 ½-year-old Sheltie, and Beau a 2-year-old Border Collie.

by snapping at Beau a little bit and was very tense. He stayed in a **crate** in the bedroom with us and slept all night.

MAY 30 — DAY 2

Fitz is very wary about the other dogs, and I found he is "pressure sensitive"— aggressive in small places such as doorways and the hall. He got into a few "fights" with Beau. They were both snapping, baring their teeth and growling. I worked on teaching him to **target my hand** and giving me eye contact. We played a recall game and the **give-and-take-it** game and worked on learning his new name. I chose the name Shadow—it seemed appropriate because he was constantly glued to my leg.

I renamed Fitz for two reasons. I really hated that name, and did not know what kind of bad associations he may have had with it; and I wanted to start fresh. I also changed most of the words that he already knew from a list given to me by the rescue group from the previous owner: sit, stay, come, wait, down, heel, kennel. I wanted to make sure that these words now had a positive association. Within 48 hours, by pairing "Shadow" and "here" (his new "come" word) with food and eye contact, Shadow was responding to his new name and the command "here" with lightning speed.

TRAINING CONCEPT

Hand targeting: I teach the dog to touch my open hand with his nose. I use this for competition behaviors to teach heeling and stands, as well as for aggression management to get him to turn his face away from something scary.

Give-and-take-it game: I have two identical toys and hand one of them to the dog while saying, "Take it." Then I show the other toy to the dog, shaking it to make it come alive so he will want to drop the toy in his mouth to get the one that I have. As he drops the toy in his mouth, I say, "Give." Then I hand him my toy, saying, "Take it." I repeat dozens of times. The purpose of the game is to teach the dog to give and not to be possessive about stuff. Variations of this game include the "two-toy game" where I throw the toy instead of just handing it over and the "two-tug game" where I tug, let it go, tug let it go, etc.

MAY 31 — DAY 3

I don't know if this is normal for him or just the stress of being in a new home, but there are major problems here. Shadow attacks Beau continually* and the attacks are increasing in severity and duration. Poor Beau is freaked out. I am upset that I brought Shadow home and have disturbed the nice balance we had with Carrie, Cody, and Beau. After only two plus days, I am questioning my sanity. Shadow begs me for petting and when I do, he leaps back as if I stabbed him with a hot poker. If I ignore his persistent solicitations for attention, he body slams me.

Shadow has been very frantic around me and Jim, although he hasn't tried to bite us. He constantly dive-bombs my face in a submissive, face licking, frantic way and I am afraid he will break my nose. (Frantic face licking is a sign of stress.) I go completely **passive** when he does, averting my face, and wait for him to get off me. I have decided to put him in the crate more and allow him to be loose in the house for only a few minutes at a time. I plan on heavily reinforcing him for calm behaviors around the other dogs and me, giving him no time to practice the aggressive behaviors he has been displaying toward Beau.

TRAINING CONCEPT

Going **passive** means that I stand motionless, giving no eye contact or any other reinforcement to the dog. I always make eye contact valuable to my dogs, so when I look away it sends a powerful message that I am not happy with what they are doing.

You may be wondering, why don't I just hit or reprimand Shadow for aggressing. The answer is simple. It wouldn't work. I am a positive trainer. It is a fundamental tenet of positive training that physical or verbal punishment is never warranted for any reason. For more on **positive training** concepts see the Appendix.

JUNE 1 — DAY 4

I am continuing to work on hand targeting, recall games, and the start of loose leash walking. During our training sessions Shadow was responsive, but in an out-of-control, frenzied way. His eyes were like those of a wild animal—pupils totally dilated, whites showing, full of fear, hurt, and mistrust.

Shadow is getting along slightly better with Beau today, but is now starting to

---

Shadow is not dog aggressive, however, in the beginning he was very stressed and lashed out at whichever dog happened to be nearby. He does tend to be a bully but that has decreased dramatically over the years.

aggress on Cody. For reasons I don't understand, he has never shown anything but love for Carrie from the very beginning. Shadow may have sensed that she is old and infirm, or it may be because they are not the same sex. I am doing management at the doorways. I have all of the dogs wait and only let them through the doorway one at a time. I am not totally brilliant—Shadow already knew the "wait" cue and was mostly reliable with it. I just used it for a worthwhile purpose.

HINDSIGHT

At this point, I still had it in my head that he would calm down within a few days and be a wonderful competition dog. I was led by the rescue group to believe that all I needed to do with him was to introduce him to all sorts of situations and he would settle in. Every rescue that I have gotten has always taken some time to relax and get used to the other dogs and our routines, so I assumed this was normal.

His behavior, however, was somewhat different than that of the other dogs. Shadow was much more frenetic and aggressive. Was there an underlying sense of aggression? Was it fear? Shock of being in a new situation, new home, strange dogs, new people?

Even Cody wasn't this bad when I first brought him home. Cody used to bite me, body slam me to the ground, mount my other dogs, and generally not stop for one second the entire day. I think I subconsciously knew I had a problem with Shadow, but did not have enough knowledge at the time to interpret what I was seeing and feeling. I was sensing this strange and incomprehensible "aura" from him that I couldn't clarify or understand and it frightened me.

JUNE 3 – DAY 6

Today I took Shadow off my property for the first time since I brought him home to get fitted for a dumbbell. We were in a narrow aisle in the store and the salesperson bent down to pick something up that had fallen. Shadow aggressed at her, lunging and growling, with no warning signals that he was about to attack. I was a bit taken aback, but was able to stay calm enough to ask him for a down, wait for a few seconds and then feed him. I asked the salesperson to move away from him. A few minutes later, in a larger part of the store, going out of his way, he lunged at her again, this time nipping her pants leg. I asked for a down again, waited until he had calmed down and fed him again. Thank goodness the salesperson was a dog person and understood what I was doing and did not get upset.

This was the first time I had seen Shadow "in action" with people and I was not happy. Although his compliance with simple obedience cues (sit, down, stay) is great, the display of aggression toward a stranger has me worried.

I have since learned that he is crate aggressive (barking, growling, lunging) towards anyone who approaches his crate other than Jim or me. I did some **counterconditioning** and **desensitization** work with two of my friends, having them approach the van (I was afraid to have anyone come to the house) while I fed him if he didn't aggress at them. We had varying degrees of success and failure. Sometimes he was quiet and calm, other times he would get frightened and bark and growl.

TRAINING CONCEPT

Counterconditioning: The use of associative learning to reverse the unwanted effects of prior conditioning. For instance, let us say you used a shock collar on your dog to get him to stop jumping on people. However, because of the association of the pain paired with the presence of people, your dog is now biting people. To countercondition the behavior of biting people, I would now pair pleasant and positive things for the dog in the presence of people, so that people become a cue that "good things are going to happen."

Desensitization or systematic desensitization: A form of counterconditioning—a procedure in which a phobic subject (human or animal) is subjected to low levels of the frightening stimulus while relaxed. The level of frightening stimulus is gradually increased, but never at a rate to cause distress. Eventually the fear dissipates.

Follow the leader: The purpose of this game is threefold. First, it teaches the dog to be cognizant of where I am, not the other way around. Second, it is a preliminary step to teaching loose leash walking on a short line. Third, it teaches the dog that being with me is the best place to be! I use the leash as a safety net, not as a tool to force the dog to be at my side. I want my dogs to want to be with me. Typically I will attach a fifty-foot line to the dog and start walking. If the dog goes to the right, I go to the left. If the dog comes toward me but then passes me, I turn around and go in the other direction. I continue this until the dog stays with me and gives me eye contact. I stop walking and feed the dog for 30 seconds. Then I verbally release the dog and continue with the game.

I took him to a park, put him on a 50-foot long line and allowed him to get within 30 feet of groups of people and children, then called him to me. Shadow seemed to be only mildly interested in the strangers and was very responsive to me. We did some **follow the leader** on a long line and he was cognizant of where I was and stayed with me quite nicely. I am heartened. Maybe I only imagined his aggression??? We also worked on his retrieving the dumbbell. His retrieve is wonderful but he only holds it for a second.

Oops, Pam! I have had him for a whopping six whole DAYS and actually felt it was important to mention that he only held the dumbbell for a second! Get a grip on yourself, Pam!

Good Doggie! Although Shadow did have a bad reaction to a stranger in the store, he was able to focus on me in a strange place (the park) with lots of new people, and have no aggressive reactions to them. He was interested in me enough to play my games such as eye contact, name recognition, heeling, etc.

JUNE 4 – DAY 7

I took him to another park with more people and walked him around. He was calm and focused. Shadow is now great in doorways, no matter how many other dogs are crowding him. He played outside with Beau beautifully today.

Good Pam! Great use of management to control aggression in the doorways! And, it only took five days! Also great use of long line training to start building my relationship with Shadow.

HINDSIGHT

I did not do as I said I was going to do—I didn't crate Shadow often enough. Sometimes I am just like everyone else and don't like using the crate while I am home. I like having my dogs around, following me everywhere I go. Essentially, I did not take my own advice—advice I give to all of my students that rescue dogs. I took my preconceived notions into this new dog situation and did not pay attention to the warning signs of aggressive behavior, nor did I give this poor dog some down time to get used to his new home. I should have kept him at home for a few months before bringing him out and about. I was still feeling ambivalent about keeping him and was very stressed myself. I was sure he was picking up on those feelings and acting out because of it.

Clueless

JUNE 5 – DAY 8

I took Shadow to my training facility and had John and Cynthia help me work with him around people. They are my best friends. We have known each other for many years and have trained dogs together in the past. Shadow lunged and growled at Cynthia without any warning or provocation. We all froze and he stopped lunging. I asked him for a down, waited for a few seconds, and then fed him for being calm.

It is VERY scary being attacked by a dog and VERY scary from my point of view as "Mommy" of the attacking dog. It is of paramount importance that the person being attacked try not to react in any way, which is why we all froze. Any movement, jerking back, pushing away, yelling and screaming by anyone in the vicinity could very well incite the dog to attack more vehemently.

John tried to hand feed him and Shadow took the food and then aggressed by backing up and lunging. We all stood perfectly still again, waited for Shadow to calm down, and fed him again. We decided to toss food on the floor, rather than hand-feed him. I played a recall game with him and even had Cynthia play a few times. He was a bit stressed, but he dealt with it. I had Shadow lie down and asked them to start walking around slowly while I tossed him food. He lunged a time or two—we froze again. Then I threw cookies toward John and Cynthia, had them ask Shadow to lie down and we all bombarded him with food. Repeated three more times. We ended the session.

Back at home now, Shadow and Beau were just playing in the doorway of the bedroom! A tight space and no one was nervous! At least a few encouraging moments now and then!

HINDSIGHT

Working with Shadow, I was starting to see increasing signs that there was a major problem here. I was working with him, but not fully understanding the extent of his issues.

JUNE 7 – DAY 10

I sent his papers in to the AKC and his name is now officially "Ewe Are Beyond a Shadow of a Doubt."

To continue the desensitization process, I had Shadow meet my friend Laurie. I had her sit in a chair, thinking that perhaps a person standing may have made him nervous. His mouth was a bit tight when I gave him treats (a tight mouth is a sign of stress in a dog), but I **clicked** him for approaching her and she fed him. We stopped after five minutes when he started to look frantic. After she left, I worked on loose leash walking, eye contact, targeting, **finishes**, **recall games**, and the give-and-take-it game. I also started to **back chain the halts** and began teaching the stand. I was curious to see if he was nervous about the vacuum cleaner and trained him while it was running. There was no negative reaction to the noise.

I am finally noticing that his pupils are huge—so huge that at this point I didn't even know his eyes were brown—and his ears are continually flat against his skull.

TRAINING CONCEPT

Clicker training/Clicked: One facet of positive training uses a marker signal such as a "Click" (also called a secondary reinforcer or bridge) to tell the dog that he did something right. The click is followed by a reward—usually food but also other reinforcers the dog finds valuable. While I do not mention "clicking" often in this book, using a marker signal is definitely part of my training process—especially when training new behaviors—whether it be competition behaviors or "calmness around humans" behaviors.

Finishes: A behavior needed in Competition Obedience. The dog is in front of you and on a signal from you, goes directly to heel position.

Recall games: I call this particular recall game "Drop the Cookie and Run Like Heck." Throw a cookie (dog treat) a few feet away to get a head start and tell the dog to "get it," as you run away fast in the other direction. As the dog is coming toward you say, "Come" (pairing the word with the behavior), then when he gets to you, click and treat with a jackpot (lots of treats).

Back chaining the halts: A behavior chain is a series of smaller behaviors that make up a whole behavior. For instance, the recall is made up of six steps: 1) I want the dog on my left 2) I want the dog to stay in a sitting position while I walk away 3) I want the dog to stay in that sitting position while I turn around to face him 4) I want the dog to come at a fast trot when I call 5) I want the dog to come in straight to me 6) I want the dog to sit close to me when he comes. When you back chain a behavior, you take the last part of the chain and teach that behavior first. In this context these behaviors are used for Competition Obedience.

HINDSIGHT

I still don't know the depth of Shadow's aggression. It was my idea to show him that if he aggressed, nothing bad or good would happen. I also wanted him to start associating that good things (food and toys), would happen when people were around. I did know that aggression, even if negatively reinforced or punished, will increase. For instance, if the dog is afraid—he aggresses—you take him away from the scary situation—aggression worked! And because it worked, it will be repeated since behavior is reward driven. I was continually training for all levels of competition, as well as taking him to new places on an almost daily basis. I was in my "Super Woman, Overzealous Dog Trainer, Hear Me Roar" identity.

An Inkling

JUNE 20 – DAY 23

Last Tuesday Shadow lunged and nipped my friend Sandy two times, with no provocation and no advance warning. She had just finished feeding him. I called him to me. As he was on his way to me, he suddenly whirled back to Sandy and nipped her. I decided to end the session. As I was leaving my training facility with Shadow at my side, he went out of his way to lunge at her, nipping her again. It has finally hit home that "Houston, we have a problem."

I have since been to a three-day aggressive dog seminar. It helped me to remember the material I already knew but ignored, since "my dog would never do those things! I rescued this dog, I am a dog trainer, how *dare* he not be perfect!" (Stamp! Stamp!) It also taught me some new information about body language and the counterconditioning process. I was ready to send him back to the rescue group last week after the incident with Sandy. I had completely and utterly panicked.

I am okay now. I am able to work with him in a more effective and productive way now that I know what I am dealing with. I want to turn him into the great companion and competitive dog I know he is capable of becoming.

I am **triangulating** between the other dogs more and heavily reinforcing calm behaviors—setting him up for success, not failure.

I am "triangulating" with Cody, Beau and Shadow

TRAINING CONCEPT

Triangulating: Because I have four dogs, the triangle isn't quite perfect in my case—more like a semicircle. Basically, I am the head of the triangle and the dogs are the base, all equidistant from me and from each other. If one of them starts to get between me and another dog, I maneuver myself so that the distances always remain the same. The reason for doing this is so that they all stop guarding me, (I am so reinforcing that they all think I am their own personal toy) and trying to repel another dog away from me, which causes them to fight.

HINDSIGHT

Looking back now—I didn't give him enough time to settle into his new home and I didn't recognize the warning signs of aggression. In failing to recognize the signs I pushed him way too fast, way too soon and was setting him up TO aggress by putting him into situations that he wasn't yet capable of handling calmly.

JUNE 21 – DAY 24

I barely sit down at all, so when I can't watch him, Shadow is in his crate. I am finding that if he doesn't understand something quickly, he gets out of control. I have to keep things VERY simple and very quick—just a few repetitions before moving on to something else.

He is giving me a weird glare versus the relaxed eye contact I would like, but I do get a few moments of calm every now and then. I am also trying to get a comfortable sit—upright, head up—not a head down, shoulders hunched, eyes scared look. I started doing the **body wrap and TTouch** on him and found that he holds a lot of anxiety in his hind end. He handled it well—no lip licking, yawning or head turns in avoidance. He stood for most of it—only tried to sit twice.

Shadow wearing a Body Wrap.

TRAINING CONCEPT

Body wrap and TTouch®: This concept and the associated techniques were developed by Linda Tellington-Jones. An ace bandage is wrapped around the dog in a particular manner, activating certain acupressure points that help to relax the dog and allow the dog to become more aware of his or her body. The actual TTouches are different kinds of touches to help with specific behavioral problems. See the Appendix.

JUNE 22 – DAY 25

Shadow and Beau were playing today and I thought it might escalate as Shadow's breathing became heavier, eyes a little wider, and his play growl became more "real." I broke it up by saying, "Who wants cookies?" and then had all four dogs do lie-downs in a semicircle around me to get treats. Thirty minutes later, Beau and Shadow were playing again, but I broke it up much sooner. Shadow is doing a lot more arcing around Cody and vice versa.

When our friend Ken came to visit, Jim tried to reinforce Shadow for calm behavior in his crate in the bedroom. He said Shadow did a lot of barking and he could only get a few seconds of quiet in which to feed. That's okay though, we will work on it. Ken has been our only visitor since Shadow has come to live with us. On hearing a stranger's voice, Shadow reacts by barking and I don't want him practicing that behavior.

TRAINING CONCEPT
Arcing, lip licking, yawning, and head turns in avoidance: These are all precursor signals given off by dogs (and wolves) to let you know they are nervous. I learned about them through the wonderful work of Turid Rugaas, a trainer from Norway. Dogs use these signals to calm you down, calm themselves down, or calm another dog down and avoid conflict. For more on Turid Rugaas please see the Appendix.

Looking Good!

JUNE 26 – DAY 29

I am getting more and more normal eyes and posture from Shadow and he is now fine for toenail clipping. I took him to watch me groom Cody. I wanted him on the table to trim the hair on his feet—he was fine although he does not like to be picked up. He got wild-eyed and scary looking. I am nobody's fool. I promptly put him down. Shadow ended up jumping up on the table himself. I will have to work on that.

Yes, I did reinforce him for his inappropriate behavior. I truly believe that it is more important to remain alive to train another day than to manhandle the dog in a "You WILL do as I say dammit" attitude. I picked him up and he freaked. Now I know that picking him up is something I need to work on.

He is doing much better overall, although he attacked Cody twice yesterday. The first attack was resource guarding—attacking a dog or person if they are near an object that the dog feels is "his"—and the second occurred when Cody circled around us. The first fight I broke up and was sorry the instant the word "STOP" came out of my mouth. When a second broke out, I just left the room. It broke up quickly.

Today I was busy and Beau and Shadow were outside when a neighbor walked by. For the first time, Shadow started aggressing by barking and lunging at the fence. I called him and he came! I then put him in his crate so I could work.

Another "stupid human" moment—allowing him to aggress at people walking by. An example of a failure to use simple management techniques to avoid problems.

Jim said that he sees a positive difference in Shadow. I guess I am too close to it and most of the time I still feel bad that I took him in…especially when Cody looks at me with those sad eyes.

JUNE 27 – DAY 30

Shadow was much better all around today. I had him up on the grooming table for a few minutes while Jim fed him. Shadow has been acting nervous if we lean over him to pet or groom him. To help desensitize him to people leaning over, I had Shadow lie down on the table. I leaned over him and fed at the same time. I leaned over, gave him a cookie, then released the physical pressure associated with me leaning over and moved my hand away from his face. I repeated this about ten times. He was fine. I also practiced this while he was sitting and standing. I am continuing to position all four dogs in a triangle/semicircle around me while I feed them all, one at a time. I am getting really good at maneuvering myself around the dogs to keep them all equidistant.

Slight Setback

JUNE 30 – DAY 33

Well, I spoke too soon. Shadow attacked Cody this morning. I yelled, "STOP," which broke it up; and then attended to Cody, who had a puncture wound on his face that was bleeding slightly. Then I had a soft chat with all of them and put Shadow away. While I was feeding the dogs cookies, Shadow was giving Cody the evil eye and I tried to get Shadow to turn his head away. It was after I released them and turned to close the container that Shadow attacked Cody. I hated to yell, but I felt if I just left, Cody wouldn't be able to trust me to protect him and keep him safe.

JULY 2 – DAY 35

I noticed today that when I smiled or even looked at Shadow, his ears were up for the FIRST time, and he thumped his tail! He also let me touch his rear end a little more whereas in the past he sat in avoidance. All in all, he seems to be

Desensitizing Shadow to me leaning over and touching him.

relaxing more. All of the work I am doing is starting to pay off. Yesterday I insisted that he train for me before allowing him to go play. Difficult at first, but then he did some really great competition heeling. I have also been running all of the dogs at least once a day and I am sure that is helping a great deal. Daily exercise seems to be a key to calmness now.

JULY 7 – DAY 40

Shadow is much more relaxed. Normal eyes at least 75 percent of the time. I am finding that if I notice his stress signals (ears flat on his skull, pupils dilated fully, hunched shoulders) and act more slowly, he then acts more tentatively. This isn't a good thing. He nipped me the other day—not really a nip, just a loose mouth on my arm and he let go instantly. I was leaning over him, my hair was down and draped over his head while he was against the cabinets. After the contact I walked away for about 30 seconds, softly asked him to come to me, petted him and then put him in his crate. He was a little weird the rest of the day. I think it upset him more than me. I am doing a lot of Frisbee throwing, adding fronts, finishes, hand targeting, and back chaining the halts.

I have started to **Premack** Frisbee throwing and touching. I have included leaning over him and petting him with one finger under his chin. This is the most touching I can do without him throwing stress signals at me. While his expression remains good—ears up, eyes clear—I throw the Frisbee. At times I ask for a straight front, touch him, and if his expression is still good, I click and throw the Frisbee. For the first 10-15 times, he looked very worried.

Today his face was softer and his ears were upright—one of the few times I have not seen them plastered to his skull. He is much calmer around the house and has even been trying to entice Cody to play. I am enthralled by how quickly he learns—no more instant frustration like he had when I first got him. He seems to understand now that it is okay to fail; he had a hard time with that before.

Good Pam! I worked on Premacking the Frisbee throwing and driving up the value of reinforcers other than food! I am seeing an inkling of a relationship starting here between Shadow and me.

Oops, Pam! I put Shadow in a position where he felt he had to bite to get me to back off, without having done more work on desensitizing him to my leaning over. I am still misreading him, or, I should say, I am not yet totally in tune to his personal stress signals.

Good Doggie! Shadow let me know he was stressed with his mouth rather than his teeth! He is trying hard and doing some good work now.

TRAINING CONCEPT
Premack Principle: Developed by David Premack, it is "The observation that high-probability behavior reinforces low-probability behavior." Essentially it means "Do this for me and I will do this for you." High probability behaviors are always what the dog wants. Low probability behaviors are always what we want the dog to do. For Shadow, if he wanted to chase the Frisbee (high probability behavior), he had to give me what I wanted: clear, calm eyes and upright ears (low probability behavior.)

Six of One, Half Dozen of Another

AUGUST 5 – DAY 69

Well, a lot has happened. At the eighth week, Shadow is much calmer all around. I am still keeping each session short because he tends to get too intense and frantic (eyes weird, dive- bombing me). I do not know if this is normal for him or not, being a Border Collie, but I am still aiming for calmness. I guess Beau spoiled me—he is very calm—probably because I got him at four months and heavily rewarded calm behaviors. I thought Border Collies were all quietly intense. Hah! Boy was I wrong!

I was petting Cody and Shadow at the same time and Shadow didn't give Cody the evil eye. Good boy! He gets annoyed and aggresses when he is in the crate if Cody walks up to him to say "Hi," but if I walk in the room with Cody he doesn't do it.

Introduced him to my friend Laurie outside the training building. I felt it would be easier for him to start in a wide open space, rather than a small building. He went up to her and let her pet him, then he looked back to me. We moved away and re-approached. He didn't greet her this time—he just looked at her, and then me, with no signs of stress, as if to say, "So what's your point?" After Laurie left, we went inside and played some training games.

I let the boys play together and Shadow let Cody bite him and body slam him while he chased tennis balls!! He is still a bit punishing to Beau and always steals his toys. Beau is acting very weird and won't come to me—he is doing a lot of avoidance. If I remember correctly, Cody acted the same way when I brought Beau home, so hopefully it will all work out.

Good Doggie! Shadow let Cody bite and body slam him while he was focused on the tennis balls and did not aggress on Cody.

AUGUST 6 – DAY 70

I introduced Shadow to Lisa D. in the front yard. Outside—to make it easier for him. I had her sit in a chair and then I brought him outside. I put the other dogs in the bedroom because they were being jerks. He was jumping on Lisa, much in the same way he jumps on us. I didn't see any major signs of stress. I gave him a few cookies and then brought out the ball. I threw it a few times and then had Lisa throw it.

He did one of two things. Either he would come in between us and lie down with the ball or he would bring the ball to me. Usually he brings the toy to whoever throws it, but he felt more comfortable bringing it to me. I felt he was ready to greet a "stranger" inside.

We all went inside the house, this being the first time we had done so when Shadow wasn't in his crate. I had Lisa sit in the kitchen. He seemed to be fine. I let the other dogs out of the bedroom and they were quiet. Lisa tried to pet Shadow on the top of his head but that made him nervous and he walked away. (Petting a dog on his head, leaning over him, pushing your face in his face, and approaching frontally are all perceived by the dog as being aggressive.) He approached her again, jumped on her and she pet his sides (this jump seemed to be a bit more frantic). He leaped again and air snapped her head. I should have stopped after just two minutes and I was actually getting ready to put him away when he snapped at her. In a quiet voice I asked him to come, and put him in his crate.

My friend Jane agreed to help me with him, so I brought him to her house later in the day. We walked back and forth (on leash) past her about six times at about a 20-foot distance. He approached her once and jumped on her to solicit cookies, but came back to me the instant I called. At this point, I did not want him jumping on people and Jane was a bit nervous.

I took him over to a baby pool and actually got him to go in it to get his tennis ball. He was very nervous at first, but he REALLY wanted the ball. Jane stood about 15 feet away and he was fine with that. I am hoping that this will transfer over to the tub.

I also learned something about him. When he starts out a training session a bit frantic, he calms down if I keep going. I think he just gets so excited at first it takes him a few minutes to relax. I also truly believe that he is an Obedience Trial Champion (OTCH) dog reincarnated. He is doing stuff I haven't even taught him yet. He is calmer than he was and is better and better every day.

Oops, Pam! Why do I let Shadow approach and jump on people when he has a history of nipping and lunging? Stupidity on my part.

Good Doggie! For doing such a good job in spite of my blunders and rushing. And brave doggie for getting into the baby pool!

HINDSIGHT

As I mentioned, I should have set him up more slowly, stopped the session with Lisa D. much sooner, and kept the other dogs away entirely. I was also starting to slide back into my "overzealous dog trainer mode," introducing him to too many people without a clear plan of exactly what I wanted to accomplish and how I was going to carry it out.

AUGUST 10 – DAY 74

And better and better! I took Shadow for his first agility lesson today with Janet and he was fabulous. Completely focused, calm, mouth soft the entire time. He solicited petting and a cookie from Janet and his body language was good. He even let Janet pet him all over and he really seemed to enjoy it. Good doggie!!!! Maybe I just imagined his aggression??? Maybe there really is no river named Denial?

Shadow ate a pen today and when Jim tried to pick the pieces up off of the floor, Shadow bit him (gently, but still a bite). Jim yelled at Shadow to go to his kennel and instead he ran into the office where I was. Jim told me what he had done and I told Shadow softly that he really needed to apologize and to suck up to Daddy. And he did! (Yelling is a hard habit to break. It does nothing to change behavior, but it makes us humans feel better.) He is letting me circle around him and his stand for exam (a behavior needed in competition obedience) is getting better. He will be standing up straight real soon. I am tickled with his progress.

> ## HINDSIGHT
>
> Well, I learned that we need to play the give-and-take-it game much more than I have been doing. We started today and will continue on a daily basis. He really tries so hard and I think he is a wonderful dog. One day I will look back at this journal and...? Laugh? Cry?

The Glass is Half Full

AUGUST 13 – DAY 77

I got together with a few of my friends at my training facility to work all of our dogs. Virginia stayed after everyone else left to help me with Shadow's desensitization program. We went outside and she walked back and forth in the parking lot, while Shadow and I were on the median. I allowed him to run up to greet her while he was on leash and he started begging for cookies. She hand-fed him and I asked her to throw the cookies on the ground instead. I think taking food from human hands is too stressful for Shadow. In the past, he would take the food, back away, and then lunge like he did with Sandy, John, and Cynthia. She started to do some hand targeting but I told her to stop because he sometimes gets too wired.

While she continued to walk, he started heeling with her. Since Shadow seemed to be quite comfortable with her outside (large open area), I decided that we could try my building (small, closed area). I had her sit while we worked. Shadow was terrific! Eyes clear, ears up, mouth soft, very focused. We did a whole host of competition behaviors. He glanced at Virginia once in a while, but it was without fear or anxiety. When, at the end of the session, he ran over to mug her for some food, I called him to me and he complied instantly!

So Virginia makes Number Five in successful introductions to new people!! (Laurie, Carolyn, Janet, Jane, and Virginia.) My definition of successful is those introductions in which he did not aggress at all.

AUGUST 15 – DAY 79

I took Shadow to the vet to draw blood for a full thyroid panel. Low-normal thyroid has been conclusively linked to aggression and I wanted to rule this out as a potential cause of his aggression. We did it outside on the grass rather than inside. When he first met the two technicians, he was pretty calm. When they wanted to hold him, he became a little nervous. One tech sat on the ground while another one approached him. He let the tech hold him for an instant, but then pulled away in avoidance, so I held him and he was fine. For more on some physiological causes of aggression see the Appendix.

Good Doggie! Shadow was nervous and moved away, rather than biting the vet tech. Wahoo!

AUGUST 18 – DAY 82

He was great today at my training facility. He is so damn smart that it is frightening! I did a whole heeling pattern and he was wonderful! I am taking him to Carolyn's for his first **private behavioral lesson** tomorrow. Our lessons will be all about developing a program to work with his aggression problems.

TRAINING CONCEPT

Private behavioral lesson: You may be wondering, since I am a dog trainer, why I need to go to someone else for lessons. When dealing with aggression, a second pair of eyes and ideas are always needed. I have also found that when the aggressive dog is your own, the emotional level involved in the retraining of the dog tends to make us hasty and therefore it is imperative to have someone watching who is not so emotionally attached. I realized I was rushing the process and training with someone else forced me to *slooow dooown.* One of the signs of a good teacher is someone who is constantly learning and trying to upgrade their skills and knowledge. They go to seminars, often work with other instructors, and know when s/he needs another pair of eyes to assess things. No one can be an expert in everything.

AUGUST 19 – DAY 82

I had a lesson with Carolyn today. We went to a fenced-in yard off leash and I just threw the Frisbee for Shadow. Then Carolyn came into the yard and threw him food. I tried to do some obedience stuff with him but he was nervous and couldn't do it. Then she just walked around and tossed him food. He relaxed slightly and was able to do a tiny bit of heeling. At one point Shadow approached Carolyn's friend (who was outside the fence) and she yawned, stretched, and turned away (giving Shadow calming signals.) He immediately moved away from her. He approached Carolyn nicely a few times—no submissive sitting or frantic, stressed looks. Then we took him down toward the house, off leash. He went swimming in the baby pool (and peed in it as well) and Carolyn fed him by throwing food on the ground. Carolyn tried to touch his hind end when he wasn't looking and he darted away.

Good Doggie! For darting away when Carolyn touched you, rather than biting her!

Carolyn sat down on the bench, bringing the water dish with her, so he could drink in her presence. An example of positive associative learning: making sure that good things—quenching his thirst—happen around people.

He was still very calm and I threw the Frisbee for him. After about ten minutes or so his eyes showed a faint glimmer of stress—the pupils were not dilated, but their shape was rounder than normal. I was able to get him out of it a time or two, by waiting for a relaxed look before I threw the Frisbee again. I put him away in his crate. I think he was tired—we had worked him for about an hour. I gave him some time to rest.

Then Carolyn and I both approached the car (side door open) and he didn't aggress! I clicked him and fed him every cookie I had left! Carolyn feels he is ready to be "flooded" with people in a controlled environment and I have set up a party for him on September 9th. Carolyn doesn't think that the thyroid test will show low-normal levels and I agree with her, but it is still nice to rule out a thyroid problem. Carolyn said that he is a nice dog and I have done a great job with him. Yippee!

Good Pam! For recognizing that rest was needed. By paying attention to Shadow's body language, I avoided a potential stress reaction.

AUGUST 20 – DAY 84

Took Shadow to my parents' house. My brother Fred, sister-in-law Jennifer, and two nephews were there. I wasn't going to introduce him but he seemed to want to say hello to everyone so I let him. He especially liked Jennifer. They all tried to pet him on the head and I instructed them to pet him on his chest. I taught Jennifer to lick her lips and turn her head away when he was dive-bombing her face and not stare at him. He responded appropriately by turning his face away from her. He gradually slowed down a bit from his initial zoomies and was fine.

Then we went for a walk in a park with all of the dogs. Shadow was great. A few times he tried to jump on Alex and Ben, my very young nephews, so I taught them how to turn their backs on him. When they did this, he stopped jumping, a successful example of **human-to-dog body language.** He was jumping because they had a ball and were doing typical boy things, making jerky movements with their arms. His mouth was a tad tight taking treats, but not bad. When we came back to the van we put the dogs in their crates and stood around talking. Shadow didn't bark at anyone.

TRAINING CONCEPT

Human-to-dog body language: Petting a dog on the head or withers region are seen as acts of aggression from a dog's point of view. So is leaning over the dog, crowding, and direct eye contact. These, of course, can be counterconditioned into meaning something quite pleasant for the dog. For more on this subject, see the Appendix.

HINDSIGHT

I don't know if, in this last entry, I was brave or stupid. While Shadow was doing a great job with a lot of our work together, he was flying off the handle in an instant and I couldn't trust him to be consistently okay with strangers. We still didn't have a real relationship yet or enough alternate behaviors for him to do instead of aggressing, or enough practice of "being calm around strangers."

AUGUST 21 – DAY 85

I gave Shadow a bath at the grooming shop today. When I tried to pick him up to put him in the tub, he urinated on me. Then I put him on the steps so I wouldn't have to bend over him to pick him up, and he urinated on the steps. Once in the tub though he was MUCH better than he was the first time I bathed him. I even put the small blow dryer on him. He didn't really enjoy it, but he dealt with it admirably—didn't try to bite or avoid it—just a little head turning, but again, not a major issue. I didn't dry him thoroughly because I didn't want to press my luck.

After grooming, we went to a park and I trained all of the dogs. Shadow had a hard time concentrating. Did a few dumbbell retrieves and a little bit of heeling. He was very distracted. Perhaps between yesterday and today it was a little too much for him and maybe I need to give him some down time (play only) between introductions, grooming, and training.

Oops, Pam! Slow down! Yes, I have had some successes, but I am still rushing the process. I am positively glowing from Carolyn's compliment and am wanting more, and more, and more...

Good Doggie! Shadow is really trying hard here and he is getting better in new areas, such as grooming and being around new people in new situations.

AUGUST 24 – DAY 88

I took Shadow for agility at Jane's and he did fine. Jane stayed outside the fence. He is so fast it is incredible. I will never be able to keep up with him! Then Jane came inside the yard and he was completely fine. He is also playing with Cody now, doing play bows, etc. Cody still isn't sure about him, but they do play a little. When I toss the ball for Shadow, Cody chases after him and bites him continually and Shadow doesn't even care.

Better Than Babe!

AUGUST 26 – DAY 90

Took Shadow for his instinct test on four sheep. He was incredible! I brought him in the pen, off leash (holding his collar) and asked him to lie down. It took him a few seconds, but he did it. Then I released him and he was fast but good. He did do some **gripping**, but nothing serious. He stopped on his own a few times, and when I asked him to lie down, he did! At an instinct test! First time ever on sheep! Wowie zowie! Then, after we were done, we walked down to the house while he was still off leash and he snuck through the fence to a bigger field (oops!) where the rest of the flock was stretched out. He lifted them off the fence and put the whole flock together, penned them all and just stood there. Incredible!!!!

To see what he would do, I closed the gate and we did some **walk-ups, theres, and get back outs**. He was brilliant! His mouth was really soft the entire time we were there. I knew I was going to be sorry that I didn't have anyone taping this. Carolyn said that he passed with flying colors and has some really good moves and instincts.

TRAINING CONCEPT

Gripping, walk-ups, theres, and get back outs: These are sheep herding terms. "Gripping" means to bite the sheep; "walk-up," means to slowly walk toward the sheep; "there" means to stop moving but keep your eye on the sheep; "get back out" means to move away from the sheep.

SEPTEMBER 1 – DAY 96

Well, I found something else I don't like—Shadow chases cars. I was walking him close to traffic at my training building when he caught me unaware and almost got hit by a car. I never walk my dogs on the road so had no clue that he would do this. Now I know what else I have to do; desensitize him to cars going by without getting a reaction from him. But he did well at the grooming shop yesterday and handled the big blower. Jim held his head and talked to him. I was so proud! He gets better and better all the time.

SEPTEMBER 3 – DAY 98

I took Shadow to Jane's again and even though there were other people there he was fine. His mouth was a bit tight at first, but then he calmed down. We did some competition behaviors and some agility.

Shadow really is getting better with other dogs. One of the other dogs was barking continuously and I just fed Shadow while the dog barked to desensitize him to it. He tends to be a bit reactive when he hears out-of-control barking. I think that is why he sometimes attacks Cody. Cody, being a Sheltie, tends to do this mindless barking, which drives all of us insane. I am so proud of Shadow—he is such a great dog!

SEPTEMBER 7 – DAY 102

Took Shadow to my training facility and worked him around traffic up the driveway. I was able to get him to lie down while I tossed him food and he started to relax about it. He wasn't completely calm but he gave me fast downs and good stays, so I just kept tossing food.

Good Pam! I am mostly relaxed when we are out and about, not sending him fearful signals with my own stress. (Probably because I am still mostly clueless...) I recognize each new problem that occurs—like car chasing and

Shadow's sensitivity to being picked up—and am addressing each one of these things, rather than just ignoring them. I am getting slightly better in reading his own stress signs—the shape of his face, eyes, and ears and am getting better in recording each session in greater detail.

Good Doggie! Shadow is really doing a wonderful job in a lot of respects. His behavior at home is improving and he is doing some wonderful work in terms of being calm in a lot of situations with new people around. I think he is incredibly brilliant!

HINDSIGHT

I was getting really cocky here. I was only touching the surface of his aggression, but thought that I "knew it all." God protects children and fools... Unbelievably, I was still rushing the process, STILL not truly understanding the "how-to's" of counterconditioning and desensitization.

Danger Ahead! Warning!!

SEPTEMBER 9 – DAY 104

Shadow's **flooding** party is scheduled today with Patrice, Margaret, Carolyn, John, Cynthia, and Diane. I am very excited! We are going to expose Shadow to many strangers at once, a situation he has found stressful so far. We discussed beforehand how many sessions we were going to do and how we were going to approach each one. It is extremely important to use only experienced people in this kind of situation—people that know how NOT to react if there

TRAINING CONCEPT

Flooding: A prolonged and forced exposure to stimulus that is or has become terrifying or frightening to the subject. With flooding, the subject is immediately exposed to a high level of anxiety-producing stimuli. Therefore, the subject must confront their fear directly and is forced to remain in the situation until the fear subsides. (My use of flooding here was inappropriate and, except in extreme cases, I would not condone the use of it with dogs.)

are any signs of aggression, and are fluent in doggie body language so they will act appropriately if and when they see stress signals.

First session. Shadow and I were in a big field and I played Frisbee with him for a few minutes and then everyone else walked up to the fence and started tossing him food. He seemed to be fine, so I had everyone come into the field and stand in a random grouping, without moving. There was no adverse reaction from him. I allowed him to approach everyone and they fed him from their hands. His mouth was mostly fine—a little nippy and frantic with his front teeth as he ate, but Carolyn said he did great. We started to throw the ball and Frisbee for him and he seemed to be okay with it all. We continued to do this for about 15-20 minutes and then we put him in his crate in the van. Everyone complimented me on how well he was doing and what a great job I had done. Aw shucks! Praise is a HUGE reinforcer for me.

Second session. We moved into the front yard and continued to do the same things. Most of us were just standing still and hand-feeding Shadow. John and Cynthia were throwing the ball and Frisbee for him to retrieve, which he did happily. About ten minutes into this session, Shadow was looking great—ears, eyes, and body posture all looked playful. He was in a play bow, waiting for Cynthia to throw the ball. I looked away for a split second and suddenly I saw a blur. Shadow attacked Cynthia! Cynthia had simply reached down (a little sideways) to pick up the ball Shadow had dropped for her so she could throw it for him again. For some reason, Shadow launched himself at her at breakneck speed, biting her on the breast, leaving a bruise, growling and biting in tandem. Let me stress, there was no advance warning growl or other body posture precursor. No warning that Shadow was going to attack at all. He had performed the same routine with Cynthia over and over again. Pick up the ball, throw the ball, retrieve the ball. It was horrible. I know now I have a **human-aggressive** dog on my hands.

Instead of reacting as we instinctually wanted to (screaming and punishing) we all just stood there and calmly discussed what had happened and what everyone had seen. I, of course, was only pretending to be calm. In reality, I was stunned into freeze position—freaked out, disappointed, and sick to my stomach. We had him lie down and after a minute of calm behavior tossed him some food to reinforce the calm behavior.

In retrospect, Carolyn said that his eyes might have been rounder than normal—it was hard to judge pupil size—it was dusk and difficult to tell. She also said that she thought he may have frozen for a split-second and then attacked. It may have been the fact that Cynthia was leaning over or it could have been

TRAINING CONCEPT

Human-aggressive dog: This problem can usually be avoided with proper socialization and training during puppyhood. The most crucial period is eight to twenty weeks, although there are additional critical periods up until the pup is two years old. It is possible to rehabilitate a human-aggressive dog but it takes time and effort and proper training under the guidance of a trainer qualified to handle aggression. That is why I'm working with Shadow so carefully, and even more carefully since this incident. That is why the extent of his training is warranted. Shadow is darn lucky to have found me. If he had ended up in a pet home, he would have bitten someone more seriously and would probably be dead by now.

There are very real physiological things going on in our bodies (in any mammal for that matter) during stress. Whether the stimuli are actually threatening all depends on the perception of the animal. We as humans know that cars are dangerous and fake plastic deer are not. Dogs may have a different perception of which is the more terrifying. To change Shadow's physiological response toward provoking stimuli, I am encouraging him to respond with his parasympathetic nervous system—the response of relaxation, of eating—rather than with his sympathetic nervous system—the response of fight or flight. When I first rescued Shadow, I was not giving him the opportunity to come completely "down" before exposing him to additional fearful stimuli, which in turn, set his stress clock higher and higher. Learning what happens physiologically to a dog in times of stress was an epiphany for me. This information made it crystal clear to me WHY it is so important to set his sessions up so he wouldn't even "think" about aggressing.

that we were all standing much closer to Shadow than we had been earlier. When I fed him, his mouth was medium tight. I gently put him away in the van.

Because Shadow gave no obvious sign that he was going to attack, such as a warning growl, it is my thought that perhaps Shadow had previously been punished for growling. A growl is just a warning that the dog wants you to back off—he may possibly feel pressured or frightened—and it is an important mode of communication. When the growl is punished out of the dog you may get a "flash-biter," a dog that seemingly bites for no reason. Dogs never bite for "no reason," but it takes time and detective work to find the cause.

We discussed whether or not we should go on to do a third session. It was the consensus of the group that we should. I was heartbroken and not really sure I wanted to do more, but in this case it was important not to end the work with Shadow on a bad note. I wanted to see if we could calm him down before ending the day. At this point my husband Jim joined us and was stunned and dismayed to hear that Shadow bit Cynthia.

Third session. I put Shadow in the barn on a15-foot tie-out and Jim and I went in first. Jim leaned over him and petted him. Shadow was very wild and frenzied. I was actually terrified that Shadow might bite him. I was relieved and able to breathe again when Jim backed away, and glad that we were all out of range. Everyone came up to him, one at a time, staying out of leash range and tossed him food. After a few minutes, Shadow relaxed. They then asked him to lie down and tossed him food. To end the session, they bombarded him with wads of food and left as he was still eating. Jim and I gave him nothing and just stood there passively as we tried to countercondition Shadow to other people—that now, good things come from them, not just us.

When we went home Shadow seemed to be okay, but as I was petting him, he started to give Cody and Beau "the eye," so I put him in his crate to let him rest and recuperate. I needed to rest and recoup too! Even though I did not create his aggression problem and am trying my best to rectify it, I still feel horribly guilty about the attack. Experts say it takes a dog two to six days to get back to normal—it will take me that long too!

I e-mailed everyone and asked for their perspective on the event. We all have different levels of expertise and I wanted to make sure that I was able to assess the incident from all angles.

Diane sent me her response to this event:

> Hi, Pam, really glad I came last night—this is what I saw and felt. Most of us kept our distance from Shadow, calling, feeding, and praising. Some in the group got a little closer, like Margaret. He ate out of her hand, but she was very quiet about it and I noticed she often turned sideways from him. She certainly never leaned over him. Now that I think of it, maybe what I really observed was how the people acted. Most of the people had a much quieter manner, except Cynthia. She was more talkative, made more gestures, and used her body much more, for example, when throwing the ball to Shadow. She used more hand movements around him. I think Shadow did wonderfully, especially given what you told me about him when he first came to live with you. It was, I think, Cynthia's forgetting or not really realizing who she was dealing with, and I think she made the

mistake, not him. She got too close and leaned over him! He was in a difficult situation last night and came through with flying colors. Also, I think you said he aggressed toward her before, maybe he remembered that or she moved a certain way again. Take heart, he is a great dog, you are a great trainer, but emotional problems in dogs, just like in people, take lots of time to heal.

Cynthia e-mailed me her response:

My perception was that in the first session we were much further apart. In the front yard, we were in a semicircle and I came out of the middle of it, directly at him, instead of on a curve, so I'm sure that didn't help. I was getting too cocky with how well he was doing and didn't think about how my body position would affect him.

HINDSIGHT

I described our "party" to Bob Bailey, a noted applied behavioral psychologist, and asked if it would be considered flooding or counterconditioning. His response, "No, that is not what I would call flooding. I would call that a mistake." Flooding can do a lot of harm if not done properly, and if done on the wrong subject. Yup. Yup. Triple yup.

After this event I felt very low, very stupid, frustrated, hugely disappointed and ready to cry. I did not see a light at the end of the tunnel and at times wished he would bite me so I could have an excuse to put him down. Of course, looking back now from a distance, he was still doing a great job in so many respects. One little setback doesn't mean much in the grand scheme of the entire process as long as you don't repeat it!

Please understand that I now know that flooding can be a bad thing and not only did we attempt to do it improperly, but it was in fact dangerous. Flooding is like throwing someone in the swimming pool that doesn't know how to swim, is terrified of water, and has no way to get out of the pool. Obviously I know now that it was not appropriate to expose Shadow to this process.

SEPTEMBER 12 – DAY 107

I did a few TTouch sessions on the bed with Shadow yesterday and he was really stressed. I also noticed that he clenches his FEET! His skin was VERY tight and his pupils huge. I pretty much left him alone or put him in his crate. He is aggressing at Cody, which he hasn't done in quite awhile.

Today, I massaged his feet and then did a lot of leaning over him while I was sitting on the ground. Then I got up on my knees and leaned over him in really obnoxious ways while feeding him. He did fine. His skin was normal today, not tight, and I could actually move his tail—it wasn't rigid like it was yesterday. When I came home from work Shadow asked me to rub his belly, which I did, but he does a lot of this paw lifting, in a submissive, frantic way, so I moved away from him. His eyes were medium-large. I plan on doing more body wraps with him, hoping to gradually desensitize him to obnoxious body movements. Shadow has, since Saturday, been dive-bombing my head again on a regular basis. I plan on giving him a few days of easy stuff to deal with so he can relax.

Reality Check, Pam! When I adopted Shadow (ONLY!) three and a half months ago, he was aggressive toward my other dogs, extremely frantic around me and Jim, sensitive about being touched or brushed, apprehensive about my body posture, nervous about tight places, submissive in frantic ways, tense about being bathed, and unstable around strangers. Today he is somewhat calmer about all of these things, and yes, even strangers.

He did have some good reactions to my family. When Jennifer petted him in ways he usually finds scary, he did not rip her face off. He left the vet tech in one piece without even so much as a growl. Shadow also did well with everyone else on September 9. I just pressured him beyond his limits at the time. He is also doing remarkably well with competition behaviors and has relaxed about learning new things. He has made tremendous progress in a very short time and I need to remind myself of that. Behavior changes are slow—sometimes it's two steps forward, three steps back! I, in turn, have learned to break behaviors into smaller pieces, read his body language better, understand more fully the physiological aspects of stress, deal with each problem as it occurs, and to slow down! (Well, not all the way...)

2

*Close only counts in horseshoes
and hand grenades.*   —Unknown

It's a Learning Curve, Not a Learning Line

SEPTEMBER 24 – DAY 119

It took Shadow a full six days to act normally after the bite incident. Needless to say, I have totally reversed my thinking on "flooding," especially since I didn't do it right anyway! From now on, I will continue to desensitize him to one person and one context at a time and then *gradually* add two people, then three, etc. I realize now that flooding him with a feared object will *not* help him to get over it, but will create **sensitization** to it.

I started doing the body wrap on Shadow again and massaging his gums. Gum massaging is one of the TTouches used to diminish aggression. Interestingly, the first time I did his gums, he was okay with it. When I was done I could definitely sense that he was happier and more relaxed.

I introduced Shadow to Diane and Vanessa today at my training facility—they stood in the median and I just worked on attention heeling with him. He approached Diane once; she turned her back to him and he came back to me. He was a bit stressed but eventually relaxed.

I also noticed that when we took an agility lesson with Janet he was somewhat

TRAINING CONCEPT

Sensitization: A case where the dog's reaction to a stimulus increases rather than decreases. It is difficult to foresee if repeated presentations of a stimulus will cause desensitization or sensitization. Generally, really intense stimuli (intense to the dog) will create sensitization to it.

okay, but not entirely okay. At one point she bent over to fix a jump. Even though Shadow wasn't even close to her, he got *very* upset and almost lunged toward her before I called him off, yet during our last agility lesson Janet was able to pet him. I have no idea why he started to aggress at her. Ten minutes into the lesson he started sniffing and I couldn't get his attention and ended the session. So, either there were some really good smells or he was really stressed.

I took Shadow to the schoolyard today and played some Frisbee and did some touching. I have noticed that he has been more stressed since the flooding party. Live and learn. I just hope it didn't cause too much damage. I really have to remember that it hasn't been that long. Keep It Simple, Stupid!!

He just has SO much talent in so many areas that the temptation to rush his rehabilitation is irresistible. I just have to come to terms with SLOWING down!

Give yourself a break, Pam! For dog's sake, it has been less than four months!

SEPTEMBER 26 – DAY 121

Shadow and I had a herding lesson. When we approached the sheep in the beginning of the lesson, I asked him for a lie-down and he actually did it! We had the sheep in a pen while we were outside of the pen and worked on balance.

He was much better than at the previous lesson. After the first 30 minutes he was more in tune with my body language, and more **balanced on the sheep**. Periodically I moved away from the sheep and it took him only a minute or two to come to me. WOW! Shadow came away from sheep to be with ME!

TRAINING CONCEPT

Balance on sheep: The ability of the dog to sense the place in which he has the most influence on the flock. This allows the dog to control, move, or hold them in the direction desired by the shepherd.

I then played with him. Once his mouth was soft, I released him back to the sheep, his reward for being calm. During the lesson I asked for a down a few times and most of the time he was able to do it. He tried to bite the sheep through the fence and grabbed some wool (thank God for the fence). His nose was a bit raw and beet red from jamming it into the fence! His eyes were clear but very round and his ears were good. He started out barking at the sheep—was it aggression/over-stimulation/barrier frustration—or just being a Border Collie? Who knows? But he calmed down after a while and, all in all, it was a great lesson.

Shadow is much calmer around the house—nothing earth-shattering—just a gradual lessening of stress. Now we're cooking with gas!

SEPTEMBER 30 — DAY 125

TED TURNER!!!

Wow! I went to a two-day sheep herding seminar with renowned animal behaviorist Ted Turner.* I learned some new things and felt validated since many of my training techniques were reinforced—I already knew a sizable share of the things Ted discussed. I spoke with Ted on Saturday and he agreed to work with Shadow and me on Sunday during breaks.

We videotaped each of the sessions. I have found that videotaping is a valuable tool in training. Being able to watch the session again helps you to see clearly what you may have missed because your focus was on something else. These sessions with Ted illustrated to me the repetitive nature of training and the desensitization process. It was difficult to analyze these videos at first viewing and it took me many months before I was able to actually recognize the progress we did make.

Ted and I discussed our training strategy beforehand and how we were going to handle any sign of aggression. We also discussed using different **contexts** and how these contexts would eventually **generalize** into Shadow's whole life.

To begin with, we did not take Shadow out of the van or out of his crate. Our goal was to have Ted approach the van and if Shadow did not aggress, I would praise and reinforce. If Shadow aggressed, we would stand perfectly still and wait until he calmed down.

For our first try, Ted stayed ten feet away from the van while I opened the side door and fed Shadow for remaining calm. I closed the door and repeated the same thing, although this time Ted tried to **reinforce** him by throwing food, clapping his hands, and verbally praising him. Shadow barked and lunged at him. Ted then stood still and after a few seconds of quiet, verbally praised him. Shadow aggressed again. We both **NCR'd** and once he calmed down, we closed the door.

---

*Ted worked at Sea World for 20 years and was Vice President for the last nine years. He is a nationally known behaviorist with wide and diverse experience working with wild and domestic animals all over the globe. He specializes in working with abnormal behavior of captive animals. Ted has been an inspiration to positive method dog trainers who have been able to take his techniques and apply them to dogs.

TRAINING CONCEPT

Context: The elements present during a training session. These include the scenario, the location, number of people present, number of other animals present, types of distractions, proximity of people and what each person is doing, and the type of behaviors I expect.

Generalize: Generalization occurs when behaviors are seen in contexts other than those in which they were originally trained. I am sure you are aware of this concept without ever realizing that you know it. You always train your dog either in the house or in the yard. Your dog comes to you in these locations 99 percent of the time. But, the instant you go to another location, the dog has forgotten that you exist and acts as if he has never before heard his name or the word "come" in his entire life. Has he suddenly become deaf? Nope, you simply did not practice in enough locations, with enough variety of distractions to develop reliability. When the dog can apply a learned behavior to a new scenario, he is generalizing.

Reinforce: Reinforcers can be food, petting, clapping, praise, games, and toys—anything that the dog likes.

NCR (No Change Response): If the dog does something you don't like, stand still, passive, and quiet. Wait for the dog to offer a behavior that you can then positively reinforce. For example, Shadow aggressed, we did nothing—no eye contact, no yelling, no shutting of the door—we gave him no feedback that he could construe as positively reinforcing his aggressing.

On our third try, Shadow was unable, for the most part, to remain calm. For the next go round, he was a little better. However, if Ted tried to toss food into his crate as a reward for calm behavior and missed the crate, Shadow would aggress at him. Each time Ted missed, Shadow aggressed. The displays were lasting longer and he started to paw the crate pad and bite the bars of the crate. At that point, any kind of movement from Ted was setting him off. We ended the session.

This is a perfect example of how to slowly, methodically and painstakingly train a dog to become non-aggressive. Shadow's aggression is most likely based on fear and was further reinforced by his success (in his previous home) at driving those feared objects away. What we are trying to do is to show Shadow that his aggression no longer works. Now only quiet, calm behaviors will be more successful for him, i.e. the presence of people is not something to be feared, but to be enjoyed.

We talked in between some of the short trials and Ted pointed out that I rely too much on food. It was obvious to Ted that Shadow was taking tremendous comfort and reward from my presence alone and the addition of food as a constant reinforcer was unnecessary. I needed to add more reinforcement variety to my training. I mentioned that Shadow had only been with me for four months and he was still only a sixteen-month-old puppy. Ted was heartened—he felt that I could turn this dog around.

A few minutes before the second session, I took Shadow out to run around a bit on leash to get his excess energy out so he would be calm for our second session with Ted. My friend Betsy approached to talk to me. I backed away, explaining to her that this was Shadow (to the untrained eye, Beau and Shadow are nearly identical) and she should stop her approach. She didn't hear me, so I continued to back away from her, keeping Shadow's attention on me. He was doing fine but all of a sudden he **tensed and stressed** when he saw her. She had stopped moving at that point. He ripped the leash out of my hand and lunged at her at top speed.

It hurt my hand and arm terribly and I whispered, "Shadow, here." He put on the brakes and whirled back to me. I had him lie down, fed him, and, as he was still stressed, quietly put him back in the van. Had my arm been okay, I would have continued until he was relaxed, but it was numb.

Good Doggie! For responding to me instantly when I called. Betsy was very impressed at his recall and the amount of relationship that was behind it.

Good Pam! For not freaking out at the potential disaster and keeping my cool.

TRAINING CONCEPT

Tensed and stressed: An essential part of training of which many people are unaware is the need to observe a dog's behavior; in other words, checking for stress/calming signals. Learning about calming signals provides us with a very important channel of communication between dogs and humans. With the ability to measure a dog's approximate state of stress, arousal, or anxiety, we have an extra foundation on which to make decisions about what to do at any one moment.

If you are missing your dog's clear signs of stress, you may push the dog beyond its limits and he or she may react with aggression. Any signs of stress at all should give you reason to stop your session and reconsider or rethink your approach. In my opinion, without the ability to recognize the signs of stress, you are missing 90 percent of what it takes to train a dog.

As I watched this video again eight months later, I saw myself getting extremely dejected, upset and choking back tears. During this session Shadow was very aggressive and reactive.

Before the second session, Ted and I discussed what we were going to do. He mentioned that I don't have to get stuck on one context at a time. He suggested I continually switch contexts but build up each one, always striving for calmness, teaching Shadow to ignore any provoking stimulus and keeping Shadow's focus on me.

On the first try Shadow was unable to lie down when I asked him to. I shut the door. On the second try he was able to look at Ted calmly and I used praise and a little food as my reinforcers.

For the next session, Ted and I approached together. Shadow was quiet, so I praised and Ted again tried to toss him food. When the food missed, Shadow aggressed. Ted froze in position and Shadow continued to aggress. Once he quieted down, I closed the door. We both noticed that he was aggressing only when Ted missed the food throw. If the throw was good (the food landed in the crate) Shadow did not aggress. I am seeing here that the arm movement has ceased to be an issue for Shadow, at least today. So there has been some improvement, minuscule as it may be.

After the second session, I took Shadow out again and used more of myself (my presence only) as the reinforcer. I got down on my knees and just petted and hugged him. He didn't try to get to the other side of my head through my nose! He was calm, cool, collected, no dive-bombing of my head or face—just hangin' out with Mom! WOW!

OCTOBER 1 — DAY 126

In this session, Ted started moving his feet and Shadow aggressed. Ted continued to move his feet until Shadow was quiet. Then I moved in to reinforce instead of letting Ted reinforce. Next, Ted sat right next to the door. I hand-fed Shadow while Ted threw food in hopes that the missed tosses wouldn't set Shadow off. No go. When Ted missed the throw, Shadow aggressed and the aggression became more "vicious" as Shadow pawed his crate pad more vehemently.

Toward the end of the day we were able to get Ted almost in the van. There was no crate biting and Shadow was less sensitive and reactive to Ted's body movements and voice. Ted asked me if I wanted to bring Shadow out of the crate and I emphatically said, "NO!" I was too afraid and knew that Shadow would pick up on my fear, which would be counterproductive. In addition, it was getting very dark out and I would have been unable to read any of Shadow's signs of stress.

At the end of the day, Ted gave out verbal awards to certain people at the seminar and yours truly got "The most determined trainer here with the most difficult dog" award!

I need to set up a more regimented and precise training desensitization program for Shadow. I noticed since being home tonight, he has been great around the other dogs—a bit wired, but in an "I have been in my crate too long" way rather than in an out-of-control wired mode. He has been very playful with the other dogs and did some zoomies, running around the house and rearranging all of the furniture.

HINDSIGHT

I finally realize here that I had not necessarily been on the wrong track, but was without the proper mentality and mindset for working with Shadow. I was still going too fast and was without definite plans for each session. In addition, the approximations that I set up were too large. Up until now, it had been a "hit or miss" kind of thing, rather than using a more systematic approach. Before the sessions with Ted, I was still in a rush, especially since I was having some successes with Shadow. My human emotions (overzealous dog trainer run amok) were still part of the process; I needed to get rid of them completely and look more dispassionately at the entire desensitization and counterconditioning process.

Just like Shadow, I learned slowly by my repetitions of mistakes and successes. When I first watched the video a couple days after it was shot, I was heavy-hearted and completely overwhelmed by the amount of work that I needed to do. When I watched this tape eight months later, I realized that we did make some progress that day, infinitesimal though it was. I am finally learning to SEE, recognize, and comprehend what I am observing and am in "tiny **approximation**" mode now. I am learning to think **"Behaviorally, not humanistically."**

TRAINING CONCEPT

Approximation: Breaking down a behavior into tiny steps. Each step can then be reinforced and built upon.

Behaviorally, not humanistically: This is a catch phrase from Ted that I fell in love with. He means that if you can get your human emotions out of animal training, it facilitates training. For instance, your dog grabs your socks and runs around the house and you chase him all over, yelling and screaming. You may think the dog is doing this for "revenge," for "spite," or for whatever human emotion you attribute to the dog or for whatever reason you tell yourself. In actuality, the dog is finding this behavior of YOURS (the thrill of the chase and YOUR ATTENTION!) to be very reinforcing. Stop chasing the dog and he will stop running away. If you can look at any behavior dispassionately, behaviorally, i.e., "What is the dog finding reinforcing?" you can very simply get the dog to stop driving you insane by not reinforcing it!

OCTOBER 2 – DAY 127

I wrote this e-mail to Ted Turner:

> Thank you so much for giving me your valuable time to work with Shadow. I cannot tell you how much that meant to me and I absolutely LOVED the entire seminar.
>
> I do have a question though—when we are teaching new behaviors we strive for errorless learning, but when we were working with Shadow's aggression yesterday, we were not setting him up to succeed. In the past, I have tried to do this—set him up NOT to aggress, not push him beyond his limits. So, I am confused. Isn't "calm behaviors around humans" a new behavior for Shadow?
>
> Which is right? Setting him up to fail, showing him that nothing bad happens and rewarding him for calm behaviors, which is where I was making my mistakes when I first got him, or setting him up to succeed and rewarding him for calm behaviors? I did do some training sessions with him in the car today at my building with two different people in almost the same context.

Later on I started a set of training sessions with Sally. Sally started about six feet away from the van. I opened the door. I praised and reinforced (P&R'd) for calm behaviors from Shadow, then stepped away. P&R again for calm behavior when he saw Sally and repeated this twice. I had her continue to move forward and gradually asked for longer quiet behavior. Yes, I asked for two criteria at the same time—a longer quiet, and Sally moving closer. He did really well, so I ended the session.

Next she started right next to the van. I praised and she reinforced by throwing cookies. We saw a pattern that if she missed the throw, he would have a tantrum, but the quality of his bark was (as far as we mere humans could tell) definitely "you stupid human, can't you even throw a damn cookie!" We NCR'd and P&R'd when calm.

Finally, Sally came even closer and was actually touching the van. Shadow got more upset and the quality of his bark changed—it was deeper and much more serious. I had her kneel down and he quieted down. Then I had her stand up and lean into the van—he did have a few moments of calmness. I P&R'd this time—not Sally. Ended the session.

Total for all of the sessions lasted 20 minutes, each session lasting approximately four to eight minutes with a break in between. My reinforcers were food and praise. I P&R'd for calm behaviors.

Two hours later we had a session with Marsha. It went basically the same as with Sally except I had her move in much quicker. Once she threw the food and missed, his barking started to become more serious than it had been with Sally, telling us how stupid we humans are. He was pawing his crate pad more and he took longer to recover after an episode. I had to close the door two times because he couldn't calm down. The last attempt was with Marsha leaning in the van, not looking at him, and me giving P&R for eye contact from Shadow, which deteriorated rapidly. He couldn't take his eyes off of her. We ended the session.

That night I wrote another e-mail to Ted Turner:

> One of the interesting things to me is that when I brought Shadow home last night, there was no residual displacement aggression toward the other three dogs and today he is fine, not crazed or seemingly overstressed (which I know because he dive-bombs my head at warp speed when he is overly stressed, and he attacks Cody and Beau). So, am I missing something? The bad food throws truly seem to set him off and I don't know if it makes sense to continue in this way.
>
> When working outside of the van, should I let him approach a person (dropping the leash) or just stand my ground, NCR and wait for him to stop being an idiot and then praise and reinforce? I don't want

to do the same "in the crate, in the van" context all of the time, but I don't want to have him outside unless I know what I am supposed to do.

OCTOBER 3 – DAY 128

Ted's e-mail back to me on October 3:

Thanks for the kind words, Pam. I've always enjoyed your energy and excitement about training. Let's keep it going! As far as Shadow is concerned, let's keep this simple.

Setting up for success! Yes. You want to follow your intuition here. We (you and I) were conducting our first sessions, which enabled us to get oriented on just where his threshold for tolerance is. We had some failures, which are no big deal, but those won't teach him much as long as we don't react AT ALL (as you appeared to have done with Sally when she kneeled down "to get him to calm down"...I'm paraphrasing here). You want to build a pattern of success now and bridge early, BEFORE the aggression is triggered. Remember, for now each new context will require starting over, although you should begin to see this process move faster and faster.

The idea of the second person throwing the food should be discontinued. There is a high degree of misses (I thought my superior male athleticism would overcome physics...which shows you why men are idiots!) Let's have you continue to hand out the food while people eventually walk in with you, although you might want them to do the bridging. The key is "association" and a process called counterconditioning. In time, it won't be a big deal to Shadow. Continue to give a No Change Response. Really work on your own behavior as well as the others involved in the session immediately after Shadow lights up. Everyone should just stop and ignore until he quits or at least slows down. You will certainly have poor sessions, an occasional poor day, and normal regression, especially when changing the settings/ context (new help, different clothes, changing conditions).

Finally, this animal is too dangerous yet to take him off lead and let him approach people, other animals, etc., on his own. Let's keep a normal loose lead on him for now with high vigilance on your part. Continue to work strong heeling under various conditions. Make it really fun to ignore things, especially the closer you walk to them. If

> he lunges at something that just means you missed an opportunity
> to redirect before he caught you not paying attention! The best No
> Change Response in this type of scenario is to simply keep walking
> (without jerking) and move on to the next reinforcement opportunity,
> instead of reacting by stopping. Follow your intuition and don't push
> him yet. Your internal confidence and experience will tell you when
> you can ease up a bit. It looks to me as if it might be a while but what
> a great animal to have. Once he's fixed, you'll be able to handle the
> worst killer whale in the world!!!!!!!!!

I worked with Claire today and videotaped the session. We were at her house.
She stayed in the fenced-in yard; Shadow and I stayed outside the fence. I had
Shadow on a 15-foot leash and let him approach on his own. If he was calm,
I praised and Claire reinforced by tossing food over the fence. She alternated
between standing still, waving her arms, running back and forth, and leaning
over. I had her ask him to lie down. I bridged and she reinforced. I started out
with a small bit of food and then let her toss food.

We did two sessions. The first one was 20 minutes and the second one was 10
minutes. I had to instruct Claire a few times to whisper "lie down" because
she was not only yelling at him but also saying it over and over again. I found
that Shadow would bark and lunge, and then go off sniffing. Once Claire made
the adjustment, they were both fine. After a few minutes he was giving her lie-
downs without her asking.

OCTOBER 4 – DAY 129

Worked with Karen today at the training facility. We were on the median and I
had Karen stand still. I heeled Shadow around, keeping his focus on me. I used
petting, food, and praise as his reinforcers for calm behaviors.

I also practiced releasing him verbally to go sniff and then, after a few seconds,
I called him to me. He started to run toward Karen two times, but it seemed to
me to be in a friendly way ("Hey, got cookies?") He came back instantly every
time and I reinforced with petting, praise, and food. I tried really hard not to
use food each time, but did a lot of praising while we were heeling and then
when I clicked, I varied the treat between food and petting. He seemed to be
pretty relaxed and there have been no redirected aggression behaviors at home.

E-mail to Ted:

> Thanks again! I had a great session with Shadow today and filmed
> it and watched it twice. I won't tell you all about it now, but the first

session we had 80 trials and 54 ended in cookies and 26 ended up in barking (67 % success). Second session was 41 trials and 26 ended in cookies and 15 ended up in barking (63 % success). I am thrilled! I'll keep you posted and e-mail you in about two weeks. Thanks a million!

Ted's Response:

Great use of quantifiable data to measure success. Now THAT'S a true Behaviorist. Those success percentages should keep creeping upward (with normal periodic slides back). If they don't—take a step backwards for a day or two, then push the envelope a little without triggering a response in Shadow. Remember, you'll see some of your best progress after a day or two off now and again (assimilation processing requires an encoding period where forgetting and as-similation are both normal). Also, start skipping the "cookie" thing on a few of your session trials and give significant attention with praise, cooing, baby talk, etc., in place.

You don't want to get on an **FR1** food schedule. It's fine to start, but it is the first one to deteriorate. More importantly, he is not doing it for the food; he is doing it for YOU (although snacks are a fun surprise now and then). Keep those reinforcers VARIABLE. He is now my pet project! Let me know next week how you're doing unless you run into a glitch.

TRAINING CONCEPT

FR1: (Fixed Ratio of One) A reinforcer is delivered at the same interval. A ratio of one means that every single correct response gets a cookie. This schedule is good for training new behaviors, but not good for making those behaviors last. **VRRV** means Variable Reinforcement with Reinforce-ment Variety. This is the strongest schedule for maintaining a behavior.

OCTOBER 5 – DAY 130

I worked with Cynthia and John today at their house. They were behind a fence, walking back and forth in a straight line, talking. We started out 75 feet away. Shadow and I were outside the fence. I worked on competition behaviors, always striving for calmness and continued to vary my reinforcers and not get stuck on food. I did two sessions, each session lasting ten minutes with a 20-minute break in between.

During the first session Shadow was nervous and, while he didn't lunge at them, he was shaking and his body was very tight and tense. He had a hard time focusing on me and would heel for a few steps and then go off and sniff. He came back to me each time, but he was worried.

The second session Shadow was MUCH better—calm and focused. I heavily reinforced him with tons of petting and praise, and used less food this time. If he did glance toward John and Cynthia, it didn't freak him out or cause him to tense up.

In the meantime they were closer than before—approximately 25 to 30 feet closer. His heeling improved and I added in additional behaviors. They said that my leaning over him seemed to stress him out somewhat (which I noticed as well) so I got down on my knees and we did some cuddling. If I did lean in, I would feed him for letting me kiss his face.

OCTOBER 7 – DAY 132

I did two very short sessions at my facility. I had some guests over and Shadow and I stayed on the median while the other people walked their dogs. During the first session he was so nervous he was shaking and mostly ignoring me. When I called him to come, it took him a few times to respond. I reinforced the recall with petting and praise. His eyes and ears were fine, but he was clearly nervous. I ended the session.

The second session was much better; Shadow responded to my recall faster and he wasn't shaking. My reinforcers again were petting and praise. After everyone left, I brought him into the building. He played with the tennis balls, chewing them vehemently, leaving them white with stress slime. I got down on the ground to coax him to come to me but I didn't say anything. He came close a few times and let me pet him, then he was off again murdering the balls.

He was a bit wired tonight at home, had the zoomies, and then attacked Cody. Beau was frightened of him and was trying to crawl up my body. I basically left him alone and when he seemed to be relaxed, I praised him quietly. Through-out the night, he calmed down and let me pet him without moving away in avoidance.

OCTOBER 10 – DAY 135

I worked with Claire again. We used almost the same context that we had be-fore. This time, instead of letting him approach the fence on his own, I worked on attention heeling while Claire was walking around erratically, doing a lot of bending over (which sets him off to aggress). Because she was going to be moving more, I lowered my criteria and started with her farther away than she was during the October 3 session. I had already decided that if he lost his focus on me and started aggressing, I was going to keep walking. The first session lasted 10 minutes. He was nervous and shaking while still in the van. At first he was biting my hand to get the food, but then his mouth loosened up somewhat. His attention on me was fantastic and he did some great heeling. I varied the distance between Claire—sometimes close, sometimes further away—he did not react at all and remained focused on me. While I used some petting and tons of verbal praise, I did use quite a bit of food as well. Put him away for about five minutes.

Shadow was MUCH better for our second session. He had stopped shaking and had even better attention than before and better facial expressions. If Shadow did glance at Claire, he would whip his head back to look at me. I gave no verbal prompting if he looked away. I used petting more this time along with food and verbal praise. His expression was a little softer. This session lasted about five minutes.

E-mail to Ted:

> I am seeing a pattern here—during the first session he is very ner-vous and in the second session he is much better. I am sure that will fade faster as I continue to work with him, so he won't be nervous even the first time. I am trying to change the context each time—do-ing the same stuff but in a new location with different people or with a fence in between or no fence in between. Have different training sessions set up for the rest of October, using different people and different approaches and the schedule of the training sessions them-selves are varied—three days on, two days off, five days on, one day off, etc. They have all been outdoors and I want to start bringing it indoors, but I will wait a week or two.

> What would be a good way to count trials? Like I did in the begin-ning? After each cookie start another trial?

> I have also been working more at home with grooming. He hates having his tail brushed and will lie down on it. When Jim is available

to help, I have him feed and reinforce Shadow while I do the handling—brushing, toenail clipping, etc. In general, he has been calmer around the house, although he does get into these punishing moods with Cody and Beau at times. I try to stop it before it happens, but I am only human and sometimes I miss those precursors...

Ted's e-mail response:

Hi, Pam. Just heading out the door in an hour so I can't be lengthy. Just wanted to tell you that you're on the right track. Don't worry about your success percentage; just keep watching for accidental reinforcement. You should see a big difference in the amount, type and frequency of the sessions where there is no aggression at all, versus the ones where there is some aggression. Don't be afraid to put him up (with some reinforcement), take a break and start again. Keep adding to the bank account; it'll pay off later.

Don't worry about the two-session pattern at this point. Stay steady, keep chipping away...you're getting there.

HINDSIGHT

I was not rushing the process, but I was still unclear at this point how to break things down into tiny approximations. Looking back now, I should have set up the sessions with Claire so that he did not aggress on her at all. Did I mention that it is called a learning curve, not a learning line? And not just for Shadow. My dear reader, I KNOW this is getting repetitive. How do you think I felt? I am not the most patient person in the world. When I want something, I want it NOW! Yesterday is even better! That is why I am very proud of myself for slowing down and taking each day as it comes.

OCTOBER 11 – DAY 136

I took Shadow to a shopping center and worked him on the grassy median in the middle of the parking lot. There was lots of traffic and some people.

During the first session Shadow was able to relax within a few minutes and was great. I trained him approximately ten minutes and then put him away. We worked on attention heeling, and rewarded with lots of praise, petting, and some food.

In the second session Shadow was even better amidst cars whizzing by and people milling around. Not too close, but close enough!

Training at the shopping center with lots of distractions.

The third session was at the park. I practiced recalls and rewarded with minimal food, lots of petting and praise. We then moved closer to the jungle gym section where there were two children and four adults. I had him lie down and we just cuddled. I did not ask him to look away from them. Shadow was great! He showed some calm interest, but it wasn't intense—just curious. Cool beans!

Good Doggie! Shadow is starting to relax in new places, with new people and is calm enough that he is now enjoying it when I pet him.

OCTOBER 13 – DAY 138

We took an agility lesson today. I had Shadow on leash and fed him and cuddled with him while Janet leaned over and adjusted jumps. In the past, this has set him off to lunge at her. He relaxed after a few minutes and was taking food gently. Once he was able to relax, we proceeded with the lesson. Shadow was wonderful.

OCTOBER 14 AND 15 – DAYS 139 AND 140

Took him to a UKC trial both days. (No, he wasn't entered!) Cody got a Second Place in Open B, High Scoring Shetland Sheepdog, High Scoring Veteran, and High Scoring Rescue dog in the whole trial—I am VERY Proud! I worked Shadow four times during the two-day show.

Great Job Cody! Yes, I continue to work Beau and Cody for competition and agility. I try to make sure that they all get equal individual attention from me. I always rotate who gets to play with me first. All of this plus I run a business six days a week. No, I don't have a life nor is my house clean.

To begin, I just walked Shadow around far away from everyone and he was very stressed. I didn't have any food on me, so I just used petting and praise. I tried some recalls and it took a few times of me calling him for him to come to me. He did lots of **displacement** sniffing.

At the next session, Shadow was much better. I used a few cookies, but rewarded his calmer behavior with mostly petting, praise, and cuddling and he was much more responsive.

The next day Shadow was even better than yesterday. I continued to use a little food, and tons of petting. His recalls were great. We tried some heeling and although it wasn't his best, it wasn't terrible. At times he would go off sniffing, but came back instantly when I called him. At one point a woman was walking back and forth and Shadow started to run toward her in what I call a "Got cookies?" way but came back to me instantly when I called. Way to go, Shadow!

TRAINING CONCEPT

Displacement or redirected behaviors: Aggression or avoidance behaviors that the dog may exhibit as a consequence of being punished or just plain nervous. Redirected aggression is usually directed toward things perceived by the animal as being smaller or more defenseless (other dogs, other species, children, the couch, the garden, etc.) often in seemingly unrelated situations. The punishment may have come from you, another dog or animal, or even the environment. A few typical non-aggressive displacement behaviors would be: sniffing the ground, turning away from you, coming slowly when called, or responding slowly to cues.

Our last session was SUPER! I used more food this time along with petting and praise. We continued to do heeling and this time he was great. I had him lie down 75 feet away from a group of people, and fed and petted him.

After a few minutes, we moved in to 20 feet away and did the same exercise—lie down, food and petting for calm behaviors. I would have moved even closer but another group of people were coming up behind us so I ended the session because I was too nervous.

I was really impressed with Shadow today. His eyes and ears were great and he was interested, relaxed, and calm. He looked back at me every few seconds without me prompting him to do so. Relationship building going on here! (I try not to prompt my dogs to look at me. I expect them to find staring at me with adoring eyes reinforcing. This doesn't just happen though. I put in a great deal of time and effort and reinforcers to make sure that they find eye contact rewarding.)

OCTOBER 18 – DAY 143

I worked at my training facility today with my friend Kris. I had her sit in a chair in the far corner. Shadow and I came into the building. I had him on a 15-foot leash and we did some competition heeling. His mouth and body started out stiff but he loosened up after a few minutes. At one point, he was lying down and I was petting him and massaging him but he kept looking toward Kris in a worried way. He wasn't looking back to me instantly, so I said his name to get his attention and he looked at me. I massaged him a bit more and he gave me better eye contact. I ended the session.

This session lasted approximately 15 minutes. Shadow was a bit jumpy, but that may have been coming from me since I was not feeling well. Or it could have been his normal over-exuberant self!

I just can't get over the fact that with all of these sessions there has been no aftermath of aggressive behaviors toward the other dogs when he is back home.

HINDSIGHT

I am getting a glimmer here of how to set up Shadow's sessions. I am going to many places and mostly setting him up to succeed. This stuff really takes a great deal of thought and practice on my part.

OCTOBER 21 – DAY 146

E-mail from Ted Turner:

Your trend seems to be moving along as I expect. I've seen this a hundred times, so don't get discouraged (as I can see you're not...a true measure of a professional animal handler). Shadow has a tough job ahead of him and he's doing as well as he possibly can at this stage. Again, don't expect fast gains. They'll come when you least expect them. Remember, REGRESSION IS AN IMPORTANT PART OF LEARNING. For the record, and to make yourself a great teaching tool for future seminars (as well as a recruiting officer for dealing with aggression!), don't forget to video comparative sessions every two weeks.

The real key now is variety in reinforcement, unpredictability in delivery of reinforcement, and timing of the session. It seems through your communiqués that you are doing it...good! In addition, continue to become "surgically precise" with your reinforcement application. Now, continue to slowly build his threshold (duration of time he will continue to stay calm, hold a stay, etc.), while you add to his session types.

Sounds to me like he's getting ample opportunity to "generalize" or learn to remain calm in a variety of contexts.

Finally, continue to look at your mathematical balance of reinforcements. Actually count the number of reinforcements Shadow gets when he has a marginal session versus an excellent session. There should be a noticeable difference. Pam, you have a natural analytical approach to your training. Very rare. You'll make progress when others won't.

Remember Pam! Ted's reminder: REGRESSION IS AN IMPORTANT PART OF LEARNING!

Good Pam! I am very proud of myself. Holy smokes! Talk about one of the greatest compliments of my life! I am thrilled, inspired, and excited!

Good Doggie! Shadow is doing a marvelous job and like Ted said, he is doing the best he can at this time.

I had some guests at my training facility—we were all training our dogs and I worked Shadow at a distance. Although we were far away, Shadow was shaking. He was glued to me and giving me great eye contact, but he was very nervous. I had no food with me but I stopped and petted him, let him go sniff and then called him back and petted him again. After about four repetitions of this he stopped shaking and then I put him away.

Shadow was great around the crowds of people on October 15. He was nervous today. I keep reminding myself, as Ted said, "regression is a normal part of learning."

OCTOBER 22 – DAY 147

Today was the same context as yesterday. I used food this time, but didn't count cookies as Ted recommended; I will try to do this in the future.

During the first session he was very nervous, although everyone was far away. Shadow was shaking again and biting my fingers when I was feeding him. I ended this session ten minutes after he relaxed. I used food, petting and praise.

The second session was slightly different. I had one person stand in the median with her dog while we heeled around her, gradually getting closer and closer until we were about 20 feet away. Then I had Shadow lie down and just tossed him food and praised him. A few times he lost focus and left me. I called him and he came instantly. This session lasted about 15 minutes. I also knelt down on the ground and just petted him and he seemed calm.

The third session was slightly different again. There were two people with their dogs on the median. I was heeling with him in the parking lot and gradually went onto the grass until we were about 15 feet away. He was great! Very calm, focused, mouth very soft, eyes soft. I used wads of food and ended this session after 15 minutes.

I am noticing that when I have the other dogs with me and I go to take Shadow out of the van he is shaking—perhaps he is nervous about what we are going to do? Even if it is just a play session, until he knows what we are going to do and where we are, he shakes.

All That Glitters Is Not Gold

OCTOBER 28 – DAY 153

More guests at my facility today. He was again stressed during our first session but relaxed toward the end of it. Shadow and I heeled outside around small groups of people and his attention to me was great. Later, I took him out when there were no people around and he was still a bit stressed.

During our next session Shadow and I did some heeling outside on the median with one person walking around, gradually getting closer and closer. He did great! His mouth was soft and his eyes and ears were okay.

Later I brought him into the building and instructed the eight people there to sit and not move. Shadow did some beautiful heeling and stands. Although he started out stressed, he very quickly relaxed. He was doing so well that I had four people stand up and Shadow was fine with that. I stopped in the middle of the room and had him lie down. I was petting him; he was starting to stress a bit and to stare at the group. I got his attention back to me and we heeled out of the building. We had gotten within five feet of the group.

Watch Out!!!! Cover Your Eyes!

You know that feeling you get when you are watching a horror movie and the heroine goes into her house at night and doesn't even turn the light on or lock the door behind her but you know the "bad guy" is waiting in the shadows…and whammo! Cover your eyes! You can't bear to watch! You cringe and hold your breath. Well that's how I feel when I read these next two journal entries…

OCTOBER 29 – DAY 154 Today I made a BIG mistake. When will I EVER learn to trust myself?? I brought Shadow into my building again. There were a few less people than yesterday and I asked them to move around slowly.

I was heeling with Shadow. Every time he approached one particular person he would lunge at her. One of the women in the group started yelling at me that I was jerking the leash (I was NOT jerking the leash!) and that I must drop it. I could tell that Shadow was very stressed during this session and I was afraid he would react to the woman's yelling with aggression. I continued to heel around the room; Shadow was still stressed but managed to stay with me. I was moving tentatively because I was completely freaked out myself by this person screaming at me. I fed him tons of food. Then, as that person was walking close to us, Shadow lunged at her again. I did drop the leash then (the other woman was still screaming at me, pressuring me to drop the leash, and it was hard not to) and as he approached her, I called him back to me. He came instantly and we heeled some more. **Good Dog!** Then Shadow lunged once again, more frenetically this time. These people were insisting that Shadow wouldn't bite the woman he lunged at, but I was sure the third lunge would end in a bite and told them so. I was starting to feel ganged up on and very angry. At that point I calmly heeled him out of the building.

Most people do not have an awareness of aggression and the counterconditioning or desensitizing process. I knew Shadow would bite if provoked further
with the yells and challenges—I was ready to bite these people too!—so I took
him out of a bad situation.

No lasting harm was done to his program, but I was angry with myself for putting him in the situation in the first place—putting him in a room with people
who didn't understand his issues or needs, or the goals I had for him.

Darn, Darn, Darn!!!

OCTOBER 31 – DAY 156

Well, today was a VERY baaad day. Carol came to my house to fix the computer. She was in the office and Shadow was in his crate in the bedroom. I
closed the office door and let him outside to urinate and eat. When he was
done, I let him inside, and stopped to stir dinner for three seconds. Apparently I didn't close the office door tight enough and Shadow pushed the door
open. The computer tech, thinking he was Beau since they look so much alike,
reached down to pet him. He lunged at her. She screamed, "He's biting me,
he's biting me!" then she turned away from him and he bit her on the elbow.
As she yanked it away, his teeth scraped her skin and drew blood. I had to call
him off twice before he could hear me and then I put him away. I did not yell,
just called him softly but firmly. If I had yelled, his stress level would have gone
even higher and he would have probably done more damage. I left him in the
crate for a few hours. When I came home from teaching, I let him out and he
was fine—no residual nervous behavior toward me or the other dogs.

Other than a bruised and sore arm, the tech was fine and very understanding.
The first words out of her mouth once I had cleaned up her arm, "What did
these people do to this poor dog to make him act like this?"

Great Pam! For not yelling in panic and staying calm while calling Shadow off
of Carol! Of course, I completely freaked out later, but by then he was back in
the crate, so my stress did not affect him.

Needless to say I was VERY upset and not thinking straight. I called a friend
and after crying on her shoulder, she helped me to refocus. I realized I needed
to work on some new behaviors: teach him a lie-down when aroused, and if

I goof again, to lie down in mid-lunge, and really work on doing crazy things with my hands and clicking him for watching them calmly.

Since Shadow's aggression is mostly sparked by rapid body movements, he needs to feel more comfortable looking at moving human body parts and have no reaction. At this point, I feel that if he is giving me solid "blinders on" kind of eye contact, there are still these scary things waving about in his peripheral vision. I don't feel he trusts me completely yet to keep him safe, but I am hopeful that he will in time. Cynthia reminded me (again!) that I have only had him for 20 weeks.

HINDSIGHT

It is obvious looking back that this was typical displacement aggression, directly related to the incident on October 29. People were yelling. I was stressed. Shadow was stressed. He had lunged at someone a few times and there was no "good, calm" session after that day in the same location with the same people. While the bite on October 31 did not have a lasting effect in terms of his entire desensitization process, it was certainly an unfortunate and horrific experience for all of us, one that I could have avoided had I listened to my heart and head (and made darn sure that the office door was shut tight!) I am extremely surprised though that there were no residual effects from this. If anything, he seems to be calmer! Do I know why he is calmer? Nope, I have no clue. Heck, he is a dog and who knows what a dog is really thinking anyway?

3

The test of a vocation is the love
of the drudgery it involves.

—Logan Pearsall Smith

The Light is on and Someone is Home...

NOVEMBER 1 – DAY 157

Took Shadow to my training facility today. I wanted to practice getting him to be non-reactive to certain stimuli. Because of the incident with the screaming women and the computer tech, I needed to make darn sure that Shadow had a super recall with major distractions—even if he was in high arousal—such as toys, sheep, or people. I had never done this before—trained a dog to come away from something during super-high arousal, so I "winged" it—and it worked!

Good Pam! Of course, I did not start with a human—I started with a toy.

 I threw a paper towel tube (no value to Shadow), told him to get it and then asked him to lie down as he was going toward it. I repeated this a few times and then raised the criteria. I pulled out a slightly higher value item (fuzzy Frisbee) and he was able to lie down in mid-chase about 50 percent of the time.

Just for the heck of it, I pulled out a tennis ball (SUPER high value) and he actually laid down about 40 percent of the time. If he did not lie down, I waited until he brought me the toy and we started over.

I also want Shadow to be calm around obnoxious hand movements. I sat down and started waving my hands in really bizarre and annoying ways. When I started, his eyes were big, but he didn't react and I rewarded him. Every time he looked at my hands and was calm, I gave him a cookie.

Marveling Pam! It is interesting to me to think of the true meaning of this exercise. I throw a toy he really wants and as he is running toward it in the typical top speed of a Border Collie, if I ask him to lie down, he will. Think about it—he can outrun me any day of the week with all four of his legs tied behind his back and yet he CHOOSES to play this silly game with me. Even if he "misses" and gets the toy rather than lying down, he is more than willing to try again. He has no leash on, no barrier, I am not blocking him or yelling at him if he doesn't lie down on my cue. This is not about "control" or "obedience." It is all about our RELATIONSHIP. Cool beans!

NOVEMBER 4 – DAY 160

Took him to a dog show and walked him around the parking lot on **harness** to work on desensitization to cars, people, movement, and noise. Shadow was a bit stressed at first and was shaking a lot. I stopped to do TTouch on him and he relaxed. We did some slow walking with eye contact and he was fine. Shadow is also getting good at letting me run my hands all over his body while he is standing still and doesn't try to stop me by turning his head toward my hand or sitting down!

Shadow was a little punishing to Cody today. At one point Cody was plastered against the wall, completely frozen. I went into the living room and softly called out, "Shadow." He growled and snapped at Cody… little baby steps. sigh…

Good Pam!! I am being much more cognizant of his own personal stress signals and in doing so, am able to control his behavior more in terms of not letting him get to the point where he would aggress. This, of course, helps me train him more effectively.

TRAINING CONCEPT

I use a sledding **harness** on Shadow when I take him out rather than just hooking the leash to his collar. He pulls less when he is on the harness and I don't want him to hurt his neck or trachea. I also don't want to get his **opposition reflex** in gear, which can then escalate into aggression. Opposition reflex is a natural reaction that causes the dog to pull or push against anything that is pulling or pushing against them. They have no control over it—like when the doctor taps your knee with that little hammer and your leg jerks. Pull on a dog and they pull against it. Punishing a dog for pulling would be the same as if the doctor punished you for "allowing" your knee to jerk!

I have subsequently learned to make no noise
ing a bully toward the other dogs. If I am com
than if I try to call him off. If I try to call him, f

NOVEMBER 6 – DAY 162

I went to John and Cynthia's house. I brought out a Boomer Ball® and let him push it around and practiced calling him off of it, without positive results. I called and he ignored me. I held the leash so he couldn't continue if he pushed the ball out of reach, and called him again. Then I just crouched down and waited until he came to me. If he came to me, I clicked him, petted him, and let him go back to the ball. Repeated this about five times. He really had a hard time doing this and never did come back to me instantly. Again, this is not about control, or disobedience, it is about building our relationship.

For our next session, Shadow and I were inside the fenced-in yard with John and Cynthia outside the fence. I heeled him back and forth and then let him approach the fence as they stood passively. If his expression was good, they praised and fed. He did wonderfully. I had them ask him for sits and downs and, if he remained calm, he got cookies. He only stressed once but with no reaction other than a tensing of his face.

Then I heeled back and forth along the fence while they moved as well. My **criteria** here was eye contact with me, no matter what they were doing. I released him verbally and let him look at them if he wanted to, reinforcing him for calmness. His mouth was slightly tight, but not bad. I put him away for about 15 minutes.

For our second session we did almost the same things. I changed the context by having John bring Mia (a dog) out while Cynthia made VERY weird body

TRAINING CONCEPT

Criteria: What I will accept in training for a particular session. For instance, let's say I am training a drop on recall and my dog has been taking three steps before lying down. My criteria for this training session may be that I will only reward those drops where he only takes two steps before lying down. If he takes three steps before lying down, he will not be rewarded and we will just start the exercise over.

ovements: bending over rapidly, stretching, arms waving wildly, cartwheels, lying down on the ground and rolling around. Shadow did not react to Cynthia or to Mia and I reinforced him for remaining calm. After a while, Shadow didn't want to even look at Cynthia—he wanted to look at me. His mouth was very soft this session. All in all, this was one of those great sessions that I wish I had videotaped!

NOVEMBER 10 – DAY 166

E-mail from Ted:

> Three important things to remember at this stage:
>
> **Stay on track with YOUR plan.** Don't get sidetracked by pressure!!!!!!! I know these folks mean well, but they don't live with Shadow, you do. YOU are the expert, Pam. When your confidence gets shaky, remember, Shadow counts on YOUR judgment and consistency, not the advice of others. You are on the right track now. It's a marathon. If you were off track, I'd tell you.
>
> **Time for some fun.** You've laid a foundation. Pick times to just PLAY!!! Play is an important component of learning. Let Shadow have some fun and don't wait till he's perfect. That will come.
>
> **Move on to other challenges.** Crate training (Shadow being comfortable in his crate while people approach) and desensitization are important but can be inhibitive if too much focus is on these types of sessions. Get Shadow into some difficult learning experiences such as agility work. Reinforce attempts to focus but don't expect perfection. VARIABILITY and ENRICHMENT are most important now. Keep up the EXCELLENT work, Pam. Have confidence and keep others out of your business if you can.

With this advice in mind I took Shadow for a long walk in the woods and he had a blast. I took him where I knew there would be no people so I could relax. The regular trail has too many people and I have to continually watch in both directions, which stresses me out. Really amazing things happened! After about ten minutes, Shadow's face softened to where I had never seen it before. He really is quite an adorable dog! I used some food, but mostly my presence and petting. He rolled in some really gooey stuff and the look of ecstasy on his face was priceless.

Ted is right, I haven't been having any "fun" with my boy and have been much too serious. Too much school makes Fido a dull boy! At this point, the process is still new to me, so having confidence doesn't come naturally—yet.

NOVEMBER 11 – DAY 167

Took Shadow to a fun match today. Everyone there was apprised of the situation—an aggressive dog in a room full of people—and instructed to remain seated while Shadow was in the building.

When I brought Shadow in, I stood by the door and had him sit facing me, and fed him. He was very nervous at first. Then I had him sit next to me in heel position so he could look at the crowd and he started to calm down. I asked him to lie down and he relaxed more. His eyes cleared, his ears went up, his mouth softened, and I ended the session. The entire session lasted about five minutes. I have to admit, I was a tad nervous myself in the beginning, but relaxed quickly.

One hour later I brought him inside again. He was calm almost from the beginning. One minute into this session he was raring to do something more than just stare at me adoringly. I took him into the ring and did some wonderful heeling with him for about four minutes. Then I had him lie down facing the crowd and he looked great! Coming out of the building he was a little stressed because we had to walk closer to the crowd, but he handled it well.

This last session was probably a bit much but Shadow handled it brilliantly! Good doggie! I am starting to slow down more, keeping the "hard" sessions shorter and I'm learning to break down behaviors into smaller pieces. Good Pam!

Rub a Dub Dub, One Smelly Dog in a Tub!

NOVEMBER 14 – DAY 170

Shadow and I took a long walk in the woods. He was very calm, happy, and having a ball! Tons of good smells and he found something disgusting to roll in. I let him, of course—how could I deny him such great pleasure? Naturally, there is always a price to pay and that came later in the bathtub!

He still has an issue with the tub, but I had him going in and out of it with ease after a few minutes and about a pound of food. Then I raised my criteria by adding the hose. He was nervous at first but went back in the tub with the greatest of ease. I raised my criteria again and added the hose running. Still okay—maybe a trifle nervous—but still going in the tub easily. At this point even though I did not change anything, he all of a sudden decided "Nope, can't do it, Mom." I tried for about another half hour in three to five minute intervals and couldn't get him to hop in and out like he had been doing.

If this were just a normal situation I would have ended it much sooner. However he really smelled BAD. Looking back, he was probably satiated with the food and/or stressed. In between sessions he drank water like a fish, which is a stress behavior. So, in the end, Jim came home, picked Shadow up and put him in the tub. Jim petted him while I bathed him. I want Shadow to eventually get into the tub on his own, hence pairing food with the tub, making it rewarding for him. Shadow was great though—eyes clear—and after a few minutes he stopped shaking. He stood there nicely and even handled the power blower very well, even on his neck, close to his head!

After the bath, I gave him his dinner. It took him quite a while to eat it and then he zonked out for the rest of the night. Maybe that is the key to Shadow—take him for long walks in the woods, give him a bath, and grossly overfeed him!

HINDSIGHT

Since the bite incident on October 31, he has been just great. Even at home his ears are up almost all of the time and his eyes are 95 percent normal. In addition, I realized that I had been letting him get away with things I shouldn't have: letting him sit on the kitchen chairs, and petting him every time he asked. Now I won't pet him unless he is "four on the floor," and if he bugs me, he gets no attention. He is now much calmer. Yet another no-brainer!

NOVEMBER 16 – DAY 172

I have been taking Shadow for walks in the woods for the last few days. Just having fun. While on our walks, I am continuing to train recalls, heeling, eye contact, and building our repertoire of reinforcers. I also started to teach him how to play tug, with rules. He is doing just fine and gives the toy instantly, not rebiting unless I ask him to. Smart doggie!

I am using a lot less food when there aren't people around. I find that at this stage, if there are people around and I try to use petting, he gets stressed, but if I use food he relaxes. I will try to add some toys, but am concerned the "toy mode" will rev him up too much, when calmness is what I am looking for. Perhaps by using some tug games at least there won't be running with tug. He is also getting a tiny bit better at **trading** stuff that is mine. Paper and my underwear are his favorite food groups.

TRADING CONCEPT

Trading for better value "stuff" is THE way to go when teaching a dog to relinquish objects.

More Interesting Than Spit on the Sidewalk!

NOVEMBER 22 – DAY 178

More long walks in the woods and yesterday he really wanted to heel rather than sniff and eat goose poo! Holy smokes! I am finally more interesting than goose poo! Now that's a real accomplishment!

I had a lesson today with Carolyn and we took him for long walks off leash around the farm. She had sheep in three pens around the farm and we just walked around. He ran around the pens a bit but when he saw me walking away he came instantly without me having to call him.

I thought the session went really well. Shadow was begging Carolyn for food in a GOOD way, not in a frenzied way. He eased up a great deal with his teeth so that by the end of the session, his mouth was nice and soft. His ears were up almost the entire time. On the next circuit of the farm, he was far away so I called him to me. I clicked him frequently for watching Carolyn calmly. We worked on lie-downs with him at a distance and he got better and better.

When we came home he was "holding" Cody; his head over Cody's neck, and Cody was frozen in place. For the first time, I walked between them (splitting) and Shadow didn't aggress—he just walked away! In addition, he is getting much better at letting me touch him in "scary" places—his hind end and tail.

I have signed Shadow up for a **Growl class**.

TRAINING CONCEPT

Growl class: A training venue where people with aggressive dogs can bring them to work on each dog's specific issues. This is NOT a "throw 'em in the ring together and let them work it out" mindset. It is a class where each dog is set up NOT to aggress, never pushing the dog beyond his limits, always striving for complete calmness in the desensitization and counterconditioning process.

Slow and Steady Wins This Race

NOVEMBER 25 – DAY 181

Took him to Jane's house to do agility. He was SUPER DOOPER! Jane is a little nervous about him, so I told her that if he approached she should turn sideways. He responded perfectly to that by walking away. He wasn't lunging at Jane—just soliciting food.

During agility, Shadow is beyond fast, which is certainly pretty to look at but in my mind not practical because wild, out-of-control zoomies are counter-productive to his mental state. So today we worked on slowing him down and getting more accuracy. He was calm, cool, collected, and very focused on me—not that he didn't know Jane was there, but he wasn't making an issue of it. I ended the session after 30 minutes when he dive-bombed my head, show-ing me he was too aroused to continue.

Good Pam! For not allowing Shadow to practice wild out-of-control behav-iors during agility. Practicing inappropriate behaviors can only get him into trouble later on. In my opinion, agility is all about calm, focused, smooth and controlled movement around the course.

At home we did some cuddle sessions (where I would lightly pet him all over and ever so gently hug him) on the floor and he was terrific! He and Beau have developed this new game of playing tug with the tennis ball. I think this is great because he usually steals the ball right out of Beau's mouth and Beau is starting to not let him do that anymore. Hurray for both of them!

Shadow still gets nervous at times when I ask him to "give" something he has that I don't want him to have. Yesterday we played the give-and-take-it game with a wadded up piece of paper that he stole out of the garbage. He was very nervous about giving it to me, rebiting the paper many times before he finally gave it up. Once he dropped it, I gave it back to him. Repeated this five times and he relaxed a little bit—not a lot—but it was a start.

NOVEMBER 26 – DAY 182

We had a lesson with Carolyn today. Our criteria and approach: the idea today was to do one easy thing, one hard thing, then back to one easy thing.

For our first easy thing we walked around the farm for 20 minutes. Shadow was calmer and relaxed faster than the previous session. His mouth was soft almost from the beginning. Carolyn was feeding him salmon and he forgot who I was. He was heeling with her all around the farm.

Then I raised the criteria. We now went into the obedience barn—a hard thing because it was inside and he had never been in the barn—and did some scent training with him, also difficult for him because he had never done it before. I think it would be great to engage his other senses—give him something else to do with that wonderful brain of his. He did quite well in the new location although he was a bit stressed, or maybe not stressed—maybe just unsure of what we wanted him to do. He kept grabbing toys and bringing them to me and trying all sorts of other behaviors. We did get him to smell the scent line for about a second or two and then ended that portion.

To finish up on an easy note (no scary location, no heavy brain work), we went outside and walked around the farm again.

NOVEMBER 27– DAY 183

Holy smokes! Shadow let me play tug with Beau and didn't bother us! At first he tried to horn in, but I positioned my body to repel him and he took the hint! Then he let Jim play tug with Beau and Cody while he sat on my lap! His heart was beating a mile a minute and he was vibrating. Jim said his eyes were VERY large, but I wasn't holding him—I was just gently stroking him, telling him what a great dog he is. He wagged his tail and let them play for a minute! A banner day!

I also worked him for a bit in the kitchen and he was phenomenal! He was STARVED to do training again! We did some retrieves, some heeling, and a few stands with me walking around him while he stood still! And he wasn't stressed about it! TRULY a great day!

HINDSIGHT

I am seeing the importance of not pressuring him (or me) with tons of precision competition behaviors, and just having fun. I have stopped my Autobahn race to get an OTCH (Obedience Trial Champion) on Shadow. Now that I am doing more and varied training, he is ready and willing to go back to the nitpicky competition training. And we are both enjoying it more.

Building the Empire State Building, One Brick at a Time

NOVEMBER 29 – DAY 185

Lesson with Carolyn today. We changed our context slightly and planned on doing one easy thing, two hard things, and end with one easy thing.

For the first easy thing (which actually turned out to be a hard thing!), we walked around the big field with sheep in the pen. Shadow ran around and around, but when I walked away and called him, he came to me. Wow! He looked at them again, but did not move away from me. I released him so he could go back to them, and then called him off again. Did some lie-downs as he was facing the sheep. He was walking up slowly to them with that really cool Border Collie crouch that is so amazing to watch (no, I did not train this as it is instinctual) and he was super.

He lay down facing the sheep and didn't feel the need to run back to me when I asked him to lie down. He stayed in position until I reinforced him! Smart doggie!

We then brought Dave (the dog) out to run around with Shadow— he did really well, except there was a tiff about a toy and Dave lost. After that, though, he was fine. Then we put Dave away.

Next, we went into the obedience barn and did some more scent training. He did much better than he did the last time. He was more relaxed about learning something new and being in a small place (the barn). To end on an easy note, we walked around the farm for a few minutes more and then put him away.

All in all, he did wonderfully—very relaxed, very responsive to me, and very calm around Carolyn and Dave while learning something new.

An e-mail to Ted:

> Just wanted to keep you posted on Shadow's progress. Nothing earth-shattering, just a gradual but STEADY reduction of stress-related "bad" behaviors. Even my husband (not really a dog person even though he likes the dogs—a good thing since we have so many!) has noticed a big difference in Shadow.

If We Both Agreed on Everything, One of Us Wouldn't Be Necessary

NOVEMBER 30 – DAY 186

Ted's e-mail response:

> A few things:

> 1. Pam, you have a systematic and thorough progression to your training with Shadow. Very uncommon. Where other people may have given up, I can tell that you won't.

> 2. Do NOT take Shadow to the aggressive dog class yet. That idea is a good one but he doesn't have a calm enough history behind him yet. Maybe six months from now. I know that you want to test him but the modeling of inappropriate behavior patterns will trigger many inappropriate behaviors in Shadow, which will linger for days (and subsequently increase the likelihood of accidental reinforcement and thus exacerbate aggression.) Remember, opportunities to rehearse poor behavior increase the probability of more poor behavior. Like an alcoholic going to a kegger after two months treatment. I would strongly recommend against it, but ALSO remember that YOU are the best judge with your animal. Weigh this decision carefully.

> 3. Although I realize your intent is to reinforce relaxation, I don't understand why you are bridging the animal for "looking around."

Shadow will look around anyway. Like it or not, you are shaping inattention—the last thing you need with an animal at his stage. Your thinking here is getting too complicated (which we all do sometimes). Stick to the basic principles of training, i.e., reinforce those things that you want to directly INCREASE and ignore those things you want to DECREASE. If you want Shadow to look at other people often, then bridge and reinforce it (and watch it increase!), however, I fail to see the purpose unless you are trying to avoid an aggressive reaction. If the latter is the case, you are going to get yourself in trouble. Better to bridge a true "relaxed" posture than shape "eye contact" with another person.

Excellent work with retrieval training. Exactly what I would do for a possessive animal. The best approach is to reinforce "letting go" with praise/food AND THEN give the object back. No tug of war...instead a party when he drops it! If he picks it back up on his own, do nothing, just wait. He'll drop it to get a positive reaction from you.

Your plan is working well. In the big picture, very little time has gone by. About the same amount of time a veterinarian would take to cure a chronic infection. Your work is a great model for others. I admire your complete dedication, discipline and focus. Many would have given up for an easy animal and would have slammed the door shut on their own expertise development. Shadow is making you a great trainer!

My e-mail response to Ted:

I read what you wrote and I have a few questions—I am not quite sure I understand.

1) The aggressive dog class will be with only four other dogs. Is this still too big a class to be in? It will be held outside on Carolyn's farm for a few weeks and then we plan to "take it on the road" and go to other types of fields, trails, etc.

2) The "looking at other people" where I praised and reinforced was not specifically for eye contact with that other person—it was for "looking calmly at another person." I thought that if his eye contact with me was so strong that he never looked at anything else, it might cause more of a problem if he did look away from me in times of stress and then got scared by what he saw ("Who is that scary baaaad person over there—I think I'll bite them and make them go

way.") My thoughts were, if I praised and reinforced him for look-ing calmly at someone else, it wouldn't be such a scary thing if he happened to notice other people. He has such issues with strangers' moving body parts that I wanted to reinforce him for looking and not reacting to people bending over, arms waving, etc. I haven't got to that part yet extensively, that will be in the future.

The bulk of my work is still building eye contact and focus with ME, but every now and then I do reinforce him for calmly looking at someone else. I just don't want him to be more neurotic about people than he already is. I have found that he seems to be a bit calmer now when he does see someone and doesn't react at all

Is my thinking faulty on this? I noticed that he still gives me wads of eye contact and attention and focus when I work with Carolyn—even yesterday she still had salmon and he gave me more attention than he gave her!

What am I missing? Thanks AGAIN!!!

P.S. Today is Shadow's six-month anniversary from the day we picked him up!

HINDSIGHT

WOW!! It has only been six months!!!! So much has happened, not only with Shadow but with my continuing development as a trainer as well. At times I feel we have made no progress at all, but I promptly squelch those thoughts. I am trying my damnedest to not concentrate on how long we still have to go. I am staying in the "here and now" and viewing each tiny lessening of stress and aggressive behaviors as unexpected gifts.

DECEMBER 1 – DAY 187

Ted's letter to me:

> Yes, I think you should wait a while. It's too soon for Shadow to be challenged near other difficult or aggressive animals when he's just starting to relax, feel safe, and understand the program. He needs a clear, secure, and relaxed environment for now. He needs to succeed often and be set up for success in order to build a new learning framework rapidly.

Point Two. As far as your eye contact strategy is concerned, I think I better understand what you mean. Not a horrible idea, but a very sophisticated one. Just be careful not to do this too often and don't make the mistake of trying to read a dog's mind...none of us get it right! (It's called "evaluator bias"—is often derived from erroneous and non-technical behavior concepts—and is usually the sign of trainers who begin to think of themselves as experts.) If you're carefully selecting these bridges based upon the criterion you've described (and not a guess of Shadow's "intentions") then it's a good idea. However, if you begin to overuse this technique, you may shape precisely what you don't want. Quit worrying about Shadow's stress level. It will go away by itself as long as you bridge appropriate behaviors and continue to have fun with him in a variety of settings. Proceed with care and watch for patterns of prolonged inattention to you, or prolonged attention to someone else when you are the primary trainer."

My response to Ted:

I realized last night (after re-reading your e-mail to me for the 20th time!) that when I write in my journal I know what I am talking about (background details), so I don't put those details in the journal. Then, when I forward them to you, I assume that you can read my mind!

I see the Growl class as augmenting what I am doing with Shadow—giving me slightly different stimuli but not that different from what I am already doing. I see it as doing more of the same, not as a higher "test." Total dog numbers/people numbers are deliberately kept low (three). Initially only two dogs are out at a time. Dog density is low—we use the whole farm and the fences to find appropriate, non-reactive distances.

The dogs that Shadow will be interacting with have some rehab history behind them or are "good" dogs. So we are not talking about complete raving Cujos here. The most provocative situation I can envision for me dog-wise initially is two dogs playing in the big field while I walk Shadow 300 yards away, clicking him for attention on me and calm observance of dogs in the distance, then refocus on me. Also, we are going to bring in "good" dogs of both sexes, different breeds, neutered and not, so dogs can have good experiences with other dogs.

Most important, the class allows me to work my dog around other people (other people are important for human-aggressive dogs!) who are sympathetic and better prepared than average to help me as I desensitize Shadow. Having extra sets of human eyeballs there to help observe is extremely useful for me as well.

In addition, in my classes, and any dealings with my dogs, my motto is always "set the dog up to be right." We always take our time and carefully watch the dogs, assessing each situation. The key is NOT to put them in a situation where they would "pop off."

As for the clicking while looking calmly at someone else—again, I don't do it all of the time ("be careful what you click for, you just may get it!"), but I have truly seen a marked difference in the way he handles himself around people. If I had to add a percentage, I probably click for eye contact with me about 97 percent of the time and three percent of the time I click for calmly looking at someone else. It all depends on the session I have set up, but that is about the ratio.

DECEMBER 3 – DAY 189

I took all of the dogs to my facility to train. Shadow and I worked on five different competition behaviors and all in all, he was fantastic!

Then some people came by (THANK GOD I lock the door when I am working Shadow) and looked in the bay window. They held up their Scottie for me to see and Shadow barked at them a bit, but was able to come to me (it took a few times of calling him) and then he was fine.

Once they left, we worked on lie-downs while Shadow was walking toward a stationary tennis ball. I tried a new way and it seemed to work. I had him on either the right or left of me and we approached the ball together. I periodically asked him to lie down, which he did.

We repeated this a few times. I raised the criteria and kicked the ball so that it was moving slowly and was able to get one or two lie-downs while it was moving slowly. He is so incredibly smart it scares me! I worked him about 45 minutes and he loved it and wanted more!

Last night he lay on the couch with me and fell asleep! He is so damn cute when he is sleeping. I am playing LOTS of the give-and-take-it game—he still seems to be possessive about objects and his jaws vibrate as he is giving me stuff, but he is improving.

Good Doggie! Have I mentioned that I think Shadow is brilliant?

Good Pam! I am taking things very slowly now, working on small snippets of behaviors, rather than lumping tons of things together. Rushing the desensitization process in the past actually drove him further away from me, instead of bringing us closer together. Now that I am TRULY in slow-down mode—not just a façade now—we are really starting to bond. The basement of the Empire State Building is now built!

All Pistons are Firing

DECEMBER 7 – DAY 193

Our first Growl class and I was proud!

First context: Shadow and I were outside of the big field, walking back and forth on the driveway. Sergeant (the dog) was inside the fence with John. Carolyn was walking all around. Shadow was very focused on me and I did not click him for looking at anyone else. He was a tad nervous before we actually began the session. He was shaking and his mouth was tight.

At one point Sergeant was on one end of the field and John the other, so we walked toward John. Shadow looked at him, but showed no reaction and then he just stayed by me. We gradually walked closer to the fence, until we were about five feet away and there was no reaction to either John or Sergeant. Total time—13 minutes.

Second context started about 15 minutes later. Shadow and I were inside the big field and Carolyn and Nell (a dog) were outside the fence. John was also walking around swinging a twig. Shadow was calm. He showed a little interest in Nell once I verbally released him and they ran along the fence together for a short spurt. Shadow came charging—and I mean charging—back to me, preferring to stay with me rather than play with Nell. He was on leash but it was dragging. Total time—ten minutes.

During both sessions he was well aware of the other people and dogs, but he wasn't making an issue about it and stayed focused on me. It was a great class all around. There was no popping off, all dogs were focused on their owners, all dogs remained calm.

Shadow still has this shaking thing going on for the first few minutes. He gets over it and I know it will take time to eliminate the initial shaking.

Last night I played the two-toy game with Shadow. I played very gently and calmly—he is now a bit wired about the game although he instantly gives when I say give. I will continue to play gently and see if I can get him to relax.

Will Wonders Never Cease?

DECEMBER 9 – DAY 195

Last night Shadow let me brush his butt while he was standing on the floor!!!!!

Today we had a private lesson. For the easy part we started walking in the big field and Shadow was relaxed. I then added the Boomer Ball and he pushed it all around as we walked. He actually pushed it up the big hill so he could be near me. Way to go, Shadow!

When he got tired, he left the Boomer Ball (!) and stayed with me for the remaining portion of the walk. As I was leaving the field, he ran back to the ball and wouldn't follow me. I went toward the house and waited, and waited. To get Shadow away from the ball, I clicked him if he looked at me. I called him—he wouldn't come to me and instead went back to the ball. I changed my strategy and stood by passively. When he stopped for an instant to look at me, I would click for eye contact and not call him. We repeated this for about ten minutes until he was more focused on me. At this time I called him and he was able to comply. I clicked and fed then let him go back to the ball. The next time he came to me much faster. At that point, I had to end the session because I had to go to work. He was completely fried anyway! We never did get to the "hard" middle part—he was beat and coming away from the ball was hard enough!

Once home, the dogs were fine for a little while. As I was preparing dinner (four hours later), Shadow attacked Cody. I don't know why. I left the room and it ended quickly (it always seems like forever but was actually about ten seconds). I put Shadow away to see if Cody had any wounds. He only had the barest scrape by one of his eyes and there was no spit on his body. I couldn't find any punctures. While I was checking Cody over, Beau came up to me and wrapped his legs around my neck, hanging on for dear life. It really upsets him when Shadow does this kind of thing. After I finished preparing dinner, I let Shadow out of the crate. Once they all finished eating, they were fine. Cody stood still with his body arced and Shadow looked at him, licked his lips and moved away. Good dogs!

TRAINING CONCEPT

You may be wondering why I didn't just wrestle the ball away from Shadow. First of all, he is faster and younger than I am. Secondly, it is my goal to become the "gate keeper, not the gate." Clicking Shadow for eye contact when he had the ball was the first step in getting him to come away from the ball. He already is possessive about objects and if I started to play the role of "the gate," then he wouldn't trust me around anything. We would end up in prey-ownership negotiations (and of course he would win—he is faster, younger AND has bigger teeth), which would increase his aggression or at the very least, evolve into the game that all dog owners love so much—"Keep Away." When he finally came to me, I fed him copiously and rather than dragging him away from the ball, I released him back to the ball. That way he could see that I wasn't keeping him from it and conversely, he would be more likely to come to me in high-drive situations since he would know that I am not a barrier or "gate." I also want him to know that just because I call him away from a toy, doesn't mean the fun is over. Au contrare, the fun is just beginning!

Please, Dear Dog Training God, tell me this will be all right in the end and Shadow will be a wonderful dog in all areas of his life! Sometimes I feel if I slow down anymore, I will be going backwards.... I know, I know, "one tiny approximation at a time." Maybe I should start a new 5,000,000 step program "ADA," Aggressive Dogs Anonymous, and our motto will be "One Approximation at a Time…"

I just let the dogs in from outside. Cody was licking his dinner bowl and Shadow went over to him. Cody tried to get out of the way but Shadow attacked. There were no puncture wounds, but there was spit this time. I did yell "Stop!" once and he instantly stopped. I then put Shadow outside again. I hated to yell, but he was really going after Cody and had him cornered with no possible escape. I know I am overprotective about Cody and either way I lose—I feel that Cody should be able to trust me and yet I KNOW it was the wrong thing to do (yell) at Shadow. Shadow hasn't done this kind of thing in a while and I thought he was over it. I KNOW this is normal doggie squabble stuff, but that doesn't make me able to cope with it better than the next "Joe." Sigh....

After this though, Shadow has been a "model" dog—very gentle and loving and not punishing to anyone. We were sitting on the couch and he was a calm, tired, sweet puppy (hard to remember sometimes that he is still only a puppy) laying in my lap and snuggling, every now and then reaching up to lick my chin. Sometimes I think he can read my mind.

For the past few minutes, I have been typing and Shadow came over to me. He had been sitting and I was petting him under the chin, telling him how much I love him. Suddenly, he STOOD UP AND PRESENTED HIS BUTT FOR ME TO SCRATCH! To the average person, this might seem like absolutely nothing to get excited about, but I am going to call it a gold star day!

Remarkable Day!

DECEMBER 12 – DAY 198

I took Shadow to my facility. We worked on heeling and stand for exams. I started to teach him to look and move to where I am pointing (I call these **directionals**), and had him walk up to a slowly moving tennis ball and lie down each time I asked him to. We also worked on recalls and stays.

He did very well with everything except the heeling—he seemed to be a bit distracted with that. I worked on touch desensitization with his front feet and touched him while he stood still, walked around him, and he was very calm about all of it. At the end of the session, we were playing the two-toy game and he could not give me the ball, so I ended the session and put him away.

Two hours later we had a private lesson. Our first easy context was to walk around the big field and then around the back of the farm. I rewarded him for calmness. He did engage with the sheep in the pen but I just kept walking. He did a beautiful outrun all around the big barn. Then he came back to me and continued with us on our walk. Total time was 20 minutes.

Good Doggie!! Holy smokes! Shadow came back to me instead of staying with the sheep! That is real progress! A few more bricks are being added to the first floor of the Empire State building.

For our second session of "doing something a bit more difficult," we went into the barn (even though Shadow is now comfortable in the doorway at home,

TRAINING CONCEPT

Directionals: If I point to the right he moves to the right, if I point to the left, he moves to the left. I use directionals as another way to make it fun for Shadow to move away from something scary.

other types of small places are still a bit scary) and tried some more tracking. Shadow really has no clue what I am asking him to do, but rather than go into displacement stuff or just go off and play with the tennis balls, he stayed with me and really tried to figure it out. He was quasi-successful, but I can tell he really doesn't understand the game yet. I worked him longer in this context than we had previously and he was quite willing to continue trying. Total time 20 minutes.

Great Doggie!! He is getting less stressed about learning new things and being in the barn. In the beginning, he would stress instantly if he did not understand something. AND, he chose to work with me, rather than play with the balls that were lying around!

Good Pam! For continuing to build that bank account, for without a great relationship, none of this good work would be happening! And good job for not pushing him beyond his limits, but steadily adding slightly different contexts with the focus always on calmness.

During the third session we did another hard thing. We brought Dave (the dog) out and Shadow greeted Dave nicely and then came to me. We then walked in the big field again. Most of the time Shadow stayed with me, but there were a few times he really alerted to Dave—legs stiff, tail held high, neck arched up. I called him to me and he came instantly each time. I got better at calling him faster, before his alert stance became more pronounced and possibly aggressive.

To work on "Shadow looking at Dave calmly," we had Dave lie down. (Lying down is a calming signal.) A few times Shadow's eyes were wide—not black, but very round. I worked on directionals, pointing toward Dave. Shadow would look down at the ground toward Dave and I would reward for calmness. Then I walked around and pointed in all directions and he was fine. Did this for about ten minutes and ended this portion. Total time: 20 minutes.

Good Pam!! My reading of his body language is improving in accuracy and speed, and I am becoming more skilled at stopping possible aggressive displays BEFORE they even start.

He was doing so well that we decided to do a fourth session. Carolyn wanted to see how all of my dogs reacted to each other, so I brought Beau and Cody out and let them run around. They did their usual stuff with Shadow chasing Beau (who had a toy) and taking the toy away from Beau. At the same time Cody barked and chased both of them, body slamming Shadow, biting his butt and back. Shadow completely ignored Cody. I wanted Shadow to leave Cody and Beau alone, so I started to click and treat him for leaving them alone. I don't really know if he understood what I was clicking for. Then I just asked everyone to lie down and fed them for a few minutes. I put Beau and Cody back in the van. Total time ten minutes. (Please don't feel bad for my other dogs, I do a great deal of work with Beau and Cody. I just don't mention it here because this is Shadow's story. Do I have a life beyond dogs yet? No.)

We ended the day with a walk around the farm for five minutes. I used much less food overall and utilized more petting. Shadow was VERY calm most of the time. A few times Carolyn leaned down slightly and he was fine with it. She even had him target her hand and he remained calm. She also did a little bit of hand-feeding FOR THE FIRST TIME! Up until today, all of her feeding of Shadow has been throwing the food on the ground. We feel that some of his aggressive behaviors may stem from a previous history of things being taken away from him in a negative, punishing, prey-ownership negotiation way, creating a possession problem.

I am very excited about today's sessions—we added many more contexts than we had previously, but they were easy enough for him to handle. I do not feel that I have pushed the envelope with him yet, which is fine with me. I am very proud of his accomplishments so far.

There have been no displacement behaviors since the few tiffs on the 9th. I do NOT think they were in relation to any of the work I have been doing with him. Shadow may have just been overly tired and cranky. Cody does get annoying and, when he was younger, Beau used to attack him. Cody reminds me of a bumbling but well-meaning guy who annoys people and then when someone hauls off and hits him, can't figure out why. "What did I do?"

Beau and Shadow were just playing tug with a tennis ball VERY gently!!!! Beau was actually trying to encourage Shadow to tug it!!!!

World Traveler

DECEMBER 16 AND 17 – DAYS 202 AND 203

Jim and I spent the weekend with the dogs at my brother's house in Massachusetts. We went up Saturday morning and came home Sunday. We left the dogs in the van at first while we were visiting. Then I had them run around his backyard for a bit. Shadow was very stressed and only wanted to chew his tennis balls. He was not interested in running after the other dogs. At one point, while stroking him lightly on the back as he chewed the balls, Cody walked over. Shadow growled—I don't know if it was directed at me or Cody but we both left him alone.

A few hours later I gave them another session in the backyard and he was still not acting himself. Then we went to the hotel, and all of the dogs went nuts! They ran around the tiny room like maniacal deranged creatures, completely out of control. I started eating some snacks and since they know that I share, they all quieted down. Shadow slept in his crate all night without a whimper.

Sunday morning we met with my friend Eve to do some training. I did not bring Shadow into the building. I felt that he was too stressed by all of the new experiences (being in a hotel room for the first time, stuck in the van for so long the day before, not being home in familiar surroundings) that I didn't want to stress him even more. We just walked around outside and I let him sniff to his heart's content, then put him back in the van and drove five hours home.

Once home, he had a tiff with Cody. I don't know the details—they were in another room, so I didn't get involved at all, just let them work it out themselves. No spit on Cody or Beau, and Cody just avoided Shadow for a few minutes. Since then he has been fine. He seems really happy to be home—kind of a big sigh, "there's no place like home!" I agree!

Good Doggie!! It was REALLY hard for him to deal with so many new things all at once, but he handled it without going completely insane.

Is That a *Good* Dog I See Under There?

DECEMBER 18 – DAY 204

SHADOW JUMPED IN MY LAP AND LET ME HUG HIM!!!!!! I did not try to lure him into doing it, he just did it. I have been very depressed and cranky today. He just leaped into my lap, sat there calmly while I hugged him and cried with joy! He will not let me pick him up—he either moves his head as if to bite me, or pees all over me, so this is an amazing breakthrough, made more wonderful because it was his choice entirely. This evening, when Jim came home I asked him to jump in my lap to show off for Daddy and he did it! We both made a huge fuss over him and he seemed to be very proud of himself as well.

DECEMBER 19 – DAY 205

At our private lesson, Shadow was stressed so we just walked around the farm and did not add too many different contexts.

Good Pam! For not pressuring Shadow and for going with the flow!

At first we walked around the farm, feeding and petting him for being calm. He saw the sheep in the pen and before he started running toward them I asked him to lie down. He did! I went over to reinforce and then released him. Then I walked away. When he stopped chasing the sheep up and down the fence, I called him and he came to me again. I heavily rewarded Shadow with food and praise. Then I released him verbally to go back to the sheep as I walked away. He came to me and stayed with me. I enthusiastically rewarded him again with food and praise. At that moment he saw the donkey and started chasing her and barking. I called him to me and he came again! MEGA rewards—food, petting, praise. The whole enchilada!

For our second context we walked around in the big field, playing Follow the Leader.

Then I showed Carolyn how he will now run between my legs without being stressed, so we added her as a different context. We played a recall game and when he came back to me, I spread my legs and threw the cookie so he would go between them. Carolyn was standing directly behind me with her legs spread so he would go through both of our legs. He did it without a problem. We repeated four times and he never stressed out. Going through our legs was great because in the past "people bending over" or tight places have scared him. Today he did not hesitate at all, nor did he stress out.

Shadow learning to run between Carolyn's legs.

For the third context we walked toward the house as Carolyn cleaned up dog poop using potentially scary utensils—I didn't know if he would react badly to a pooper scooper. Shadow and I played the give-and-take-it game with the tennis ball. He was fine and was eventually able to put the ball into my hand rather than dropping the ball on the ground. I see some trust building here! Wahooie!

During the fourth session he found the Boomer Ball. We walked to the sheep pen. He followed me, pushing the ball. When he took a breather and looked up at me, I called him to me while I was standing next to the sheep. It took him two tries before he could leave the ball to be by the sheep and me. Then I walked back to the ball and when he relaxed around the sheep, I called him to me to get the ball. We rotated between the sheep and the ball a few times and each time he came to me faster and faster.

At that point I walked away to another part of the farm. When I could see that he had stopped for a moment, I called him. He couldn't find me at first, but kept trying until he did. We did not do any work in the barn, nor bring out any other dogs. Carolyn fed him a little bit and he only jumped on her once in a frenzied sort of way. The rest of the times he either sat or lay down automatically and waited patiently. I think he was still stressed because of our weekend trip. His pupils were normal, but his eyes didn't look calm and his body was tighter than it has been in a long time.

He had a big sticker bush embedded in his tail but he sat down for me and let me untangle it without moving at all! He is still sensitive about his hind end, so this was fantastic.

Once home he was completely fine. No redirected aggressive behaviors at all. I crated him while I typed this. I don't want to push my luck!

HINDSIGHT

The purpose of the fourth session was again to show him that I am not a barrier to his fun. If he comes to me, he gets more "stuff," such as sheep, balls, playtime, and food. He certainly could have chosen to stay by the sheep (he was off leash and let's face it, no one can outrun a Border Collie!), but by now we have built up our relationship so that he WANTS to play the "game" with me.

DECEMBER 21 – DAY 207

We had our second Growl class today and he was a good boy!

First session. Shadow and I were outside of the big field, walking back and forth next to the fence. Sergeant and John were inside the fence. Carolyn and Cynthia were walking all around the outside of the fence with me.

Carolyn approached us and in a loud voice, started talking to Shadow and me. He ran towards her, soliciting food. I called him, he came, but then started to go to her again. I called him twice—he didn't respond, so I ran away. He came flying after me. Once he was more focused on me, I allowed him to go visit. Carolyn and Cynthia were able to feed him without incident. A few times he seemed to be interested in Sergeant, but when I called him, he instantly complied. Then he just started running up the fence line so I ran away again. I did not call him, but he ran after me at top speed. Shadow was very focused on me after that and I did not click him for looking at anyone else.

We did a round-robin kind of thing with all three of us calling him, asking for a lie-down and feeding. He was very calm and his mouth became really soft. During this session, I let the leash drag the entire time. Toward the end, Carolyn leaned over slightly and fed him while he was in a down. Then she kneeled down, continued to feed him, then pointed away from her, tossing cookies so he would leave her. She did this about eight times (pointing for him to go away) and he was great with it.

Carolyn was reaching down to pick up a cookie she had dropped. Shadow ran over to her but wasn't nervous about her leaning over to pick up the cookie!!!!! Total time for this session was 30 minutes.

Good Doggie! Shadow is starting to relax more when people lean over, even amidst a few distractions—people and another dog.

Brave Pam! For trusting our relationship enough to drop the leash!

For the second session, Shadow and I were in the big field. Carolyn, John, Cynthia, and Nell were outside the fence. Shadow was relaxed. He showed more interest in Nell then he did last time. I called him—he couldn't do it—so I ran away and boy did he come flying! I love to watch him run! I heavily rewarded him with massive petting and cookies and released him again. He and Nell ran back and forth, up and down the fence line, having a grand old time. When I sensed that he would respond (watching his body language and speed of the chase slow down), I called him and he came instantly. I heavily rewarded again with petting and released him to play. Each time he came back faster and faster and then didn't want to leave me. I used a little food in this context but not as much as in the first session—and much more petting.

Cynthia and Carolyn came up to the fence and were feeding him for lie-downs. Most of the time he will automatically lie down when they call him. They started out by tossing him food, then Carolyn leaned over and hand fed him through the fence. His mouth was soft, but Cynthia said that even though his eyes were clear they widened just a tiny bit the closer Carolyn's hand got to him. Then Cynthia did the same: leaning down and feeding and he remained calm. His mouth was like butter during this session and pretty much remained soft the entire time. Total time for this session was 25 minutes. Again, he was well aware of the other people and dogs, but he wasn't making an issue about it and stayed focused on me.

Wow! Shadow responding positively and calmly to other people!

When we came home I let him run around outside for a few minutes. I let him in and he seemed a bit nervous. He dive-bombed my head and his body seemed a bit tight. He looked nervously at Cody and Beau, so I put him in his crate and he is now napping. Will see later (I'll probably give him about an hour nap) if there is any residual displacement stuff.

Will There Be Coal In Your Stocking?

DECEMBER 22 – DAY 208

Nope, no residual stuff yesterday. He and Beau were playing very nicely, doing their tug game with the tennis ball. Today I worked the boys in the building and did a few competition behaviors with Shadow—he seemed unsure and then decided he would rather play with the ball. I ignored him until he dropped the ball and came to me. We did a little heeling and some recall games, and his mouth and body softened. He has this initial zoomie thing going on where he gets all revved up for the first few minutes and then relaxes.

We played the two-tug game and he did great. I dropped the toy after about two to three tugs before he started to get too wired. As soon as he dropped the one in his mouth, I encouraged him to take the other one. Periodically I threw it rather than have him retake it from my hand. We played for a few minutes and I ended the game. He did not have any problem with me reaching down to pick up the other toy.

DECEMBER 23 TO 25 – DAYS 209 TO 211

On the 23rd, Shadow was completely wired—not attacking the dogs but he seemed to be very needy of me. If I ignored him he went around and stole things. I tried to do TTouch on him and he just couldn't calm down.

The next day was somewhat better, although he was constantly stealing things. Where did this come from all of a sudden? So I kept putting him in his crate for a few minutes at a time. He did better with TTouch and calmed down nicely.

On Christmas he was very needy again. Shadow was in the crate from 10:30 a.m. until we got home around 6:00 p.m. I was trying to type and he kept stealing stuff, so I closed the door. WELL—he became angry and started banging on the door to come into the office. I asked him to lie down and he did (I could hear the big sigh and THUNK!) and then he attacked one of the other dogs—don't know who. I know it was hard for him to be in the crate that long. Usually when I know he has to be crated for long periods of time, I try to give him some really vigorous exercise to counteract the inactivity.

I did TTouch on him and he was rubber boy; he lay down on his back and went to sleep. I truly understand the old adage "Let sleeping dogs lie!" Merry Christmas, boys!

DECEMBER 26 – DAY 212

We had a private lesson today and for our first session we just walked around the big field. He kept going back and forth between stress and calm. Although it was subtle, I could observe it. This is how he'd been at home for the past few days, so it wasn't a surprise and I did not feel like this was a setback in training. I feel it was a direct result of inactivity due to very cold weather and my resistance to going outside.

Because Shadow has a hard time letting me reinforce Cody or Beau (he horns in, pushing them away or aggressing at them) we worked on name recognition as well as having Shadow remain calm even if I wasn't reinforcing him. During this session I let all of the boys run around and practiced calling them one by one, only reinforcing the dog whose name I called, whether or not they all came to me (which they did). I could say "Banana Come" and they would all come. They all did wonderfully and Shadow was super. He had been having a bit of a problem with being so needy and I thought that this would be a good way for him to relax. I also realized that I am on too much of a 1:1 ratio of reinforcement and am truly going to make more of an effort to be more variable.

At one point, Shadow was in mid-chase after Beau, I called him and he came back to me at warp speed. Sometimes I feel that I do so much work with him and sometimes I feel I don't do enough. Carolyn feels that I do "just right."

Give Yourself a Break Pam! Am I an overachiever or what????

Came home, put him in his crate for half an hour and then let him out. He has been absolutely super—very calm, not needy. While I cleaned the closet, all the dogs lay on the couch TOGETHER and went to sleep! Good doggies!

Later, as I was trying to type a little bit, Shadow started stealing papers, so I played the "calling one dog over and ignoring the other dogs and feeding the dog I called" game and he relaxed. It was so cool—he was just cuddling with Jim with this sleepy-eyed look on his face. I did some TTouch on Shadow and he was fine, and he even let Beau play with the ball. They have been playing tug with the ball every day now and although Beau always lets him win, I see this as a great improvement.

DECEMBER 28 – DAY 214

Today was Growl class. Sherilyn was our guest "dog bait." (Yes, we all have a sick sense of humor.) We started with Shadow and me, Carolyn, Cynthia, and Sherilyn outside of the big field, walking back and forth next to the fence. Sergeant and John were inside the fence. We told Sherilyn not to feed Shadow from her hand or make direct eye contact, but rather to arc around him and to throw the food towards his rear if he approached her, so that he would turn away from her to get it. While everyone was just milling around, I kept Shadow occupied with toys and downs and eye contact with me. I released him a few times to approach them so they could feed him. They all had him lie down and then threw the food behind him.

To change the context slightly and add some noise to the session (we have always been pretty quiet up until now), Carolyn started talking in a REALLY loud and obnoxious voice, "Hey lady, can I pet your dog?" while she approached us. I, of course, replied, "SURE and you can kiss him on the face too!" Yes, we really do have a sick sense of humor… We repeated this a few times, with me verbally releasing Shadow to approach her and then calling him back to me.

A few times when Carolyn and John called Shadow, he wouldn't go unless I released him. Interesting! At one point, Sergeant ran up to him and Shadow turned away and started sniffing; a calming signal to Sergeant. Shadow was very focused on me and I did not click him for looking at anyone else. He was very calm and only in the very beginning was he nervous and shivering.

Cool Beans!!! Shadow won't go to anyone else unless I release him and give him permission!

I again had the leash dragging the entire time. Sherilyn was surprised at how well Shadow behaved. She said that she never would have known that he was aggressive if we hadn't told her. Total time for this session was 20 minutes.

For our next session, Shadow and I were in the big field. Carolyn, Cynthia, John, Sherilyn, and Nell were all outside the fence. Shadow showed some interest in Nell, but was looking to me much more. Only once did he have a hard time coming to me when I called, so I ran away and he came to me right away. A few times I didn't call him to me and he came on his own. He and Nell ran back and forth and up and down the fence line. The funny thing is that both dogs can fit through the gate but they prefer to run back and forth on opposite sides of the fence. I called him, he came, and I heavily rewarded with petting and released him again to play. Each time he came back faster and faster and then didn't even leave me at all. I used a little food in this context but not as much—much more petting.

John and Cynthia came up to the fence and were feeding him for lie-downs. His mouth was soft, and his eyes were very clear and normal—no widening of his eyes this time. His mouth pretty much remained soft the entire time.

At the end of the session Carolyn came over, fed him, and then got down on her knees to hand feed him. He stuck his head through the fence to sniff her face and was calm. She started to wiggle her arms and he did fine. She did it again, wiggling them a bit too vehemently this time. He didn't do anything to her, but he became tense, so I asked her to stop.

Shadow was calm all night. He let me clip his toenails and trim his feet and brush him. He was also nice to the dogs all day. Jim was home in the evening and he said that all of the dogs just laid around and slept. Eve (my friend from Massachusetts) called and "yelled" at me for thinking I don't do enough with him! She said that I am doing a wonderful job. Sometimes I get lost in the notion of all the work that still needs to be done with Shadow and get, not discouraged, but a bit overwhelmed. I have to remind myself to "throw out the BIG picture and focus on the small steps."

TRAINING CONCEPT

Whenever my students have a dog with issues, I tell them, "Picture your perfect dog. Imagine each and every detail of this perfect dog. Got it? Now forget it and work with each issue as it arises. If you focus on your perfect dog picture, you will never move forward and you will get depressed. If you work on each tiny approximation, one day you WILL have your perfect dog." Good advice, eh?

At the end of the day I wrote an e-mail to Ted:

> Hope all is well with you! All in all I am pleased with our boy's progress. I have learned that he does better all around with a little "crate time" thrown in periodically throughout the day. Otherwise he just gets too stimulated—although how stimulating Jim and I are is suspect! Even if his crate time is just five minutes at a time, I think it helps. He doesn't seem to know how to quiet himself down like the other boys do—but then again, they didn't know how to do it at first either.
>
> I am sending you a video of four training sessions. You don't have to return it—I made an extra copy for you. One night when you can't sleep, this should make you pass out within minutes! (Grin.)

He That Dare Not Grasp the Thorn, Should Never Crave the Rose

JANUARY 3 – DAY 220

Shadow has been mostly fine over the past few days. I took him to Carolyn's on New Year's Eve day just to play with the Boomer Ball and we both had a blast! We walked around the big field and he followed me with the ball. The snow was about a foot deep. Then it took me about 20 minutes to get him away from the ball. I clicked him for looking at me and if he seemed focused, I called him. Nope, can't do it. I left the field and hid behind the truck. He kept looking around for me, but could not leave the ball. He finally got it stuck between the fence and rubber snow fence, so I came back to him to help him get it. At that point he was completely frantic with his eyes wild; growling and attacking and biting the fence. I picked up the ball and did not give it back to him. He did not try to get the ball. His eyes spoke volumes—"THANKS for taking this away from me, I just couldn't stop!" His mouth was bleeding and running rivulets of blood—he must have bitten his tongue. Before I put him away, I did some TTouch on him, and he relaxed instantly. Amazing that he actually let me take the ball. Good dog Shadow!

JANUARY 4 – DAY 221

Private lesson today. For our first session we were in the big field and there were two flocks of sheep in pens at opposite ends of the field. We started walking around, reinforcing him for being with me and giving me eye contact. We did a round-robin between the two flocks. I called him to me, rewarded heavily, and we did some "walk-ups" and "lie-downs." Then I either released him to see the sheep or called him back to me to go see the other flock. There were a few times that he couldn't lie down—as he was running towards the sheep—but when I called him, he came back to me instantly. Cool beans! I was very proud of his walk-ups and lie-downs. Carolyn was too! We had been practicing this with a rolling tennis ball. My reinforcers were food, TTtouch, and letting him go back to see the flock. I am going to continue to add tennis balls and other types of toys to be more variable in how I reinforce—yes, I finally realize I have become a bit too predictable. Session lasted about 30 minutes.

Second session. We added Cody to the equation and Shadow found it harder to listen to me with Cody chasing after him. So, Carolyn fed Cody and Shadow got his hearing back. Did the same round-robin game that we did in session one. Session lasted about 20 minutes.

Third session. I put Cody away and brought out Beau. I then became "invisible" to Shadow—not on purpose of course! We walked away to the other flock as they "churned butter"—like the fairy tale about the tigers that ran around the tree and ended up being butter. Beau was the first one to come all the way to me. They both looked at me quite often, but when I called they just couldn't do it. After a few minutes, they were both coming to me, eating food, and as a mega-reward, got to go see the sheep again. They came back to me faster and faster each time. To end the session—they were both exhausted—I left the field and waited by the van until they actually came up and touched me. Then Shadow found the Boomer Ball, but thankfully got it stuck under the truck. Funny how I can (mostly) call him away from sheep, but can't call him off of that ball! Session lasted about 20 minutes with another 10 to15 minutes waiting for them to come to me. I came home, put Shadow in his crate to rest for half and hour, and then let him out for half an hour. We all took a nap.

Later that night Shadow was a model doggie —very calm, clear, content, relaxed. I did some group stays in the kitchen with the boys and they did well.

JANUARY 5 – DAY 222

While he was still in the van, just before starting the session, I fed him a few handfuls of food and did some Ttouch on him. When I first took him out of his crate he was shaking, but after the food and TTouch, he relaxed a bit.

John and I got together to work on Sergeant and Shadow. He and Sergeant were in the big field and Shadow and I were on the driveway. Shadow was a bit startled when Cynthia walked up behind us. He barked at her three times and started to run toward her in a crouchy, fearful manner, but when I called him, he came instantly. I started to walk away and he stayed with me and we practiced heeling. Then I released him to "go visit" and he gave Cynthia some nice lie-downs for cookies. He jumped on her a few times, but in a "What kind of cookies do you have?" way, nosing her fanny pack. He instantly lay down when she asked him to and then stopped jumping completely. I went back to practicing heeling, and he was just super. His facial expression was tight at the beginning, but his mouth was very soft and his face smoothed out quickly.

Once we came home, I put him away for half an hour, let him out for half an hour, and then we all took a nap. He was out of the crate for the rest of the night. Again, he was a model doggie! I think I am finding out some valuable information here, in terms of how to manage him after a training session for optimum calmness at home. Very exciting! Cody on the other hand was a big pill, but Shadow did NOT react!!!!!!!!!

JANUARY 6 – DAY 223

Worked on scent articles a little bit and I think there is the barest glimmer of understanding.

I took him to the vet in Yardley again to get blood drawn for the thyroid test (they lost the other blood in the mail…) and a rabies shot. He did quite well, considering. He wasn't as relaxed as he was the first time, probably because I was more nervous. I held him and the vet drew blood from his hind leg. He struggled a bit but calmed down. He wasn't shaking, nor did he try to bite. His eyes remained clear and weren't excessively round.

When it came to the exam part, the vet had to listen to his heart. I had him between my legs, facing the same direction I was. She came up behind us and reached down to put the stethoscope on him. He was okay with that for a few seconds and then he urinated on me. He wasn't shaking, nor was he trying to bite at all. He let me hold his mouth open and show the vet his teeth—good doggie! And good Pam for training him to accept that! There have been no residual displacement behaviors. In fact, he has been very subdued and calmly lovey-dovey.

TRAINING CONCEPT

Accepting handling calmly is an important skill that every dog should learn. There are so many dogs that need to be put under, or muzzled and wrestled to the ground by five football players, just for clipping their toenails! I teach my dogs to accept all types of handling, including complete grooming, ear cleaning, eye drops, mouth exams, etc.

JANUARY 8 – DAY 225

The goal of the sessions today was to change the context very slightly, continuing to shoot for calmness. We added different people and gave him the opportunity to interact with new dogs and new locations, having the leash drag in some instances. (In the desensitization process, it is important not to get bogged down by keeping the sessions exactly the same all the time. So while it doesn't look like we were doing anything noteworthy, these contexts are all adding to the construction of the Empire State Building.)

In our first session, Cynthia was in the front yard, kneeling down. Shadow and I approached her with Carolyn walking behind us. Shadow ran up to Cynthia and jumped on her. She ignored him until he lay down. At that point he stopped jumping up completely. Shadow and I walked back and forth. When I told him to "go visit," he approached Cynthia and Carolyn. I decided that I didn't want them calling him to come if I was working with him on eye contact, and I don't want him to rush up to people anyway. We did some heeling toward them and then away from them and he was super. I used toys, food, petting, and praise. Put him away after about 30 minutes. The break between sessions one and two was very long—probably about one hour.

Second session. Shadow and I were in the big field; Nell, John, Cynthia, and Carolyn were outside the fence. I had him off leash. Shadow did not seem that interested in Nell—he wanted Cynthia and John and their food. He did some fence chasing but then was doing some very wide arcs, lots of sniffing, scooping up snow, and was just generally unfocused. His body seemed tense to me and I tried to get him come to me. He came a few times, but would only let me touch him for a few seconds and would then leave me. When he did not come, I walked away in hopes of getting him to follow me.

It took him longer than usual to come to me as I was leaving. In the beginning, Cynthia suggested that I take the leash off and leave his harness on. His face, mouth and body seemed very tight. I was able to loosen up his mouth a bit, but he just looked weird. Hard to describe it—just a feeling. So, I tried a few things to regain his focus. It only worked up to a point, so I ended the session.

Cynthia felt that by taking the leash off, I had changed the context, but didn't lower the criteria enough. We also realized that during the first session of each class, he never really sees John because John is working Sergeant. In the second session, we "seem" to be adding a new person. Next time, we are going to have John join us without Sergeant.

I felt that he was very unfocused today, especially in session two. Normally he doesn't shake in the crate before the second session, but today he was shaking before I took him out again. His mouth was very hard and never loosened up. Could it be from the vet? We were just there two days ago. Could it be from taking the leash off? I normally let it drag so I don't know how much bearing that had. It is on his harness so it doesn't pull on his neck—he could know when it is there and when it isn't. Could it have been that he heard Cody barking? Could it be that he is just a dog? I don't know at this point, but I will continue to think about what was so different to cause him to be so nervous. There was no aggressing though, no barking or lunging, his eyes were a perfect shape and color, and his ear carriage was great. It was just a feeling and I am learning to trust my feelings. **Good Pam!**

We came home and I let the boys outside, Beau and Shadow were playing. When they stopped, I called them in, gave them cookies, and took a two-hour nap. I think I will crate him a bit more today, just in case there is any residual stuff going on.

JANUARY 9 – DAY 226

He has been great today. John, Cynthia, and I went to my building tonight to train. I put them behind some baby gates at the end of the building. I brought Shadow in and we stayed about 40 feet away. I had him on leash and tied the leash to my waist so my hands were free. I had him lie down next to me and massaged and fed him. At first he was shaking and very tight. After about ten minutes, he finally relaxed. Total session: 15 minutes and half a pound of kielbasa.

No residual stuff with Shadow tonight—very lovey-dovey, without being obnoxious. I took a cookie out of the box for ME to eat. Shadow took one look at it and ran into his crate, thinking it was for him. Silly boy!

JANUARY 11 – DAY 228

Took Shadow to my training facility again. Cynthia was there. I had him tied to my waist and I stood this time. He relaxed very quickly and his mouth was soft. Glanced occasionally at Cynthia, but no big deal. I tried to do some touching but he didn't want to be handled and sat in avoidance. We walked around a little bit, staying far away from Cynthia, and practiced attention heeling. Played a recall game. He saw a tennis ball but I didn't want to rev him up, so I ignored it and then he ignored it. Total session lasted about seven minutes.

At this point I didn't want to use toys because he gets too excited when we play. I can use toys on the farm, but that is 65 acres. My building is only 30 x 58, and I don't want him, in the full arousal of play, to get scared and possibly lunge at a person.

JANUARY 18 – DAY 235

I haven't been doing much of anything with him since the 11th. Today was Growl class. First session. All of us humans walking around the big field—no other dogs. Me, John, Cynthia, and Carolyn. We just walked around and if Shadow approached any one of them, they would ask him to lie down. If he jumped, they turned, and someone else called him and asked for a lie-down. Food was thrown behind him. At times they would do some directional pointing with him. He didn't get it right too often but he wasn't stressed about it at all. We did this for about 20 minutes. He also found a toy and I threw it in all directions. He was calm, cool, collected. When we all walked out of the field, Carolyn and Shadow walked out through the gate at the same time and he didn't have the slightest issue with it at all! His whole posture was fantastic the entire time. His mouth was very soft almost from the beginning. I remember, a short seven months ago, Shadow was aggressing in tight places with the other dogs. This time, people were squeezing him, so this was a super dooper event.

Second session. All the people were outside the fence, along with Nell. Nell was being silly today and she came into the field with Shadow. She was very frantic (barking and other types of obnoxious behaviors) and he avoided her. We walked off and she left us alone and went back to Carolyn.

At the end of the session, Nell ran into the field again. They both had toys. Nell was really being stupid, pestering him and trying to steal the toy out of his mouth. He told her what for, I kept walking and didn't look back. Shadow acted completely appropriately—he held Nell down only using his body position, but had his face pointed toward me. Practicing proper doggie etiquette without leaving puncture wounds or blood is a new thing for Shadow. I am so proud! (Miss Manners would be proud, too!)

The Good News is "Behavior is Not Static." The Bad News is "Behavior is Not Static."

JANUARY 25 – DAY 242

My 45th birthday. Yucch! Growl class.

Wasn't great but wasn't terrible. I tried feeding Shadow in the van, closed the door, opened the door and fed, then shut the door. Repeated five times with a minute or two between feedings. I would like him to be more relaxed before taking him out of the van because he still does a lot of shaking. Didn't work well. We were on our way up to the big field to walk around—at least that was the plan. He was very nervous, his cheeks were blowing, he was very frantic, his face looked funny and his body was very tight. I knelt down to do TTtouch on him.

I asked everyone to go back into the house while Shadow and I just walked around until he could focus on me. I tried to pet him, and after a few strokes he would leave me. Even his running around was frantic. It took about 20 minutes for him to focus on me and relax somewhat. Then the gang came out of the house, I told them to stay on the other side of the fence and about 200 yards away. I heeled him around for a minute and put him back in the van. We did not do a second session.

Came home, let him out for a bit, brought him inside, put him in his crate for about ten minutes, let him out and he was still weird. I gave him some balls to chew on, he relaxed and I put him away again.

I think the problem was that I haven't worked him at all in anything since my last post in the journal, or taken him out for runs. Ted's reminder…RE-

GRESSION IS A NORMAL PART OF LEARNING. I am trying to look at it this way—I recognized the signs and did not push him. I gave him some time alone with me in the field. Had we been clueless, there is no doubt in my mind that he would have bitten someone. When I was doing TTouch on him I felt that he would have even bitten me had I continued. I have to remember that I have bad days and he is allowed to have a bad day too.

So, I plan on giving him a little more downtime in the crate, more exercise, and some more bonding time alone with me without the other dogs. He went after Beau a few times yesterday. I had noticed that he was getting weird a few days ago and yesterday he was just nuts. Very scientific term, "nuts." Very out-of-control and very tense.

Tonight I separated the dogs, paying attention to each dog individually. Shadow was very stressed. I was gently petting him and gave him random cookies and we played ball. Then he started with this frantic, wild-eyed bark. I happened to touch him as he was moving, and frankly, the look in his eyes scared me. I put him away in his crate (silently and gently) and let him stay there for a few minutes. I just let him out and he is fine—not bothering me or the other dogs. He is lying down in the hallway as I type this. I was going to schedule a lesson on Saturday but I think I may have to put it on hold until I see how many days it takes him to recoup.

He is acting like today is his first day here and the last eight months never happened.

REGRESSION IS ALL A PART OF LEARNING, REGRESSION IS ALL A PART OF LEARNING, REGRESSION IS ALL A PART OF LEARNING, ad infinitum…..

Good Pam! For taking things slowly. I am a bit frustrated here, but I am not taking it out on Shadow and I am handling his behavior appropriately.

JANUARY 26 – DAY 243

Belated birthday present from Shadow. He has been a model dog today. He was crated from 8:00 a.m. until 6:00 p.m., an unusually long time. He has been calm, cool, collected. While the other boys were out, I started training some tricks and he loved it! I worked on weaving between my legs, which is hard for Shadow because of my leaning over and his having to go through my legs. He handled it beautifully. I also worked on getting him to spin to the right and left.

I want to work on some nose work with him—he is a natural tracker. The other day he followed my tracks in the snow, which were all curvy. It was so cool! I really need to keep his brain more active. I also need to rework how I handle his obtaining inappropriate objects. I have started doing two things: If he has some paper (his favorite food group) or some underwear (second favorite food group), I either clap my hands, telling him he is wonderful and then leave the room without trying to trade for it; or completely ignore the fact that he has something he shouldn't and pay tons of attention to another dog. Don't know which one is better but I am sure to find out soon! This morning he stole almost everything out of my underwear drawer. Cheeky little bugger! Of course, I was an idiot for not closing the drawer.

JANUARY 27 – DAY 244

Private lesson today. Unbelievable progress! Carolyn and I both noticed the difference in him immediately. Calm and cool, his mouth was soft within the first few minutes. We walked around the big field, then we went toward the lower sheep pen and he alerted to the sheep, and did a wonderful outrun. He was sniffing the donkey and standing with his feet up on the fence when Carolyn touched him!!!!!!! AND he didn't react!!!!!!!

We walked around the pen and I threw the Frisbee for him. We went into the lambing barn and he sniffed the new mommies and babies. Some of the moms stamped their feet at him. Shadow reacted appropriately by backing off. This barn is very dark and close and he was just fine.

Then we went outside again to the big field and did some more Frisbee playing. He didn't jump on Carolyn at all while soliciting food. He has this habit of not bringing toys close to me, so we tried this: I threw the Frisbee, he retrieved it and if he did not bring it within five feet of me, I turned my back on him and walked away. If he brought it close to me, I clicked, gave him wads of food and threw the Frisbee again. It was very hard for him to do because I had changed the rules on him and it was hard for me because I REALLY wanted to **help** him! But I knew I had to let him work this out. If I helped him, I would end up slowing down the learning process. He was a bit confused and frustrated, but it wasn't bad and he didn't overreact.

Total session was about 75 minutes. Came home, let him outside for a bit and then crated him for 45 minutes and he has been really fine since then.

Good Everyone! Patience is sometimes rewarded! By not pressuring Shadow, his "good" behavior is now back on the rise.

TRAINING CONCEPT

It is very important to not always **help** the dog. The dog will progress faster if they are allowed to think for themselves. I am not a child psychologist, but think about it this way—if you always help your child, you will end up with an adult who doesn't know how to solve problems on his or her own. They will think "I don't have to do this because someone will come and help me."

JANUARY 31 – DAY 248

Private lesson today. I vowed to use as little food as possible, instead trying to add more **reinforcement variety**. It is so hard to not rely on food exclusively! We went into the big field and he ran toward the sheep in the pen. I walked the other way. He came to me, and I heavily praised and petted him, and then threw the Frisbee. Then we did the same as we did before with the Frisbee—he had to bring the Frisbee to within four feet of me and drop it. If he didn't, I walked away. He was only mildly successful doing this. After a successful try, I decided to end the session, but he decided that he would rather run around the sheep pen.

At one point, I called him and rewarded with food, petting, and praise, and let him go back to the sheep. Then he wouldn't come away from the sheep. I left the field and he went looking for me— but still couldn't come all the way to me. I finally tricked him into coming to me because I had to leave—otherwise I would have left him there permanently. (Not really…) For most of the lesson his mouth was soft, but there were times where it was hard. I only used about a quarter cup of food!

Came home, let him out. Put him in his crate for about ten minutes and he has been fine.

TRAINING CONCEPT

Using **reinforcement variety** is so vital to good training. Use only food to reward your dog and he will only work for food. It is tiring sometimes to use other things because we then have to plan out our sessions and use our brains, but it pays off later on.

HINDSIGHT

Today it is eight months since I brought Shadow home. For the past three months, the biggest differences I have seen have been on my end. I have slowed down and not been frustrated (well, maybe a little). Changing my mental attitude and behavior was the first step in being able to change Shadow's behavior. My understanding of training has matured and grown. No longer do I think that constant drilling is the way to build strong behaviors. Small context changes, new kinds of games, more cognizance of body language, new ways of looking at behavior are what my foundation is now made of. Am I getting frustrated at times? Sure I am. It is very hard for me to not listen to the naysayers: "Why would you put so much time into training him, you'll never be able to completely trust him," "Couldn't you have just given him back to the rescue group?" "Can't you just give him away?" "You should put him down," ad nauseum.

Whenever I hear these kinds of things, I think of Ted Turner. At Sea World they have predator and prey working in the same shows. Killer whales—predator—which tip the scales at anywhere from 5,000 to 15,000 pounds along with Pacific white-sided dolphins, bottlenose dolphins, and California sea lions—prey. So, if Sea World can do these things, I can certainly train a mere 40- pound Border Collie to like people again and show in Competition Obedience!

Shadow has also evolved. He hasn't even come close to biting anyone recently (GOOD Pam for not pressuring him), he is responding to people in a positive manner, and he is playing nicely with Beau and Cody. Shadow has had some "bad" days, but the percentage of good days far outweighs the bad ones. It took six months for Carolyn to hand feed him for the first time. A mere one and a half months after that she was able to touch him for the first time.

4

Serendipity is the ability to make fortunate discoveries by accident, without expecting them.

—Unknown

There Is a Light at the End of This Tunnel

FEBRUARY 1 – DAY 249

Growl class. I practiced "go visit" with John and Carolyn. Shadow approached without jumping and gave them record-speed downs. The first few times, he wasn't patient and his eyes were funny —I called him back to me and we started again. Then we walked around and we played the "Bring the Frisbee to Mommy game." Carolyn tried to reach down to pick up the toy, but Shadow couldn't handle it and raced in and stole it. This could become "race in and bite," which I do not want, so I changed the "game." I have now added: (1) bring me the Frisbee (2) drop it within four feet of me (3) lie down (4) get back, a sheep herding term that means to go away from me (5) lie down again and (6) reach down and pick up the Frisbee and throw it for him.

At first we clicked him for moving back slightly and he very quickly understood what we wanted. This first session lasted about 15 minutes. I stopped it before his tongue was hanging down to the ground and BEFORE his "point of no return" where he just can't stop himself.

Second session. I repeated the same context as the first one. I didn't feel like changing anything and really wanted to get the logistics of the game down in my own mind. Shadow was wonderful overall and I used MUCH less food— probably about a quarter of a cup. I am really trying to use other reinforcers.

Later on, no displacement stuff at home. I am doing a lot more "focus on Mommy" games, while the other dogs just stand around. I also enrolled him in an aggressive dog seminar for the second time. Very controlled atmosphere with tons of safety nets in place (fences, leashes, etc.) where we can practice with more new people, but in the same comfortable location.

Here Comes the Serendipity Part

FEBRUARY 4 – DAY 252

Over time it has become apparent to me that Shadow still gets upset and nervous and could potentially aggress when people bend over. He does it when they are leaning over him, or a toy, or just in general—at any distance from one foot away up to many yards away. So, thinks I, why not make "leaning over" become a **cue** to him to "get back out and lie down?"

We have been doing this for a few days with the Frisbee and tennis ball and he is doing really well with it. Today was the pièce de résistance—he had a spoon in his mouth, I called him to me, had him lie down, leaned over slightly, and asked him to give (I did not reach for it), get back out…and drum roll…he did it. WaHoo! A few hours later we were outside with the Frisbees. He ended up with both of them and as I was leaning over, before I could say, "get back out," he backs up and lies down!!!! Methinks he is starting to equate the "cue" with the behavior!!!!!!

Later he stole a knife, we did the same thing and he did it again. MEGA-jackpot! He has this major issue of not wanting to give me the inappropriate objects that he steals, so this will be great.

Brilliant Pam! For taking a previously provoking stimuli (people bending over) and changing it to mean something different and incompatible with biting (get back out and lie down). Give yourself a hot fudge sundae—make it two!

TRAINING CONCEPT

You can do this with your dog—make anything a **cue** for any behavior you want. For instance, you can make the sound of the doorbell a cue for the dog to go to his crate, rather than maul your guests. You can make a person approaching your dog a cue for the dog to sit, instead of jump. In this case, I taught Shadow to "back out" when I leaned over him—something that had often caused him to aggress. I have subsequently also taught Shadow that a person touching him (as in the stand for exam exercise in competition obedience and Rally obedience) is a cue to "lock eyes with me and don't move," which is also incompatible to biting.

Lean over means...

Get back out!

FEBRUARY 5 – DAY 253

Just worked on getting Shadow to go into the tub. He did it once, got scared, then frustrated, and started whacking the wall with his paw. All of a sudden he jumped in and out of the tub repeatedly and wasn't nervous! Reinforcers—the tennis ball and yippees! Clapping and cheering. The first few attempts were hysterical—he looked like he was "testing the waters" with his paws, although there was no water in the tub. I really have to get a video camera that straps to my forehead! Also did some more get back outs when he stole my mitten and he instantly complied!!!!

FEBRUARY 6 – DAY 254

Private lesson today. We started out by walking around the farm, visiting the new moms and their babies in the dark barn, calling him off the sheep in the pen, playing the "lean over means get back out and lie down" game. We have three cues for this right now: (1) lean over (2) hand gesture and (3) verbal. I want to make each a separate and distinct cue so I can use them for different things such as sheep herding, agility, competition obedience, and don't bite people.

His body was soft and relaxed. I could tell he was really concentrating on the new game. If I leaned over and he didn't move back, I gave him a helper cue (verbal and hand) and if he still didn't move back, I stood there for 30 seconds and then tried again. I ultimately want him to move back about 10-12 feet.

Toward the end of the session, he was backing up about six to eight feet. Session lasted about 45 minutes. He has been great at home since then.

FEBRUARY 8 – DAY 256

Growl class. For our first session we did a very short walk up the driveway with me, Shadow, John, and Carolyn. He was very calm almost from the outset—mouth soft. Practiced a few recalls and used variable reinforcement type—talking, petting, and a little food. When petting, I would release him only if he was looking AT me rather than AWAY from me.

I brought the ball out and we did the "lean over is a cue to get back out game." I gave him no helper cues—only my body reaching down and he did it! There were two times that he didn't move, so I stayed bent over for about 15 seconds. If he didn't back away, I stood up, counted to 30 and then tried again. He got it instantly. I repeated this about six times and with no other cue than my bending over, he got it right. Total session lasted about 15 minutes.

For our second session we repeated the same context as the first one. Shadow was distracted by the sheep and ran toward the pen. He came back to me on his own and I was able to engage him. Then he started air sniffing, and since he can't pay attention to me if he is too focused on sniffing, I stopped the session.

FEBRUARY 10 – DAY 258

Well, my boy has been a model of good doggie-ness. Took him to my training facility today and did heeling, stand for exams with me touching him, retrieves on the flat and over the high jump, "leaning over means get back out," some fronts and some directed retrieves of the gloves. I also did the weaving around my legs game. All in all he did wonderfully. He didn't get anxious if he didn't understand something. Shadow has been great all day—cuddly and calm.

He stole a few things, but much less than his usual raids and he was able to give them up and get back out after a few tries. I have been heavily rewarding him with praise and petting when he has an appropriate object. I realize that I haven't been rewarding him often enough for being a good dog. So, if he is lying down on the bed or couch or playing by himself, I walk by, wave, smile, and praise him. I have seen a decrease in his stealing things. He still does, but not as much. Oh! And he has been bringing the balls and toys to within inches of my feet!

Holy Smokes!

FEBRUARY 13 – DAY 261

Private lesson today. A banner day!!! Shadow's mouth was soft the instant I took him out of the van. He still has this shaking thing going on at first, but I have decided not to dwell on it anymore. We walked around the farm and Carolyn tried to get him to "get back out" by pointing—he wasn't quite sure what she wanted and kept targeting her hand.

We changed tactics and added the ball. I threw it for him, he retrieved it, dropped it at my feet, I leaned down, he got back out, I threw it again. I repeated this a few times and then Carolyn leaned down behind me as I was leaning down. She was also talking REALLY loud, saying really weird things and making very obnoxious noises, probably to get me to laugh so I wouldn't be nervous and then hold my breath. Shadow didn't react other than cocking his head and having a quizzical expression on his face. One time he went up to sniff her.

Good Doggie! Make that brilliant doggie! We were trying to get him used to someone else leaning down. In the beginning he would aggress at anyone leaning or bending over—no matter how far away they were. Today, Carolyn was able to bend down right next to him and he handled it wonderfully. Way to go, Shadow!

We took Shadow to the lambing barn for the second session and changed the context in two ways. We closed the barn door so it was darker and "closer," and Carolyn was in one of the pens bottle-feeding a lamb. He was fascinated by the babies and was actually calm.

His mouth was soft most of the time. I like the idea of getting him really calm and serene around sheep before we ever actually do more herding. The last time he was gripping (biting) and pulling out wool. We left the barn and started walking around the farm. He left me and did an outrun around the sheep pen but came right back. I tried engaging him with the ball, but he wasn't interested so I ended the session.

I am getting really good at ending sessions before his breaking point. Later on, we went to a park and played with the tennis ball. He loves to sniff in the snow and bury his head and dig! He was great all last night although I still crate him when we go to bed. Shadow still sleeps all night in the crate because he cannot yet control himself. I can ignore and sleep through a 40-pound dog dive-bombing my head in the middle of the night, but Jim cannot!

Good Doggie! For not biting Carolyn when she bent over!

Good Pam! For keeping the sessions easy enough for Shadow to succeed, yet constantly changing them slightly, so that he will eventually generalize calm behavior.

I am very proud of myself for being relaxed enough to see this through and not give up!

FEBRUARY 14 – DAY 262

Took Shadow to the park and walked around for a while. I brought all of the dogs to the building and just let them be dogs. Shadow chewed on his tennis balls. A man came up to the door and Shadow did NOT react! AT ALL!!!!

Did I Mention That Behavior Isn't Static?

FEBRUARY 15 – DAY 263

Growl class. His mouth was medium soft from the get-go. Played the "lean over means get back out" game. Carolyn stood next to me and leaned down also. I threw the ball and she threw snow because not only does leaning over affect him, but arm movements have also set him off in the past. Shadow approached and she asked him to get back out and he did, but not as far as I would have liked. Then he just sat there and looked at me, so I called him to me and ended the session.

Next, we repeated the same context, but this time John joined us. After a few minutes, Shadow asked, "Why are you all looking at me?" I laughed and he relaxed. I was still the only one picking up the ball. This session lasted about eight minutes.

I asked the group this question: "I have noticed our second sessions have been decreasing in length. Is this because he is stressing faster or because we are stopping it long before he is even thinking about being stressed?" It was the consensus that we are stopping them sooner and are reading him better.

We came home and took a three-hour nap! Boy I must have been tired! He was a bit of a pain this afternoon. He was barking to go outside, which I don't allow. After dinner, I was cutting up some food. Cody was pacing and Shadow attacked him. This scuffle was the shortest yet—just about six seconds. I waited a few seconds and then put him in his crate. I let him out after a minute or so and he was still being weird so I put him away again and shut the bedroom door.

I tried to kiss his face (I always ask him if I can kiss him and he lowers his head for me) and he put his teeth on my jaw—just for an instant, but I am not happy with this at all. Just when I think that things are going well...I know, I know… REGRESSION IS A NORMAL PART OF LEARNING…(I really hate that!)

TRAINING CONCEPT

Why do I want to kiss his face? Because human faces coming toward a dog's face is seen by the dog as aggressive. I want to desensitize him to this because I don't want him to bite anyone that happens to try to kiss him. You would be surprised how many people, on meeting a dog for the first time, try to kiss that dog. Plus, I just like to kiss my dogs on their faces.

FEBRUARY 16 – DAY 264

Shadow took a plastic lid off of the counter. Jim asked him to give and tried to take it from him, he bared his teeth at Jim. I really wish Jim would listen to me and do this the way it should be done. He just doesn't get it yet and if he undermines what I am doing, we will never progress.

HINDSIGHT

Looking back at this now from a great distance, Shadow baring his teeth was a good thing. Why? Because he gave Jim a warning and did not just bite him.

FEBRUARY 18 – DAY 266

Took him to a park and played the "get back out" game with a new twist. I am now asking him to also "look back" at the same time to break his eye contact with the toy (person). I don't want him to be even more obsessive than he already is. He did really well with it. He started to run away from me, which is different than hopping backwards, and a few times he turned his head. I stopped when his tongue was hanging down to his knees. I also changed the context by not having the harness or a leash on him!

Last night we were watching a movie and he was nice and relaxed. All of a sudden he started to get this crazed look, so I asked him to get the ball and he relaxed. I can find nothing that would stimulate this look. We can be sitting there nicely and all of a sudden he flings himself on me backwards and does this scary bark noise. If I touch him, he leaps away from me. If I ignore him, he does this backwards fling thing and the cycle continues.

I don't let it go on more than once before I put him away in his crate at the first sign I can't redirect him with a toy. Last night he even lay down on the couch and let Cody cuddle with me on the loveseat! Then I groomed Cody while Shadow watched. Later, he jumped on the table and let me brush his tail, cut his front nails, and trim the fur on his front feet!

Do I know why he is suddenly displacing at home? As I look back on the last few journal entries, I can see no reason for it. But then again, I am only human…And he is just a dog and who knows what a dog is thinking anyway?

FEBRUARY 21 – DAY 269

Private lesson today. We did more of the same stuff. Nothing overly noteworthy other than calmness. Carolyn did not lean over. No food except to assess his mood. Worked on petting him and releasing him only if he looked at me.

Received an e-mail from Ted Turner:

> Your video was excellent. I hope you are taking some pictures (stills) of your work with Shadow. You'll need them for articles and books. He is such a great subject.

My response to Ted:

> I was wondering—you had mentioned that when you work with killer whales, if they grab you in their mouths, you have to go limp. That if you struggle, they would then think you are prey and do some not-so-nice things to you. My question is this—HOW did you train yourself to not be scared out of your mind and to go passive?*

> By working with Shadow continually in a familiar place, not only is he practicing not being aggressive, but I am also practicing not being tense and worried. While I try my damnedest to set up every situation he will be in, we don't live in a vacuum. And, because I am human, even though I know "calm is best," I still have a tendency to tense up and I know I need to work on it.

FEBRUARY 22 – DAY 270

Growl class. For the first session it was just Cynthia, the video camera, and me. Played the "bend over means get back out" game. He did well. Then Cynthia bent over behind me. His get backs were slower and not as far away. I think he is still nervous with someone other than me leaning over him. I also worked on getting him to turn his head away. Eventually Cynthia was able to reach down for the ball and Shadow did get back out a few feet and sat down.

---

* In a later email Ted responds: "It's not as hard as you might think when you're paralyzed with fear the first time. It's the fifth and sixth time that begins to unnerve you."

Session lasted about 15 minutes and then I ended it when I saw him lip licking.

Good Pam! I am using his calming signals, or lack thereof, as a guide to end or continue sessions.

Carolyn was able to join us for this session. To work on his stealing of inappropriate objects we threw gloves and wads of paper all around, clicked him for looking away from them, and then threw a toy. If he grabbed or looked at a glove, I walked away. He seemed a bit unfocused, as if he wasn't sure what we wanted.

Toward the end of the session he wanted to play by himself, so I walked away. He dropped the toys and came to me. We ended the session after ten minutes.

Shadow has been great for the rest of the day, although he was back to stealing some stuff. I threw some items on the floor and played the same game that we did earlier today. If he grabbed the knife, bottle top or magnet, I walked away. When he dropped the object, I gave him a cookie. Repeated a bunch of times with each thing and he seemed to be trying to figure out this new game and what he was supposed to do. Kudos for Jim! Shadow had a magnet and Jim didn't try to take it away from him! He told me and I was able to get him to drop the item.

FEBRUARY 25 – DAY 273

Trained at my facility today. Cynthia and Karen were there sitting down behind a baby gate. I did some heeling with Shadow and he was very stressed at first—shaking, wild-eyed, tense. After a few minutes he relaxed. I had the long line tied to my waist. At one point he moved toward Karen and made a face at her. I couldn't see it, but Cynthia told me his face was pushed forward and his eyes were big. He came back to me instantly and we resumed heeling. He did not go to the end of the leash nor were there any more problems. During the evening he was fine.

FEBRUARY 26 – DAY 274

He just had a tiff with Cody. God I really hate that. I left the room and it stopped within seconds. I then put him away in his crate and though usually he is quiet, now he is whining.

FEBRUARY 27 – DAY 275

Private lesson today. My objective was to teach him to **play tug**. I feel that his possessiveness might be alleviated if I can play tug with him. I started to play with him and he got stressed and left me. I realized then that I was asking too much of him. I was expecting him to play tug like the other boys do—actually tugging with me, growling, and all of us having fun. He isn't ready for that. It stresses him out entirely too much and he doesn't know how to handle it.

Good Doggie! He was stressed by the game and instead of doing something "bad" to me, he moved away!

TRAINING CONCEPT

Why would I want Shadow to learn to not only **play tug**, but to enjoy it? Jean Donaldson says it best in her book *Culture Clash*: "Played with rules, tug-of-war is a tremendous energy burner and good exercise for both dog and owner. It serves as a good barometer of the kind of control you have over your dog, most importantly, his jaws. The game doesn't make the dog a predator; he already is one. The game is an outlet." She further states, "The big payoff is in lowered incidence of behavior problems due to under stimulation."

He saw the Boomer Ball and played with that for a while. He actually started out very calmly with it and I got some lie-downs from him. I was able to get him to move away from it so I could kick it for him. Then he became frantic about the ball and I walked away. After a few minutes he brought it back to me. Even though he was spent, I threw it for him a few more times because he brought it back to me. At that point, I took it away and put him in the van for about ten minutes.

I had videotaped the session, so Carolyn and I went inside to watch it. I wanted to time exactly how long he played tug with me before getting stressed. Two minutes and ten seconds was his limit. My idea was to take him out again and play for one minute and 30 seconds and then end the second session. In addition, I was to pull him toward me, let go of the toy and ask him to drop it (instead of letting him pull me toward him).

He did so well with it that I inadvertently ended the session much sooner by throwing him wads of food because I was so excited. After that he didn't want to play with the toy, so I did some heeling around instead. Then Carolyn fed him some cookies and touched him while feeding—THREE times! This was a first!!!! Wowie-zowie!

Carolyn touching and feeding Shadow.

Good Doggie Again! Shadow tried very hard to play with me, and again, when he had enough, he did not aggress in any way—he just walked away. Which, now that I think about it, is a calming signal. Perhaps he felt that I was getting stressed by the game? In addition, he let Carolyn touch him three times! And he did not displace on her even though he had been nervous about the tug game!

FEBRUARY 28 – DAY 276

Trained at my facility. Took Shadow to the far end of the parking lot while Lisa was working on the median with her dogs. His mouth was very hard and tight. It took about 15 minutes for his mouth to soften up. He heard some dogs barking and became more nervous. We did some heeling and eye contact work and toward the end of the session I did some TTtouch. His eyes went back and forth between fine and not-so-fine. Total session lasted 25 minutes.

He was a bit frantic tonight, going back and forth between fine and frenzied. When he started to become agitated, I massaged his gums to try to calm him. If he calmed down, fine. If not, I put him away for a few minutes and then tried again.

MARCH 1 – DAY 278

Growl class. For our first session Cynthia, Carolyn, Shadow, and I all took a walk. I am trying to teach Shadow that "running up and instantly lying down" is the proper way to greet someone. I am calling this behavior **go visit.** We worked on get back outs and lie-downs using just a hand signal. Toward the end of the session (about 15 minutes) we all stood by the gate in a very close group.

Carolyn leaned down toward him and tossed him food. She repeated this a few more times, gradually lowering herself closer to him. Instead of tossing the food between his front legs, she delivered it directly into his mouth and continued to hand-feed him. Her glasses fell off of her face and Shadow got a little nervous when she bent over to pick them up, so we took a one-minute walk and ended the session. He is also getting good at visiting on my cue and not on his own whim!

TRAINING CONCEPT

Go visit: Go to the person I am pointing to and lie down, it is also about taking a previously scary thing—approaching people, and turning it into something more fun and incompatible with biting. He can't be biting if he is lying down.

Our second session lasted two minutes. We tried to play tug in the front yard. I am used to pulling and pulling with the other dogs, but with Shadow I have to drop it as soon as there is tension on it. He is still a bit unsure of the game and doesn't seem to like it yet. That is why the session was so short.

Carolyn leaning over, feeding and petting Shadow

HINDSIGHT

Shadow and I did quite a bit of good work in the past 30 days. I changed lots of contexts, always watching for signs of stress, trying not to push Shadow beyond his capabilities. While he did have a small setback mid-month, he recouped quickly. I am proud of myself for not getting overly panicked or worried, and about taking it in stride "as a normal part of learning…"

Shadow had some memorable "firsts" this month—Carolyn fed him with her bare hand on numerous occasions and she was actually able to lightly touch him! He learned that people leaning over isn't a bad thing. He is somewhat better overall with Beau and Cody, and is slightly better with grooming. He is practicing being calm around sheep and the general public if they are at a distance.

Zip-a-dee-doo-dah, Zip-a-dee-ay, My Oh My, What a Wonderful Day!

MARCH 3 – DAY 280

First day of an aggressive dog seminar; I videotaped and took pictures. These were all new people for Shadow to meet, but in the same controlled atmosphere that he was comfortable in.

For our first session, seven people were outside of the fence, while Carolyn, Shadow, and I were inside. We stayed about 300 feet away and played Frisbee. He did well with get back outs but when Carolyn did the throwing, he became a little nervous, so we ended the session.

Carolyn, Shadow, and I inside the fence, new people walking outside the fence.

Between sessions we played some recall games, and verbal marker signal work. (By saying "yes," and giving a cookie numerous times, the word "yes" becomes valuable.)

For our second session with the group we stayed inside the fence while everyone else lined up outside. A woman named Angel was off to the side. We were much closer this time—only about 15 feet away. We played Frisbee for a few minutes. Then Shadow and I went over to Angel, who was armed with a whole bag of treats. I told Shadow to go visit and he went over to her. She asked him to lie down, which he did, and she threw cookies behind him. Angel did this many times and he was fine with it. Then I told him to go visit Carolyn and he did. She was able to feed him out of her hand numerous times and he was very relaxed. Everything about him was perfect—mouth soft, and a supple and relaxed body. Only two days ago he was sensitive about Carolyn leaning over, and today he was unruffled by it!

Carolyn with Shadow, a student armed with treats outside the fence.

I noticed that during the first session, Shadow's get back outs were not as far away as they normally are during private lessons, but in the second session they were much better even though we were closer to everyone. At first he was watching the group with an alert (but not stressed) look and then he ignored them.

MARCH 4 – DAY 281

A SUPER DOOPER day!

Day two of the aggressive dog seminar. Seven people were stretched out along two sides of the fence, with plenty of space between them. I played Frisbee with Shadow. Carolyn also threw the Frisbee a few times and he was outstanding. Then I moved closer to the fence and tried giving him food but he wasn't interested—he wanted the toy, so we played a bit more.

Angel was off by herself again and I had him go visit. He did some nice lie-downs for her. Carolyn fed him by hand a few times. We asked everyone to congregate into one large group. Shadow and I approached them. He was more receptive to taking food and each person asked him to lie down and tossed him food. I periodically called him to me and reinforced him when he did. Then they all moved en masse toward a corner of the field and occasionally threw him food as they walked. He was super—eyes, body, mouth were all perfect for the entire time. No signs of stress from any body part! To end the session, I had the group leave while I took him farther into the field and played with him until they were all out of sight.

I did not do a second session with Shadow today for a couple reasons. The snow was getting so bad you couldn't raise your head up without being blinded and, more importantly, I felt he had done such brilliant work that I really wanted to stop there. I was getting tired and was concerned that I wouldn't be as sharp and aware as I need to be with him.

Good Pam! No more "greedy trainer" for me! Great use of judgment! The contexts were similar to what we had been doing previously with Shadow. They were different in that we had so many new people present, but not so hard that he couldn't handle them.

I just watched the video and saw something I had missed. At one point a woman was tossing Shadow food for lie-downs. She dropped a cookie on her side of the fence and bent over to pick it up. He saw her bending down and HE DID NOT REACT!!!!! And she was only about five feet away from him!

Good Doggie! Shadow did particularly well this weekend, I was so elated and proud!

Once home, Shadow was totally relaxed. I put him in his crate to type this. I am really excited about this weekend and really glad I did this seminar again. I plan on doing the next one as well—maybe by that time, the crowd can be on the same side of the fence?!

Waiting calmly to be fed at the fence.

Just had another thought. There were people all around the van this weekend, talking and walking, and he did not bark once!

This evening he did have a sort of thing with Beau—Shadow had him pinned under the breakfront. Cody was in my lap and we ignored them. They broke it up after about five minutes. Since then he has been gentle and good.

HINDSIGHT

While thinking back to the first aggressive dog seminar, the improvement is incredible! Even with a leash on and fences in between, he and I were both distraught and stressed. I had cotton-mouth the entire weekend. I was terrified of his aggression, which of course, did nothing to ease his mind. I am extremely proud of his accomplishments, not only in his increasing calm behaviors, but also with my own composure. The people at this second seminar were very impressed with Shadow and me as a team, and found it hard to believe that a mere 10 months ago we were both basket cases!

MARCH 7 – DAY 284

A SUPER DAY!

Took the boys to the facility today and played "two-toy tug" with Shadow. At first he did not want to play. I persisted and he relaxed a bit. I offered him a toy and told him to get it. When he grabbed it, I instantly let go of the toy, told him to give and held out the second toy. Continued for a few reps. I started to tug slightly, drawing him into me and releasing the toy, saying, "give" before he actually gave me the toy, and he dropped it instantly. Repeated three times and ended that portion of the session.

Next, we did some heeling with turns and go-outs without a target, and he was amazing. The last time we practiced go-outs he did not understand the game and was frustrated. Today the light was on!

I also did some touch desensitization while he was standing. I touched his tail and pulled it gently, picked up all four feet, and he stood very calmly. He did not really want to be touched, although he put up with it. I have been more perceptive to when he is being touch sensitive versus when he wants to be handled.

He really likes it when I talk to him, so I have been touching less today and talking more. I noticed that he was calm from the beginning of today's session, whereas in the past it would take him five to ten minutes to calm down. His eyes and face were clear, although his mouth was a tad tight. Session lasted about 20 minutes.

MARCH 8 – DAY 285

ANOTHER **SUPER DAY**!

Growl class. Taped the first session only. I was throwing the Frisbee and Shadow was a bit stressed—eyes weird, body very tight, didn't want to interact with me very much. I ended the session after it was clear that he wasn't going to work himself out of it. Looking back, I see from the tape that I let it go on too long before I ended the session. That is the wonderful thing about videotaping our sessions. I can look back and see the good things that happened, and also see where I may have made an error.

I put him away for about 15 minutes and then took him out alone in the field for a bonding follow-the-leader type of walk. I heavily rewarded him with food for staying next to me. At times I added touch in between feeding. At one point toward the end, Carolyn and Cynthia came toward the fence. Shadow alerted to Cynthia's voice and I could see his body tense up so I had her go back into the house. I put him away for ten minutes.

Next I had Carolyn, John, and Cynthia come out of the house and stay outside the fence. I did a little work with him and then released him to go visit. He was much more relaxed for this session. He did great lie-downs for food. John and Carolyn both leaned over and fed him from their hands through the fence. They also did some get back outs and he was super. We did some heeling and finishes and a recall while Carolyn was talking loudly and being obnoxious. Shadow was terrific! Then I threw the ball a few times and ended the session.

It was nice to see that he was able to pull himself together after a ten-minute break, and great that we got to do three sessions with him.

He was really good tonight. I think it is because I overfed him—one pound of tortellini, one and a half cans of chickpeas, and dinner! He just lay around all night and even put himself in his crate for about an hour. Jim and I kept asking him if he felt okay! Poor baby!

While this was a good day; I am feeling very discouraged about his progress (because I am anal and at times STILL wonder if this dog will ever be normal.) Carolyn has been reassuring me that he is doing remarkably well overall. I decided to keep a diary of how many minutes he is in the crate at home versus how many minutes he is out. That way I can see if giving him more "down time" has any bearing on his behavior.

TRAINING CONCEPT

You may be wondering why I called today a "**super day**." As I mentioned, even though the first two sessions were less than stellar, he was able to pull himself together for the third one. To me, one sign of a healthy (temperament-wise) dog is one that can recuperate quickly after being nervous. Recuperating quickly is a new behavior for him, so I am seeing this as a very positive step forward. Like a dry, brittle rubber band that breaks at the slightest pressure, the work I have put into Shadow's desensitization program and our relationship has now added elasticity back into his "rubber band."

MARCH 9 – DAY 286

SUPER DAY NUMBER THREE!

Private lesson. Richard was our guest "dog bait." Richard and Carolyn were in the field; Shadow and I were outside of the fence. Richard asked Shadow for both lie-downs and get back outs. Shadow couldn't seem to get back but he was very calm and soft. We even had Richard hand-feed him and his mouth was very soft. Did that for about 15 minutes. I also did some competition heeling and stays right next to the fence and Shadow was stupendous!

Good Doggie! Wow! Within minutes of meeting, Shadow let a complete stranger hand-feed him, and was calm and relaxed enough to do competition work with me! Only one month ago Carolyn hand-fed him for the first time. I am starting to see some INCREDIBLE progress here!

During our second session we walked around the front yard. Carolyn hand-fed Shadow as well as petted him lightly along his sides and he handled it calmly. She continued for a few minutes. We were "supposed" to go into the barn but Shadow had a different plan. He ran into the junk field and raced around a small pen that had sheep in it. He couldn't leave, so we worked on balance for a while. I tried to lure, bribe, plead, beg, block, grab—anything to get him to come to me—but he could not leave the sheep. He was bumping into Carolyn as he was whizzing by at top speed, "around and around and around the pen he goes, where he stops, nobody knows!" At times he stood right next to Carolyn, touching her leg and actually laid down on her foot briefly! Carolyn held out her hand with cookies in it to try to slow him down. He zoomed by at 100 miles per hour, grabbed the cookies without missing a beat, and kept going! Hysterically funny! It took us about half an hour to get him away and I had to practically tackle him—there was no other way to stop him and I had to leave.

Once we got about ten feet away from the sheep he was completely focused on me again. This was fantastic overall though—new person, feeding from his hand within a few minutes of the first meeting, Carolyn petting him, me doing competition behaviors while he was completely relaxed the entire time. Even the sheep thing wasn't totally out of control until the end—he was just wired and couldn't stop himself. Carolyn felt that he did good work with the sheep and could easily have displaced any aggression he may have been feeling by biting her leg but he didn't.

He has been calm all night. I went to the facility to train with Cody and Beau and left Shadow at home. I felt he had done enough good work today and didn't want to push it.

MARCH 15 – DAY 292

SUPER DAY NUMBER FOUR!

Growl class with new student Eileen. For the first session Eileen preferred to stay outside the fence. John, Cynthia, Carolyn, me, and Shadow were all inside the fence. When I first took him out, his mouth was great and he wasn't shaking. Carolyn tried to feed and pet him. He looked frantic AND BACKED AWAY! He did not try to lunge at her.

Good Doggie! Shadow is learning that if he is frightened, he does not have to respond with barking, growling, lunging or biting. He can simply move away. YAHOO!

Carolyn stopped trying to pet him and we walked around. I tried to have him go visit but he was too nervous, so I played Frisbee and he loosened up. After a few minutes, I sensed that he was able to visit. He approached each person calmly. No one tried to pet him. His lie-downs were fast and everyone threw food behind him.

We had a discussion—why was he so stressed? We concluded that the context was different because we were all moving, whereas most of the previous times we were stationary.

For the next go-round, we did almost the same context except we added Eileen and deleted John (not permanently!). He was super dooper this time. We played Frisbee, did some go visits with lie-downs (food still being tossed behind him), some hand-feeding from Carolyn.

Cynthia and I played Frisbee with Shadow. Only once did he look a bit nervous. He took a few steps toward us, so Cynthia and I turned sideways and walked away.

We started to walk toward the car, he heeled with Cynthia (!) and she was feeding him from her hand. Then, she was able to get her fingers IN HIS MOUTH, and said his mouth was like velvet! I praised him heavily and she said that as I was praising him his mouth got just a teeny bit tighter, but was still soft. Once Cynthia and I were outside the fence, I did a whole host of competition behaviors right behind Cynthia and he was FANTASTIC! Then because I REALLY wanted to do more, I put him away so I wouldn't be tempted! **Good trainer, Pam!**

He has been great all night—very calm. We are putting up a privacy fence and that should help considerably since he won't be getting aroused anymore when people or cars go by. It will be interesting to see if there is a noticeable difference (for the better of course) in his behavior in all contexts due to this change. I have also noticed that he does better around the house if he is crated for just a few minutes at a time. If he is in the crate for long periods of time, he goes insane. Short snippets of downtime suit him.

MARCH 16 – DAY 293

Private lesson today. Ali was guest "dog bait" for the first few minutes. We all walked together. Shadow was very nervous and couldn't seem to focus on me at all—he just wanted the Frisbee. I put him away for a few minutes and brought him out again once Ali left.

Evening—he was great all night—I wasn't home and had the other dogs with me. Jim said Shadow came over to him, lay down in his lap, and fell asleep! I don't want to know why. I do know why, but don't want to admit it… and I don't even want to write down why. Guess I'll have to explain it. I "should" give him more alone time with Jim and me, without the other dogs and I hate to admit I am not doing something I should. OK, I SAID IT. THERE!

MARCH 20 – DAY 297

Took the boys to the park today. Walked/heeled Shadow about 75 feet away from Cynthia with Boomer (a dog), and 75 feet away from kids playing with skateboards. He was super—absolutely no reaction to the stimuli—great heeling, medium tight mouth but the rest of him was soft.

HINDSIGHT

HUGE amounts of progress in the past 14 days! To say that I am extremely excited and ecstatic is an understatement! The second and third floors of the Empire State Building are finished, complete with the furniture! I am truly enmeshed in the "process." In the beginning, the small approximations were KILLING me. Painstaking, meticulous, exacting work, requiring enormous amounts of patience had (note: past tense!) never been my forte. NOW, I love it! Does that make me anal???

5

Climb High Climb Far, Your Goal the Sky, Your Aim the Star.

—Inscription at Williams College

Holy Smokes

MARCH 22 – DAY 299

THE BEST DAY IN 10 MONTHS!!!!!!!!

Growl class. I wanted to try something new—instead of having Shadow approach people, I wanted people to approach him. I took Shadow into the front yard. I stood with him on leash and each person approached, asked him to lie down, fed him a few cookies, and walked away. I had Cynthia, John, Eileen, and Carolyn doing this. If he got up, they walked away without feeding. If he stayed in position, they fed. He learned very quickly that staying down was more beneficial. Started out with them approaching slowly, then had everyone come in faster. Cynthia also reached down and fed him by hand (she was turned sideways). In addition, they were also walking around and around us, rather than remaining static. Did this for about 10-15 minutes and he was SUPER relaxed.

For the second session, we repeated the same context but I had him sit instead of lying down and stepped up the speed in which everyone moved around him. I was so proud that I had tears in my eyes!

Shadow has been great all day. John and Cynthia keep telling me how great he is getting (and I almost believe it!). It is hard to see sometimes because I am too close to him.

Give Yourself a Break, Pam! Shadow is doing a terrific job and so are you!

Good Doggie! Shadow is becoming very brave and learning to be calm in more and more difficult contexts.

MARCH 23 – DAY 300

Took Shadow to the park. He was scared of the playground stuff but relaxed after a few minutes. I reinforced him for being calm around the "scary" slide. When he saw people walking on the bridge he alerted to them—not vocally, just by his posture. His mouth was a bit tight for a few minutes after that.

MARCH 25 – DAY 302

Took Shadow to my training facility. Cynthia and Marsha were there, sitting down behind a baby gate. His body was shaking. I couldn't let him off leash to play with a toy to release his tension, so we worked through it by doing attention walking, stopping to do TTouch, and petting. It took about 15 minutes for him to chill out and even then he was a bit nervous. When he was calm for five minutes, I ended the session.

Yesterday he spent most of the day in his crate, so I can understand him being a bit wired. Shadow **growled** at me the other day when he had a glove in his mouth and I touched it while asking him to get back out. This is bad and good. Bad because he didn't do what I asked him to do, and good because he gave me a warning! In the past there was never a warning, so this is a good thing. I promptly walked away. I put him in his crate for a few minutes, let him out and he was fine for the rest of the night.

TRAINING CONCEPT

A **growl** is just a warning—nothing more. It is obvious to me that Shadow had been punished for growling by his previous owner. It is very important not to punish the growl out of a dog because if you do, you end up with a flash biter—a dog that bites with no warning. A growling dog doesn't want to bite—that is why he is growling. Punishing the growl out of the dog is like telling a police officer that he doesn't have to say "Stop or I'll shoot." A growl is a wake-up call to YOU, to show you that you need to work on desensitizing your dog to whatever it is that he growled at. The important part is to not take it personally, a "How dare you growl at me!" kind of attitude.

MARCH 27 – DAY 304

Private lesson today. He was super! We were in the big field and did many small context changes. The first context: Carolyn came toward him out of nowhere. If he approached her with his "bunny-hop alert stance," I would call him back to me. If he approached calmly, I would let him continue and Carolyn would feed him. Well, he bunny-hopped, I called and he came instantly. For the second context, Carolyn was jogging and I reinforced Shadow for ignoring her. For the third context, Carolyn started out petting and feeding him simultaneously. She changed to petting him first and feeding him if he remained calm. He did wonderfully. She then petted him without any food and he was absolutely terrific! For the fourth context, we took him in the front yard and he was showing the barest glimmer of nervousness, so we put him away for five minutes. I brought him out and played Frisbee with him for five minutes, then ended the session. We both realized that we should have put him away a few minutes sooner. No big deal and sometimes I think it is okay to push the envelope slightly, as long as there is no backlash. It wasn't anything terrible, just a one percent reduction in calmness. Carolyn said he is coming along very nicely and that I am doing a really great job with him. **Good Pam!**

Two hours later I took him to the park and we walked around. I had him do lie-downs in front of the geese (they were across the river) and then we just sat on a bench and communed with nature together. It was so cool! We went home, took a nap, and then I was gone all night with Beau and Cody. Jim said he was very relaxed all night.

We Are On A Roll Now!

MARCH 29 – DAY 306

Second most super dooper day in 10 months!

Growl class. We started in the big field. I worked on eye contact and calmness while the usual complement of people jogged around us, waving their arms. He handled it like a trooper! His face and body were great although his mouth was a bit tight. Everyone stopped jogging while I heeled around them in a big figure eight and Shadow was AMAZING! As a release for him, I threw the Frisbee. He rammed into Cynthia's leg by accident and it was no big deal at all (for HIM anyway…)

For our second session I took Shadow into the front yard. I stood with Shadow and had him in a down-stay. One at a time, John, Cynthia, Eileen, and Carolyn approached. If Shadow remained down, they LEANED OVER (!) and fed him, either by tossing cookies between his legs or hand- feeding him. After feeding they walked away, made a big loop and came toward him again. If he got up they were to walk away without feeding. He stayed the entire time. I continued with the down-stay for a few minutes, then asked him for a sit and repeated the whole process. We did this for about 10-15 minutes and he was SUPER relaxed, even with everyone walking around in a steady stream. Carolyn petted him a lot today and when she reached down to pick up a cookie off of the ground, he DID NOT REACT!

John leaning over and feeding Shadow.

Good Doggie! Holy Smokes! So many good things, I can't even count them all!

APRIL 3 – DAY 311

I videotaped our private lesson today. For our first session, I had Shadow next to me and was working on eye contact. Carolyn asked me to release him from such a formal stance. He remained calm while she approached. She waved her arms around and he was fine with that. She threw food at him if he remained calm. Carolyn also asked him for some "get back outs" and Shadow actually turned his head away from her!!!

We repeated the same context during the second session. At one point his eyes were starting to get round. I walked off with him and he was fine after a minute. I used a lot more petting as did Carolyn. I noticed that when she pets him and the food is gone, he will come right back to me. Not really a bad thing at this point.

A few hours later, I took him to the park. We walked around for a bit and then communed with nature on the bench. I worked on kissing the side of his face and gave him a cookie if he was calm. I think he really enjoyed just hangin' out with mom. I know I did.

APRIL 5 – DAY 313

Growl class today. For our first session we all went into the big field. Shadow was a bit stressed and his mouth was tight from the beginning. I tried to get him out of it by throwing cookies to get him moving. He relaxed enough to accept petting by Carolyn. After 10 minutes, he was fine. Shadow and I approached everyone, they did some food throwing and then we ended the session.

Second session. We were in the front yard. I had Shadow next to me. Everyone approached and fed him while he was in a down. Cynthia got down low and relatively close to take still photos. (To some dogs, cameras can feel threatening.) Everyone fed him by hand, and his mouth was like butter. Carolyn came up later and he was just wonderful.

Third session. We all walked and ran around waving our arms and Shadow was amazingly calm. No reaction to moving body parts. I had noticed in the past that if someone stopped feeding him, he would come back to me for more cookies. This time, after Carolyn petted him, he went to the closest person for more cookies—it isn't just "Carolyn pets me and then I go to Mom for more"—he is now indiscriminate about who feeds him. Carolyn also petted him on his head! Three times!!! He was really relaxed these last two sessions. The first one wasn't terrible by any means, but I see a "raising of the bar" and I am not the one pushing it!

Great Doggie! Shadow is progressing in leaps and bounds now and my head is almost spinning! He is moving calmly through new contexts and bouncing back quickly from any stress he may be feeling.

Carolyn feeding Shadow.

APRIL 8 – DAY 316

I took Shadow to my training facility today and we played tug for a few minutes. He is still unsure about the whole concept of the game. I held a toy out to him, told him to take it, put a very slight pressure on the toy and then I released it, said, "give" and handed him the other toy. We played for a few minutes and then did some heeling. I started to teach him directed jumping and the broad jump. Later I had him up on the window seat and we communed for a few minutes.

Tonight he was really wired and went crazy stealing things, which he gave up readily. Jim went to bed early and took Shadow with him. Good riddance!

APRIL 10 – DAY 318

Had the boys out in the yard yesterday with the Boomer Balls. Shadow was lying down in the baby pool, saw some kids walking by, and calmly looked at them and then looked at me. Tons of praise and I threw the ball down into the yard for him to push around. He was also giving me some get back outs and lie-downs away from the Boomer Ball!!!! A short while later, Shadow got out of the yard from a hole under the deck and went next door. I don't know if he was barking at the two dogs that were tied up or their owner, but I called him to come and he instantly complied!!! It took me a few hours to come down from that one! WHEW!

Good Doggie! You came back instantly when I called even though you were aroused! THANK YOU!!!!

APRIL 11 – DAY 319

Shadow got out of the back yard again today (same place—Jim REALLY has to fix it). Once Jim realized he was out and called him, he came right back. Shadow had rolled in something really smelly, so we had to bathe him and he was the best yet. He still won't go in the tub on his own, but Jim was able to pick him up and although Shadow was nervous, he didn't try to bite or urinate. His pupils were large, but the shape of his eyes were normal, his face looked good, and his body wasn't tight. Toward the end of the bath, he was calm enough to eat cookies while I was blowing him dry!!! Then he rubbed himself all over the furniture, jumped on Jim and me, ran into his crate and stayed there.

Shadow has been really good these past few days, even though I have had no time to train him. When I don't have the time, I let him play with the Boomer Ball, which tires him out quite nicely. He is still stealing things but giving up most of the items with less stress. Yesterday he stole something then brought it right to Jim and gave it up.

APRIL 12 – DAY 320

Growl class. We started the day with a walk in the big field with Cynthia, John, and Carolyn. Shadow was a bit nervous for the first few minutes. Carolyn was right outside the van when I let him out, which was a new context, but he was fine. Carolyn was touching him and everyone else hand-fed him. I also did some TTtouch.

For the second session we all went into the barn. Carolyn petted him, everyone else fed him, working on leaning over while he was either sitting or lying down. He was great. I had everyone stand around while I tried to do some heeling but he was too distracted. I tried one more time to get his attention and when I couldn't, I ended it. No sense beating a dead horse!

APRIL 13 – DAY 321

A private lesson today. We walked around for a few minutes. Shadow was fine almost from the beginning of the session. Carolyn did a tiny bit of petting around his neck and some touching of his sides and hind end. We went into the barn and I did some competition heeling and he was great!

For our next context we went to the front yard. He seems to be more nervous in that area, so we keep things simple for him when we work there. I had Carolyn bend over to pick up objects and he showed no reaction whatsoever! Then I played some fetch with him and did some directionals; he was relaxed and happy.

About a half-hour later I brought him to the park and we sat at the picnic table while I ate my bagel, and he was very sweet. There were a few fishermen walking around and he only reacted to two of them—just a raised ear set and slightly higher head set, so I gave him **something else to do**, i.e., practiced directionals. He calmed down and refocused on me instantly. A paper flew off the table and I asked him to retrieve it, he went over and licked it instead. After repeating the cue two more times (I don't think he believed that I actually WANTED him to get the paper. After all, I have been trying to get him to NOT pick up papers!) he brought it to me, sat, and gave it up instantly! We sat there for 40 minutes and he was super. Shadow has been a model of good doggie-ness.

He got out of the backyard again, but came instantly when I called him. Then

TRAINING CONCEPT

Doing something else: When working with a dog that has issues, it is imperative to teach him all kinds of incompatible or alternate behaviors to do instead of aggressing. So far, Shadow has the following incompatible and alternate behavior repertoire: eye contact, heeling with attention, sit, down, stay, come, name recognition, targeting my hand, directionals, weaving around my legs, retrieving, roll over, go visit, chasing a toy, lying down in mid-chase, get back out and lie down when someone bends over, drop on recall, chase Mommy (but don't chase other people), and he will let certain people pet him.

Jim fixed the broken fence. Whew! Shadow is lying down next to me while I type this, not annoying me at all! Wahoo!

APRIL 19 – DAY 327

Growl class—newly renamed "The Breakfast Club." We renamed it because Growl class is a misnomer since there aren't any growls going on. We had some new people in class today. Jen and her husband Bob and their two dogs, plus the usual complement of people and dogs.

We started in the big field and Shadow was very stressed. His mouth was very tight and his body was stiff. I was able to get him to relax somewhat. Carolyn petted him and, after 20 minutes, I ended the session. I am sure he was stressed because we added two new people. Also, I didn't use his harness—he always has it on during lessons or walks in the park and today I chose not to use it. Plus he could hear Sergeant barking in the car. Sometimes he is still reactive to strange **dogs barking mindlessly**.

Because he was nervous for the first session, I repeated the same context since I didn't want to push him. The change for the better was instantly apparent. He was calm from the moment I took him out of the van. We all walked around and I had him go visit everyone. Carolyn petted him and then I ran around and he followed me. I had everyone spread out and do funny body movements, and he ignored them. Shadow was marvelous!

> ### TRAINING CONCEPT
>
> **Dogs barking mindlessly:** If your dog is reactive to barking dogs, you don't have to "just live with it." You can change your dog's reaction to the barking by reinforcing your dog for quiet, calm behavior. When I first got Beau, and then Shadow, they both reacted terribly to Cody when he went into a barking jag. I heavily reinforced them for NOT reacting, and now they (mostly) don't beat Cody up. I reinforce them when strange dogs bark as well, so that the behavior will generalize to all dogs, not just Cody.

We went into the front yard and did the tie-out exercise—everyone approaches him and feeds him while he remains in a stay. I had him start in the down position, progressed to a sit, and then to a stand! This was the first time we did the stand in this context. Jen and Carolyn were able to pet him and everyone said his mouth was like butter. This session was about 40 minutes.

My friends approaching my calm dog who is in the down position!

I practiced sit-stays with all three dogs in a row in the living room—they were within two feet of each other and did well. I don't normally train them together because they get jealous of each other, forget that I just gave one a cookie, and now he thinks "he's getting one—where's mine?"

APRIL 21 – DAY 329

I took the dogs to a pet fair. At the end of the day, I took Shadow out when there were only a few people scattered around. He was calmer than I was! No stress whatsoever—he was great! I gave him a few cookies when bringing him out of the van and after that I had no more food. We just walked around for about five minutes and then I put him away.

Brought them all home, let them play with the Boomer Balls, and got them to "swim" in the kiddie pool. Took a nap and Shadow has been very calm for the rest of the day.

This Is One Brilliant Dog!

APRIL 24 – DAY 332

Took all of the dogs to my training facility. I worked Shadow on competition behaviors. I can't remember how long ago we worked on these but he was remarkable! We did heeling, figure eights, halts, the stand for exam with me touching him all over, retrieving the dumbbell, recalls and directionals. I forgot, because of all the behavioral work, how truly amazing he is in competition. And today was the first time that he was excited but calm. His mouth was medium soft and he wasn't frantic about working. I didn't have to work him out of being stressed!!! Session lasted for 20 minutes.

We went to the park and I walked him around on a collar (instead of the harness) for five minutes. We saw some kids up on the bridge and he alerted to them—head high, ears up, but his tail stayed down (a sign of relaxation—conversely a high tail or "gay" tail in a Border Collie is a sign of arousal). We went down to the river and then heeled all the way back to the car. I have been letting him play with the Boomer Ball on an almost daily basis and today, for the first time, he came off the ball when I called! He wasn't in mid-play with it, he was just lying down next to it, but hey, it's a start! I also left the back door open and he came in a few times, ran around the house looking for me (!), then ran out again.

He has been mostly good all night. We had one little incident where I was bending down (but not over him) petting him and he dive-bombed my face, licking, and then jammed his front teeth into my lip. After that I let him outside for a few minutes and when he came in he was breathing heavily. Since I don't think it was from exertion, I massaged his gums and he visibly relaxed. He lay on the floor next to me while I watched TV (a very rare occurrence—I never watch TV).

There are 52 Cards in This Deck!

APRIL 26 – DAY 334

Session with John at his house today. We were going to start with John outside the fence while Shadow and I were inside. Shadow was so completely unconcerned with John that we had him come right inside. We played with the ball and switched from me doing get back outs to John doing them. The first time John leaned over, Shadow rushed the toy, so we both stood up and walked away. John tried again and Shadow moved away so John could throw the ball.

I had been working last night on getting Shadow to get back out using my eyes instead of voice or arm movements—for no particular reason, just for the heck of it. We tried it today and he did amazingly well—even with John doing it! He went back and forth between calm and nervous, although the percentage of calmness was greater. I also noticed that he was holding his tail very high, so I made it a criteria that he lower his tail before I would throw the ball again. I whispered, "lie down," a few times until his body would relax, and then threw the toy. He caught on very fast.

For the next session, John was sitting in a chair. I told Shadow to go visit and he didn't jump! John fed him mostly by hand and then encouraged Shadow to jump in his lap. JOHN WAS PETTING HIS WHOLE BODY WHILE FEEDING HIM!!!!! THIS WAS A FIRST AMONG FIRSTS! (Brave John!) Shadow was completely fine with the handling. He came back to me and I fed him. John and I did a round-robin kind of thing between us. I sat on the ground and Shadow got a ball and laid down between me and John, then we all hung out for a few minutes. John commented that Shadow looked more relaxed than ever before.

Came home, took a nap and now all of the dogs are outside with the Boomer Balls. I have a nine-hour day tomorrow and he is going to be stuck in the crate for most of that time so I want him to get his excess energy out now.

Good Doggie! Need I say more? I am bursting with pride!

APRIL 29 – DAY 337

I took Shadow to the park and worked him for about 10 minutes in the parking lot. A few cars and people were going by. I had him doing attention heeling and directionals. Although he was a tiny bit nervous for the first few minutes, he relaxed quickly. I am really starting to do more petting and TTouch with him as a reward for calmness. It is so hard not to use food all of the time! I was going to bring him down into the park, but there were too many people for me to feel comfortable.

Then we went to a different park and he was sensational again! Did some dumbbell work (brilliant as usual) and then directionals. I started—again—to teach him to roll over, something I hadn't practiced in almost a year. In teaching roll over, I lean over the dog. Shadow still has a problem with this at times.

After that, we went over to where there were tons of people playing softball, and we sat and communed with nature. During both sessions he was quite calm and his mouth was very soft.

APRIL 30 – DAY 338

Shadow and I went to the park today. We worked on tug. He handled it well—much less stressed than previously and I ended it sooner. Also did some directionals and heeling, both of which he did wonderfully!

Shadow saw two men working with heavy machinery about 100 feet away. He didn't make a big fuss about it and remained very focused on me. I am finding that if I engage him in some activity, rather than having him sit and stare at me, he is calmer.

Later, at home, Shadow had one of my socks, and paraded around with it. Jim ignored him and Shadow came over and dropped the sock in his lap! Outstanding!!!

MAY 1 – DAY 339

Today Gets the "HOLY SMOKES" Award!!!

Carolyn and Lois (our "guest dog bait" person) were in the big field and Shadow and I were outside the fence. We did some competition heeling and I allowed him to go visit. Carolyn hand-fed him, Lois threw food. We did some get back outs. There was no reaction to Lois, so after 10 minutes, Carolyn and Lois came outside the fence. Shadow was fine. We ended the session.

For the next session, Carolyn was sitting in a chair under the tree and Lois was standing next to her. We approached and Shadow did some nice lie-downs for food. Then Carolyn fed Shadow and petted him all over his body. Many times! Shadow was sniffing her and rubbing himself on her legs like a cat does. He walked away from Carolyn, returned to her, and she continued to pet him without the use of food. She also did some TTouch on him. He was so incredibly relaxed it was beyond wonderful. I WAS SO CHOKED UP, I STARTED CRYING!

As if that wasn't enough, Lois asked him for lie-downs and he responded wonderfully. Then, John came up out of nowhere and got down on his knees and Shadow kissed his face (John has a beard and so does Jim—Shadow likes beards), then he fed him. This was a new thing for him in many respects:

1. Someone approaching that he didn't see coming

2. Someone kneeling on the ground

3. One new person

4. Carolyn petting him all over and doing TTouch

5. Being completely and totally 100 percent relaxed for BOTH sessions!

Lois said that she couldn't sense any reason to be afraid or nervous about him—she felt only calm vibes from him and she thought he was quite wonderful. He has been super the rest of the day. I am tickled beyond belief with his progress!

MAY 3 – DAY 341

Incredibly Enough, AN EVEN BETTER DAY!!!!

The Breakfast Club class. Shadow and I went into the big field and Eileen, John, and Carolyn followed separately. People "coming out of nowhere" is a new context for him, but he was fine. He jumped on them a little bit, but it was very soft and gentle jumping, not his usual high speed ramming of his front feet into your abdomen (so he can get a kick out of hearing you go "Oomph!"). I wanted to start desensitizing him to what John Q. Public might do, so I had them wave their arms in weird ways once he had approached them and was lying down. He was quite calm for this and just looked at everyone quizzically. Then Shadow went wading in the baby pool. There were cookies at the bottom and he stuck his head in the water and was blowing bubbles! Very funny!

For the next context, Carolyn was sitting, John and Eileen were kneeling, and I was standing. We were all feeding him and Carolyn was petting him—he was fine. Carolyn started to teach Shadow to balance a cookie on his nose and then catch it!!!! To do this, she gave him one cookie to keep his head still and put another one on his nose!!!! HE WAS COMPLETELY CALM about her hands approaching his head AND when she was done, he waited patiently for her to do it again! She repeated this at least 12 times. When he was successful in catching the cookie, we all cheered and applauded AND HE DIDN'T GET NERVOUS!!! THEN, EILEEN AND JOHN BOTH PETTED HIM AND HE WAS FINE!!!! This was a first—everyone petting him.

For the third session we did more of the same—petting, and balancing the cookie game. I did some tricks with him. During this session, Carolyn was in a chair, John and I were both kneeling. After 15 minutes he saw some goats and went toward them. Luckily they were fenced in and after about one minute he came roaring back to me without me having to call him!!!! He was aroused by the goats but recovered quickly. I tried to get his focus for competition stuff but he couldn't do it. We continued for awhile and then put him away for a few minutes.

He was calm from the outset of the first session and it continued all the way through. I am proud of him, and proud of me, for not rushing after the success we had on May 1. It was tempting, but I held myself in check! I am very careful to change each context slightly rather than dramatically. I am watching his tail more and we are waiting for it to lower before throwing balls or food. He is doing a phenomenally great job!

Good Doggie and Good Pam! Shadow is really turning the corner here into normalcy. Proud, elated, rapturous, exhilarated, happy, thrilled, euphoric, doesn't describe how I am feeling!

MAY 4 – DAY 342

Here are two e-mails I received from Ted Turner today:

> Your "Holy Smokes" awards are becoming legendary. It's great to see that by sticking to the basic principles of patience, perseverance, and positives, an animal this far in the hole is now climbing Everest. No doubt, he's there already, and learning to like people again. In the big picture, you've turned this animal completely around very quickly. You are truly a savior!

> Outstanding stuff! Very impressive, Pam. I have yet to run into someone with your determination and commitment. The videos are excellent. I don't know if you've had a chance to compare his current mannerisms with the first video but it is remarkable.

My e-mail back to Ted:

> Thanks for the kind words!!! They truly mean so very much to me! Be well and I hope to hear from you soon! And thank you again for the "clicks." Praise is a HUGE reinforcer for me.

MAY 5 – DAY 343

Took the boys to a pet fair. Lisa P. was standing about 15 feet away. I fed

Shadow and kept his attention on me, his mouth was soft. I told Lisa to get some food for Shadow to greet her. As she was reaching for some, his mouth became very tight, the look in his eyes was funny, and his nose got big even though she was nowhere near him. I asked him "do you have to pee—what is the matter?" as I looked around to see what might be bothering him. I couldn't find anything amiss and he ran into his crate in the van. I have no idea what was bothering him. I was calm, so it wasn't me sending him fearful signals.

I had him stay in the van for about 20 minutes, then brought him out again, and he was fine. Had him visit Lisa with a lie-down and she tossed him food. He was pretty calm. I didn't want to push it by letting her pet him because of his previous reaction. After a few minutes of Lisa feeding him, I put him back in the van. I left the van door open so he could see Lisa and he stayed completely calm.

I think he did great overall—tons of people and dogs were there and a dog across the parking lot was barking the entire day. Shadow was really tired all night.

Good Pam! For again, not pushing Shadow beyond his limits! It is so tempting to push the envelope and rush the process.

MAY 6 – DAY 344

I took him for some agility at Jane's—not a lesson, just playing around. He did everything very nicely and calmly. Once home, Shadow had a tiff with Beau—they were playing when all of a sudden—whammo! It ended within five seconds. He has been a tiny bit needy today and is stealing things for attention. I was too busy to deal with it, so I let him outside more than I usually do. Hey, we do what we can…

MAY 8 – DAY 346

Private lesson today. We did our usual walk around and then we went into the barn. Shadow wasn't as relaxed and calm as last week, but I wasn't expecting all of our sessions to be perfect, so I wasn't upset. He did some great competition behaviors, but when Carolyn tried to pet him he moved away from her.

Good Pam! For not expecting the learning roller coaster to smooth out into a learning line. Sure, we are getting a tiny backslide here, but the percentage of calm behaviors outweigh the stressed behaviors. I am tickled with his progress!

MAY 10 – DAY 348

Breakfast Club. We started out by walking around the front yard. He was nervous the instant he came out of the van and wouldn't let me massage his gums. I told everyone that he was nervous, so they all acted accordingly, not hand-feeding or touching him. I practiced having him roll over three times. We walked around the farm and we all threw a toy for him and he was fine with that. Eileen and John and Carolyn were bending over and he backed away appropriately. We ended the session.

For the second session we went right into the barn. He did some nice competition stuff—heeling, recall past a toy (!), and a stand for exam. Everyone came up and fed him and he was fine. Carolyn touched him and Cynthia made an abrupt movement as if to touch him and he remained calm! Then Cynthia and Eileen were both petting him and feeding at the same time. We all did the "balance the food on the nose" trick and he was VERY relaxed. He really loved Eileen today. I REALLY REALLY REALLY wanted to do more but I ended it then. God, that was hard! I still have a problem mentally with my "greedy trainer syndrome," but I know when I push it I am ALWAYS sorry—whether it is with Shadow, Beau, or Cody. Part of his stress in the first session today was because he was crated for most of yesterday and didn't get a chance to get his ya-yas out.

I am trying to add more "stuff" other than just walking around—competition, freestyle, agility, stupid pet tricks—whatever—just to bring new dimensions into our sessions and he is doing wonderfully. Sometimes I think "Yikes it has been almost a year and this is all I have gotten to so far," and then there are other times when I think, "Wow, look how much we have done and it isn't even a full year yet." Shadow isn't even two years old. I tend to forget how young he is.

When we came home I let the boys play with the Boomer Ball for about two hours, then we took a nap. Shadow actually asked me if we could take one! He looked at me, then very slowly walked into the bedroom, periodically looking back at me to see if I was following.

After dinner I took Shadow out in the front yard and worked on scent articles and heeling. He did really great! This is a new context with him—working in the yard. I had three articles out and one of them had my scent and some peanut butter. We did around six reps and he was a bit hesitant at first, not sure what I wanted him to do, but each time the pickups got faster and more accurate. His heeling was pretty good and we even had a mild distraction—a new neighbor boy was walking across the street. I did not want to push my luck and did not want him to start barking at the little boy, so I ended the session. I am trying really hard to stick to only one or two behaviors in each training session and I see that it is paying off.

I put him in the crate so I could work the other dogs and when I let him out he was wired!!! Jim and I tried playing with him but he was too fired up. I let him outside for a minute and he smashed into the screen door, telling us he wanted to come in. Methinks he needs a "cat nap," so I put him in his crate to chill out.

MAY 12 – DAY 350

Took him to a match show today and brought him out three times, each time a little closer to the crowd. He was great—very calm the entire time, no signs of stress, body supple.

MAY 16 – DAY 354

Private lesson today. We took him to the Appalachian Trail. He was a bit stressed. Heck, I was a bit stressed! At first, he was fine, then we saw some people and even though we were about 100 yards away, he "glommed" on to them with his eyes and I couldn't get his attention. So, we walked off into the woods. His mouth was very tight most of the walk although he did seem to enjoy himself. I did some heeling with him and he was great. We saw a person walking a dog off leash, so we backtracked through the woods to avoid them. There were people around my van—Carolyn moved it so we could get in. Our goal for this first VERY new context was to have no overt signs of stress— barking, lunging, etc. He did one bit of blowing in the beginning when he saw the first group of people, but after that the only sign of stress was a very tight mouth, which came and went.

We will continue to do this for many weeks until he is really relaxed. Then we will NOT go out of our way to avoid people.

MAY 17 – DAY 355

Shadow's second birthday! Breakfast Club.

We played in the front yard for a few minutes and then went into the barn. He was very nervous. Tried to do some heeling, and while he did that well, he was very tight. Tried to get him out of it by playing ball, but he couldn't relax. No one tried to pet him.

We did almost the same context for the second session. I realized Shadow really needs to get his ya-ya's out before getting down to business. We threw the ball for him and did work on directionals, with John throwing the ball. We did not go into the barn again nor did I have anyone pet him. He was very relaxed.

Later on I took the boys to the park. Shadow did very well. We did eye contact, heeling, and directionals. We were about 300 yards away from Laurie and Lisa and their dogs. There was no reaction from Shadow when Lisa's dogs were barking in her van. Then all of a sudden millions of vans drove up en masse and parked next to my van! Yikes! I had Laurie move my van so I could put him away because suddenly all of these screaming kids were racing around. Shadow handled it very well—he was very focused on me and not nervous at all. And I forced myself to breathe!!!

Later tonight I was brushing Beau when Shadow asked me to brush him. I got down on the floor and started to brush him. When I lifted him up to brush his butt and tail, he attacked Cody who was just walking by. A case of displacement aggression because he still doesn't really like to be brushed. I didn't say anything, but ran out of the room and Shadow stopped. Once that was over, I put Beau and Cody in the bedroom and brushed Shadow. He was lying down and I fed him while I brushed. Then I massaged his gums and petted him gently and he seemed to relax. Brought the other dogs out and everyone was fine. Shadow was so tired that he fell asleep in the middle of the kitchen floor. When he woke up, he and Beau played nicely.

Looking back, he has been sort of nervous for the past few days—ever since last Thursday's Breakfast Club. Don't know why though, nothing has changed around here and that class was a great one. I am planning to take things a little slower—not that I have been rushing anything but if he is nervous, it is time to slow down even more. I do NOT want him to regress—I know I am not God and can't control everything, but I would feel terrible if I caused him to "lose it."

HINDSIGHT

One of the pitfalls of rescuing a dog is that I miss seeing them as puppies. They "look" like adults and it is difficult to remember just how young Shadow really is. Most dogs don't fully mature until they are three or four years old. It is amazing to me, notwithstanding the behavioral issues he has, how much Shadow knows already, at only two years of age! Give the dog a break Pam!

MAY 20 – DAY 358

Great day! Took all of the boys to a pet store. Worked outside with Shadow first. He was INCREDIBLY wonderful! Very calm from the outset. I worked him at competition heeling on the grass first, then on the parking lot, about 100 feet from people and other dogs and cars. His face was VERY soft and his body was supple and relaxed. He let me pet him without jumping on me and he was extremely responsive.

Looking back on the last journal entry, Cody has been VERY barky lately and I think that is starting to annoy Shadow a bit. So, today when we came home, I fed Shadow for about 5 minutes while Cody was barking.

MAY 22 – DAY 360

Took Shadow to my training facility today. Laurie was there and I had her sit down while Shadow and I did some competition behaviors. We played a recall game and he seemed to be very relaxed, so I had him "go visit." Boy, is he getting good at that! I tell him to "go visit" and he looks toward the person, walks up a few steps and lies down with the speed of light. I had Laurie throw food at his butt to get him to turn away from her. Did that for a few minutes and then I had her toss food between his front legs. I called him to me and fed him and his mouth was like butter! Total session lasted 15 minutes.

He has been a bit wired at home—I think his displacement stuff is because of Cody's barking. I also have been clicking Shadow for dropping things out of his mouth. My reasoning is threefold: 1) if he steals things, he will bring them to me, instead of going off and devouring them; 2) he will give them up readily rather than multiple rebiting or devouring even faster in an attempt to hide the evidence; and 3) to eventually get him to stop stealing things in the first place. I did this with Beau and it worked. I am also going to be clicking him more for NOT having anything in his mouth at all. Don't know if he will understand why I am clicking him for that, but heck, it is worth a try.

MAY 23 – DAY 361

Tracy was our "dog bait" person today. We did some heeling and dumbbell work and then I took Shadow off leash. Had him go visit and his lie-downs were very fast! I had Tracy throw food toward his butt and then at his front feet. His recalls were great, mouth was medium soft. He was doing so well I ended it after about 15 minutes. Tracy said that if she didn't know he was aggressive, she never would have guessed it and remarked on how talented he is. That's my boy!

MAY 24 – DAY 362

Took Cody, Beau, and Shadow to Carolyn's for fun. Had them all in the big field with me, throwing the Frisbee for about 45 minutes. Then let them all meet Dave and Meg (the dogs). They were all true to form—Beau did a belly up to Meg and Dave, Shadow charged in and split them up, and Cody completely ignored them after initial sniffing. Meg and Shadow had their tiff, Dave got in the middle to stop them, and Beau went off in avoidance. Lots of teeth baring, lip licking, posturing, growling, snapping. It was fascinating to watch, especially since it wasn't a real fight! I walked away, Shadow followed. Then I brought them all back together and fed everyone, and no more "fights" ensued.

I JUST REMEMBERED! A few days ago, I was sitting on the back porch and encouraged Shadow to jump in my lap and he did. And sat calmly for about five minutes while I gently stroked him!!!! He was great all evening, letting me clean without going into attention-seeking, stealing behaviors. WAHOO!!

MAY 29 – DAY 367

Our first anniversary! So much has happened in the past year, in terms of his training process and my growing expertise as a trainer. This is such hard work! There have been horrible days, incredible days and everything in between. I have cried with frustration and cried for joy. Am I sorry I kept Shadow? Nope!

MAY 30 – DAY 368

Took him for the second time to the Delaware Water Gap trails today. He was okay, although his mouth was very tight—about a ten percent reduction of stress over the last time we were here. I had him on harness this time, and practiced heeling and directionals while we were walking. He calmed down immensely. We ran into a man on the trail, so we made a fast beeline for the woods. (I do wonder what people think of us doing that. They probably think we are nuts!) I kept Shadow's attention on me, and once the man passed, we proceeded back to the trail. This is good practice for me too—I am VERY nervous, which is probably why Shadow is nervous. I am practicing breathing, but I'm sure I am sending off stress smells. His body was a tad softer than the last time. I have noticed that the amazing calmness we had gotten in the middle of

May hasn't returned yet. A slight regression period, which I hope will soon pass…

JUNE 4 – DAY 373

Took Shadow to John and Cynthia's. For the first session Shadow and I were in the yard with THREE Boomer Balls. John and Cynthia were outside the fence watching. After an initial tense moment, Shadow relaxed and I was able to get him to lie down for the ball. Cynthia brought out her bike and was riding up and down outside the fence. Shadow was calm and did none of the fence chasing he does in our backyard. She also brought Midget (a dog) out with her and they sniffed noses through the fence and were fine. Ended the session with John leaning over him over the fence (John is VERY tall) and feeding him.

Second session. Brought Shadow out with Beau. Then we brought Little Pam (a dog, and yes, she WAS named after me) out and threw the balls for all three dogs. With each new context, he was totally composed.

JUNE 6 – DAY 375

I realized the other day, if something were to happen physically to Shadow before we were ready for a vet visit, he could very easily be traumatized and ruin all we have accomplished so far. In that case, it would either be kill him or me! So, I have started to desensitize him to the muzzle. I took him out for a run to get his ya-yas out and then started our session with the muzzle. I wadded peanut butter in the wire muzzle and let him eat it. Repeated this six times. I put peanut butter in the muzzle and while he was licking it, fed him cookies from the side of the muzzle. After a few reps, I put nothing in the muzzle and just held it out. He rammed his face in it. It was very funny!

Repeated about 12 more times and we both got better at it—Shadow in ramming less forcefully, and me in getting the food in his mouth better, while holding the muzzle steady. A few times he ripped the muzzle out of my hands with nose and flung it (I did NOT laugh!) I had him retrieve it and we started again, always letting him make the choice of putting his face in it.

Tonight he has been really good. Shadow seems to be slowly getting over whatever it was that was bothering him. Jim helped me to brush his rear—Jim fed, while I brushed. He didn't even know I existed.

JUNE 8 – DAY 377

I worked Shadow in the front yard. We did go-outs to the baby gate with just my head and eyes as the signal and he was superb. We did some heeling, turns, and a stand for exam with me touching him all over in obnoxious ways. I showed Jim how he does his directionals and we did some more muzzle work. He now places his nose in the muzzle and waits calmly for me to clip it closed. Jim was suitably impressed! My Calm Boy Is BACK!!!! WAHOO!

JUNE 12 – DAY 381

AND… ANOTHER HOLY SMOKES DAY!!!!!

We met Carolyn at the Delaware Water Gap trails. Shadow was super-relaxed from the get-go. Carolyn fed him while he was in the van and he was perfectly calm. We walked, and he was a normal dog in every respect!!! He was giving me eye contact, walking calmly by my side, not pulling on the leash if he went on ahead, checking in with me every few seconds. His face was super dooper soft, as was his mouth and body. He played in the water a little and I worked on desensitizing him to hands doing obnoxious things to his head while Carolyn and I had a half-hour discussion on the difference between counterconditioning and desensitization. Funny what we talk about for entertainment.

We saw someone on the trail so Shadow and I veered into the woods. When we came back onto the trail, Carolyn was standing there. Shadow went up to her in a very friendly manner and sat down in front of her in greeting! Then we ran into a man with his dog and since the trail was very wide at that point, we did not move off of the trail. Carolyn moved to "split" between the other person and Shadow, she was on the left and I was on his right and he STAYED COMPLETELY CALM!!!!!! I sang "Happy Birthday" to make sure that I was breathing. We both did really well!!! I used a fraction of the amount of food I usually do and did lots more praise and petting.

The really neat thing is that I thought we would have to work for months in this context (trail) before getting to where we were today. This was only the THIRD session. Carolyn said we both did the very best we have ever done and gave me wads of compliments AND ice cream! When we got home, Shadow asked me if we could take a nap—he kept looking longingly at his crate and then back to me. He has been incredibly calm all night, very gentle and sweet.

Good Everyone! Wowie-zowie! Such amazing progress in such a short time!

JUNE 13 – DAY 382

Took the boys to the park and let them "swim" in the river. Shadow doesn't actually swim—he wades out to his chest and retrieves sticks that I throw. He also really likes to put his entire head under water and blow bubbles. I think he would make a great water rescue dog—he sniffs the surface of the water and then dives under to get sticks.

JUNE 14 – DAY 383 And Yet Another Super Amazing Day!

Breakfast Club today. Before we started, we were all standing around the van with the side door open and Shadow remained calm. First context. Shadow and I played by ourselves. I was throwing the Frisbee and doing directionals. Cynthia came over and Shadow jumped on her in a nice way, getting her all muddy. Cynthia petted his sides! Then I put him away for a few minutes.

Brought him out again and continued to play. Carolyn, John, and Cynthia joined us. Carolyn was very impressed with his directionals. There were also two new people working on the farm. I was nervous at first because he was off leash, but Carolyn and Cynthia said that he was up for it. So I sang Happy Birthday and I was fine. A few times he alerted to them—head up high and a slightly stiff-legged gait, but I called him to me and he ignored them. He was getting tired so I put him away.

For our third context we were all in the front yard. I tried to do some heeling with him but he wasn't interested so I did very simple things—like having him in heel position, waiting for eye contact and then releasing him to get the ball. Once I could tell he was concentrating, I had him "go visit" everyone and they all fed and petted him all over his body—all of them! A few times, Cynthia was feeding and Carolyn was petting—even his rear! Wow! I had him weave between my legs and Cynthia's legs, and then I worked on "roll over". He was super dooper! This session was about 15 minutes.

The entire time his face was soft. His mouth was a bit tight at first but he relaxed almost immediately. We all feel that he has truly turned the corner and is an "almost normal" dog. The key point now is to get ME calm.

Received two e-mails from Ted:

> I had one reviewer who said he teared up when he read your log. Pretty powerful stuff in context! You're really on track with Shadow. Simply delightful to read your progress from my end. I can't wait to watch this animal live!

In his second e-mail Ted responded to my question of whether or not it was okay to publish our "disagreement" about Growl class:

> Reality is what makes for compelling reading. I would feel comfortable including the facts, regardless of outcome. It's YOUR book. I don't mind being wrong...in fact I'm rather good at it!

JUNE 15 – DAY 384

Another letter from Ted:

> Excellent stuff about Shadow. He is generalizing fully now and seems to be at ease in all surroundings. Isn't it amazing how confident one gets when criticism is replaced with support! As you are doing, don't forget to reinforce him for socially appropriate behavior in all contexts...especially the behavior that most take for granted.
>
> You're right about your behavior as well. If you get too tight, you'll be too anxious to provide immediate reinforcement. Go girl! Have a great summer with Shadow...now the real test begins!!!

An Incredible, Extraordinary Day!!

JUNE 16 – DAY 385

Enrolled in the aggressive dog seminar for the third time. Before we started, I took him out in the big field and played with him for a few minutes. Then everyone (Jen, Bob, Carolyn, and Christine) came into the field and walked around while we played. He was completely focused on me. I had Jen and Bob throw the Frisbee for him and he was super dooper. Even with them leaning over the toy! I had him "go visit" and he was fine with that. The really cool thing is that the people were new and he didn't care!

For our second session we all went into the barn. We did some recalls past everyone and then did a stand for exam where everyone was circling him and feeding while I stood in front of him. The stay part lacked a bit of "staying," but he was calm, and that was more important. Then everyone was petting and touching him and he was fine. We did a figure eight around Bob and Jen— Shadow was amazing! I had him weaving around my legs and then taught him to do the weave poles in about 30 seconds, he did them perfectly about four times in a row. What a sensational dog!

I wanted to start working on some of the different components of the CGC (Canine Good Citizen) test. In particular, the supervised separation part where he has to be with a stranger for three minutes while I am out of sight. I had Carolyn hold the leash while I left the building for 15 seconds. We did three trials, gradually increasing the time I was out of the building to 30 seconds. They were all feeding him, and on the last one, Jen and Carolyn were feeding him while Bob was leaning over and petting him!!!

He has been SUCH a great dog at home tonight. Leaving me alone so I can work, letting me pet him when I can and not annoying me further when I release him, being nice to the other dogs, very relaxed and CONTENTED! I am truly sensing that he is HAPPY—proud of himself and thrilled that I am proud of him.

HINDSIGHT

Just for the heck of it, I looked through Shadow's journal and came up with some interesting things:

May 29. Rescued him.

December 12. Carolyn hand-fed him for the first time (seven months after I got him).

January 27. Carolyn was able to barely touch him for the first time (one and a half months after the first hand-feeding).

June 16. Complete strangers were able to pet him all over his body while leaning over him, throw toys for him, hand-feed him (six months after the first touch by Carolyn).

Stupendous growth the last three months! My head is spinning! Perseverance and positives DO pay! Am I proud???!!! You bet!

6

There are two ways to live your life.
One is as though nothing is a miracle.
The other is as though everything is.

—Albert Einstein

Such Stuff as Dreams are Made Of

JUNE 17 – DAY 386

HOLY SMOKES days are becoming the norm! One session today at the Breakfast Club class. We went in the barn with Carolyn, Christine, Bob, and Jen. Shadow and I practiced many competition behaviors and his attention was almost perfect.

I had Shadow "go visit" a few times and he was fine. We did figure eights around everyone, directionals using my eyes and not my arm, heeling, drop on recalls, finishes, weave poles, and the tunnel. I had Carolyn kneel down so her face was close to his face and she petted him. Since he was fine, I had Jen do the same thing. We practiced the stand for exam where everyone came up to him and fed him. We did another round and everyone petted him as well. His mouth and posture were all perfectly normal from the beginning and never wavered.

JUNE 18 – DAY 387

Took Shadow to a different trail. Totally new context for Shadow:

1. Cynthia instead of Carolyn

2. Different trail

3. Cynthia had Mia (the dog) with her

Shadow was slightly nervous. His mouth was a bit tight but after a few minutes his body relaxed. We did directionals and lie-downs and kept the walk to about 10 minutes—five minutes out and five minutes back. As we were approaching the van, two people drove up on a motorcycle. I remembered to breathe and did not have to sing Happy Birthday. On a stress level of 1-10, 10 being fainting in fright, I was about a five! Shadow was a one…In addition, Cynthia and I stood by the open van door and she fed Shadow through the crate and his mouth was soft. He started out sitting in his crate, but then was able to totally relax and lie down! His eyes remained calm as Cynthia threw him cookies. He has been great since we came home—just lying around like a good dog!

JUNE 19 – DAY 388

Private lesson today at the trail we normally go to. Well, it was just another HO HUM day walking in the woods WITH MY NORMAL DOG! 'Nough said?!!! WAHOOIE!!!

JUNE 21 – DAY 390

And yet another ordinary session with my NORMAL DOG! I took Shadow in the big field by myself and played Frisbee with him to get his ya-yas out. I left the gate open even though there were people and dogs walking around the farm. I even walked him back to the car off leash!

About 10 minutes later, I took Shadow into the barn. John, Cynthia, and Carolyn were there. We stood around and Cynthia was petting him without using food. John started feeding him and GOT SHADOW TO ROLL OVER— MANY, MANY TIMES! John also had Shadow crouch down and go under his legs, and then petted him all over.

I did some competition heeling and weave poles. Cynthia sat on the floor and we heeled around her. He started kissing her face and then he paid attention to me. She wiggled her fingers at him and he did not lose focus on me. Carolyn stood and we heeled around her. Shadow was tired so I ended the session. We all feel that Shadow is definitely in the "normal range" of normal dog behavior.

Later that day I took the boys to the grooming shop. He was relaxed getting out of the van and going into the shop. There were some people around (not too close) but there was no reaction. I realized that I wasn't breathing and so sang Happy Birthday on the way into the shop. I wanted to groom Cody, and start really desensitizing Shadow to getting in the tub on his own by using the steps. Familiar place, familiar people and he was completely and utterly calm. The shop is very small but he was fine. I had brought Beau as well and Cody

John getting Shadow to roll over!

I'm heeling with Shadow around my friend Cynthia.

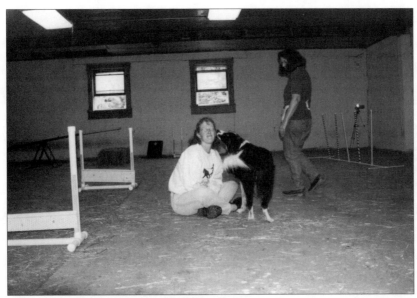

Taking a break from heeling to lick a friendly face.

was in the back being dried, barking continually (as usual). Shadow went up the steps with ease, with no prompting from me. It took him a while to actually put his front feet in the tub. Once he felt comfortable, he was doing it faster and faster. At no time did I try to force or hold him in the tub. I did have some strategically placed cookies and tennis balls so he could reinforce himself when he got to certain points. I stood there passively, to make sure he did not fall off the steps. I was just about to end the session when I turned to Cynthia and said, "I wonder how long it will take him to actually get his whole body in the tub?" She pointed, I turned back and looked—voila! There he was, in the tub!

On the way back to the van I was relaxed and did not need to sing.

I have also noticed that he has finally learned how to CHILL OUT! He is now lying down and resting or napping even if I am not paying attention to him. It has been a dramatic change since June 16th. It is almost as if the light bulb went on his little brain—"OH, this is what you wanted! I can do that!"

On the Ball!

JUNE 25 – DAY 394

BANNER DAY FOR MOMMY!

I was up at Carolyn's today just bonding with each of the dogs separately. Played with two Boomer Balls and worked on relationship exercises. If they went to one ball, I went to the other one, and waited for them to come to me. Then I would kick the ball for them and immediately go to ball number one again and so on. Shadow came off of the ball very fast. At only one point did I have to call him off a ball and he came to me instantly—the other times he came to me of his own free will.

At the end of the session, I left the field, leaving the gate open. I walked to the house, sat down on the bench and waited for Shadow to come to me (which he did) **Brave Pam!!!** I was breathing and didn't need to sing one note! I went into the house to tell Carolyn, she got the significance of that instantly and was very proud!

I sent this e-mail to Ted:

> I just keep thinking how one could learn to stay calm if they were so unfortunate as to be in the mouth of a killer whale...

Ted's response:

> It's not as hard as you might think when you're paralyzed with fear the first time. It's the fifth and sixth time that begins to unnerve you. Having a great time reading your progress!!! You're an impressive woman!

JUNE 26 – DAY 395

We went for a walk in the woods with Carolyn. I started the session by taking Shadow out of the van and let him approach Carolyn while she was across the parking lot. He was very happy to see her and had great body posture when approaching (head down, body wiggling in delight). At one point there was a group of people in front of us and a group behind us. I was ready to stay on the trail, but Shadow was nervous, so we walked off into the woods.

Once I thought the coast was clear, we started to come out of the woods. One of the women in the front group was coming into the woods toward us. (Why would she do that? Maybe she thought we were doing something weird and just had to see for herself.)

Shadow alerted and barked once. I got his attention back to me and he was fine. I think the only reason he barked was because he was startled. After that we went back on the trail and followed the large group of people up the hill. He was perfectly calm and remained so for the rest of the walk.

He was checking in with me every few seconds. I only called him to me once —after that he was checking in on his own. I used food a lot in the beginning, and then used only petting and praise. Carolyn was able to pet him all over his body many times—with no reaction from him—very clear eyes and face.

I want to teach him a new behavior, "stay as people come up to us," so Carolyn went into the woods and came back and approached us. I had Shadow in a down-stay, he did not move and remained calm.

JUNE 27 – DAY 396

Had a short session at my training facility today with John, Cynthia, and Marsha. I brought Shadow in and did some competition heeling, visiting, back to heeling, back to visiting. His face and body were great. John came up from behind and petted Shadow. He was startled and became nervous. It is amazing how fast Shadow's face can change! BUT he did not aggress—just moved away, so I had John approach from the front and Shadow was fine. I threw some food to Shadow while John was petting him and Shadow relaxed after that. John tried to get him to roll over but he did not want to do it. Marsha hand-fed him—didn't do any petting. All in all, it was a great session.

JUNE 28 – DAY 397

Growl class today. New person—Patrice. Because of Shadow's startle reaction to John the other day, I wanted to practice having everyone there "pop up out of nowhere." I walked around the farm and they jumped out from behind bushes, cars, the house, the grill, the ATV. Shadow was fine and utterly calm through all of it. I kept his attention on me (he was able to see that some-one was there) but there was no startle reaction. After I fed a few cookies, I had him "go visit" each person. He hadn't seen Patrice seen since September 9th and I am sure he didn't remember her, so she was a new person for him. Carolyn had a worker wandering around the farm doing chores and Shadow ignored her completely. He was cool, calm, collected.

For our second session we repeated the same things except I had everyone pet him more.

JUNE 29 – DAY 398

I did two training sessions with Shadow today. Our first one was in my front yard. We did some heeling and I had him do a stand for exam. I brushed him while he stood and he did not move!

For our second session we went to my building and worked for about 20 minutes. We practiced heeling, freestyle behaviors, go-outs, and the directed retrieve. Then I threw the tennis ball, petting and relaxing him between each throw. He was great for most everything.

There has been a gradual lessening of "stealing things for attention" and he is chilling out on his own much more. If he does steal things, he is giving them to me slightly faster and with less re-biting of the object. I do not put my hand out to him—I just ask him to give and then wait.

JUNE 30 – DAY 399

Took the boys to a match show today. I didn't enter—just walked around, praying that Shadow would choose to heel with me and he did! There were lots of people by the van but not one peep out of Shadow. Took him in and out of the van and he was super dooper calm from the get go—his mouth was like velvet the entire day. We got within 15 feet of people and dogs and he was great. At home he is better and better every day.

Piece of Cake!

JULY 2 – DAY 401

Took him to the park and we worked on the dumbbell retrieve. He loved it and had apparently missed it very much—wow is he fast! There were tons of kids there today and while he seemed interested, it wasn't in a bad way. We worked on a few competition behaviors. All the while, Beau and Cody were arguing in the van and the kids were wrestling and he was a NORMAL dog! I had him on leash—it would be silly to press my luck, but he never went to the end of it and was always responsive to me. His face and body were soft. I find that if he is nervous and I engage him in some activity, he settles quickly. It doesn't matter what it is as long as either his brain or muscles are engaged.

This evening, I worked each dog in the front yard. I worked him last. He had heard me with the other boys and he was screaming in his crate—he was super-charged! I petted him and spoke to him softly until his breathing rate slowed down and then he was amazing—directed retrieve again, go-outs, stays, heeling, a cuddle session, and then release to the back yard for a session with the Boomer Ball. He was great all night. Very calm, relaxed, sweet, and loving.

JULY 5 – DAY 404

Didn't do much these past few days other than work in the front yard. Yesterday, my neighbors were walking by in droves when I brought him out so I kept him busy with different behaviors and he was fine. Worked on heeling, directed retrieve, go-outs and just cuddling. I had to force myself to stop the session.

This morning was Breakfast Club. Would you believe it took me 10 minutes to remember what we worked on last time because he was SUCH A NORMAL DOG!?! I threw the Frisbee around and had everyone kneel down and pet him. After a few minutes, we all took turns and threw the Frisbee for him. He was very calm.

Our second session lasted about three minutes. I wanted to start desensitizing him to strange dogs. We started with Dave (the dog) who is very non-reactive. I tried to throw the ball but Shadow was not interested in retrieving, so I did some other competition behaviors and he was HOT! There was no reaction to Dave—he just wanted to work with me. Good doggie! Ended the session.

For the rest of the day he was very relaxed, lying around the house all day LIKE AN ORDINARY DOG! I am working on a great deal of brushing; at least five days per week. I brushed him yesterday and again, he was fine for the upper portion of his body but he wouldn't stand for me so I could brush his butt and tail. I put him on the bed and chatted while I brushed his butt and tail and he was fine with it. He wasn't happy, but his eyes did not change. He seems to like it when I talk to him, so I continued to do so. I am also brushing him when he is alone in the room—he does better when the other dogs aren't there.

JULY 6 – DAY 405

I have noticed that in the past, his face would be clear for small snippets of time. Now it is the opposite. There are only small snippets of time when his face is not clear.

I enrolled Shadow and Beau in a "Chase Class." Not because either one of them chases anything, but because I want to get them out more in varied contexts with new people. Did one session tonight with Shadow—all strangers, all in a small pen where he had never been before. It was almost pitch black out. Four completely new people, standing and walking around AND HE DID NOT CARE ONE IOTA!

We played Frisbee and when I asked him to go visit, he did not want to—he wanted to play with me. He went up half-heartedly once and lay down, but his eyes were on me.

On the way back to the car he kept looking at me with this expression "Mom, aren't you proud of me?!" (I do NOT let my anthropomorphizing get in the way of my training!)

HINDSIGHT

I have come to the conclusion that in the end, Shadow will be my most reliable dog! Why? Because I am working on our relationship, rather than drilling, drilling, drilling for competition. I never gave my other dogs the choice to work with me like I do with Shadow. I am actually in the process of retraining Beau—lots of play, tons of attention and focus on Mommy exercises, maybe a few steps of heeling or some other such exercise interspersed between the playing, but no pressure to "perform." I already see a difference!

JULY 10 – DAY 409

Private lesson on the trail with guest "dog bait," Sue. For the initial greeting, I had Shadow approach her and lie down and she threw food down to him. After a minute, she was able to hand-feed him. We started to walk and he took turns heeling with each of us! There were lots of people on the trail and we walked off into the woods to let them pass. I felt that by adding a new person, staying on the trail in the same session would be too big a context change. At the end though, I had Shadow on my right, Carolyn and Sue on my left, and we passed two people who were 10 feet way. I only had to sing half a verse of Happy Birthday!

A few hours later, I introduced Shadow to Andrea. I started out about 40 feet away from her. Shadow saw her and then ignored her. After I had him go visit, Andrea tossed food at his rear end, and then was able to hand-feed him. We just stood around talking and he was SUPER! Very calm, soft mouth. Then we stood by the van, he was fine and she was even looking at him! Shadow's face stayed perfectly calm!

JULY 11 – DAY 410

I took Shadow to my training facility today to work on competition behaviors. The tennis balls distracted him, so I sat down in the middle of the floor and waited for him to come to me to tell me that he wanted to work. I did not take the balls away—I want him to want to be with me. It only took about five minutes and then we were able to do go-outs, directed jumping, dumbbell retrieving and heeling. Some things he did great, other things he did terribly. But it was no big deal. No pressure, no impatience, no anger—not like when I used to train using punishment.

All of Our Ducks Are in a Row!

JULY 14 – DAY 413

I took the boys to a herding trial. When it was over, I heeled Shadow around Cynthia and Sue in figure eights in the front yard. He sniffed them, then ignored them. To make it a little more difficult, I had him sit right next to them and stare adoringly into my eyes. Lots of people were there, some sitting at a picnic table, some walking around the farm with their dogs. He was incredibly calm. I was incredibly calm! Cynthia gave me a pat on the back for breathing!

Shadow has been marvelous all night—very calm and relaxed, not bothering anyone. I also noticed that his stealing of things for attention has decreased about 75 percent.

JULY 16 – DAY 415

I did multiple sessions with Shadow today. For the first one I took him to a supermarket parking lot. We stayed at the far end, away from most of the pedestrian traffic. I wanted to see how he would react to shopping carts—he was fine—no nervousness at all. I moved a cart gently—no reaction, so we took a walk with it and he was fine. We did some heeling and directionals and he was focused on me. He noticed the people walking around but did not go into an alert stance.

For our second session we went to the park. I sat on a bench and petted

Shadow while I ate breakfast. We went over to the river and played "fetch the stick in the water." There were a few kids and a mom with a stroller about 200 feet away. He was very calm and gentle.

Received an e-mail from Ted:

> Make sure you have 100 percent recall response under these new conditions. If Shadow's recall begins to weaken, even a tiny bit, stop what you are doing, and spend a few days strengthening and reinforcing fast and immediate returns. This will keep Shadow moving in the right direction and give him a place to go BEFORE he gets uncomfortable and perhaps aggressive. This should now become your priority behavior, especially considering Shadow's recent past. I have seen many a trainer neglect this critical aspect, only to be very sorry later on. Good Luck!

My response back to him:

> Thanks! Except for the rare occasions—like yesterday in the park with the Frisbee, or when we are in a fenced-in area with no people around or at Carolyn's (except at the herding trial where he was on leash)—he is always on leash. I may not mention it in my journal entries, but instant recalls are always part of each and every session as well as name recognition. Carolyn feels I can have him off leash at most parks, but I don't feel comfortable with it yet. Although he comes to me instantly 98 percent of the time, I feel it would be a major mistake to completely trust him yet. Don't worry! "Slow and steady" is STILL my motto—even with all of the wonderful successes we have had. Each context change is well within his ability to handle them calmly. And when I REALLY want to do more in a session because he is doing so well, I force myself to stop. I don't want to get this far along in his rehabilitation program and then screw it all up because I was stupid and in a rush! My middle name is now "Turtle."

For our third session we went to a different park. We were walking around when all of a sudden he started barking and barking. I looked around—there was absolutely nothing to bark at. We were completely alone in the park, notwithstanding the bugs. What was he barking at? The bridge, which he has seen umpteen million times! Silly boy! I walked him over to it and stood there quietly until he relaxed.

We worked on standing while letting me brush and comb his tail and hind end.

He did rather well with it. I also fed him while I picked up each one of his feet and placed my arm underneath him (as if to hold him up) and he remained calm. Then we walked around a bit and did a few steps of heeling. He wasn't interested in doing anything else competition-wise, so I ended the session. Worked the other boys and then brought Shadow out again.

We sat on the bench and communed with the gnats. There was a man at the far end, hitting golf balls. We walked up the side of the field, closer to him. Shadow was fine. We got to about 100 feet and while Shadow's body and face remained calm, his mouth got very tight, so we left.

I was going to do more stuff with him tonight but he is really tired. We did enough things today, with a lot of different contexts.

JULY 17 – DAY 416

Private lesson today. I let Shadow out of the van and he found the Boomer Ball. When I called him—he came to me without hesitation! We went into the barn and practiced weave poles, heeling, approaching Carolyn while she was walking around—his eyes were glued onto mine. She added cookies in her hand, waving them over his head as she walked by us and still his eyes were glued to mine! I did some ball throwing for directionals, and then Carolyn did some ball throwing for lie-downs.

I wanted to start working on behaviors for the Canine Good Citizen test (CGC), so I stood right next to Carolyn with Shadow in between—very close quarters—and his eyes were locked onto mine. Did some recalls, and had her do some petting and touching his ears, lifting each paw. He had a tiny problem with the ears, so we stopped that part. We also worked on the "supervised separation" part of the CGC test where I leave him with a "friendly stranger." We did two **short training sessions**: one for 20 seconds and one for 40 seconds. When I returned on the first one, Shadow's eyes were big and his mouth was tight. For the second one, his eyes were almost normal and his mouth was soft. We had worked for an entire hour without stopping.

TRAINING CONCEPT

Short training sessions: I don't normally work my dogs for huge chunks of time—smaller sessions work better. Will they work for an hour or more? Sure they will, but how much are they really retaining? As my training with Shadow progresses, I am actually shortening his sessions even more and seeing faster learning.

We went to the front yard. Sue and John were there and Shadow ignored them. Then he saw the sheep! Oops! He didn't get into the pen (Whew!) and after a minute, I got his attention and tossed him the Boomer Ball. He was actually pushing it to me and lying down so I could kick it for him. He had a hard time coming to me, his tongue was down to his knees (past his "point of no return, please help me Mommy, I can't stop"), so I ignored him and walked away. Shadow came to find me instantly—I told him to go back to the ball and hung around for a few more minutes, and then he came to me and stayed with me.

Carolyn feels on an Empire State Building of ten stories, he is well past the eighth floor. I feel he is at floor number five. Better to be safe than sorry! At home, Shadow had a small tiff with Cody…I did nothing, and then put him away in his crate. Could it have been over-stimulation with the sheep and ball? After the tiff he has been fine all night.

JULY 19 – DAY 418

A super day! Breakfast Club class—one session only. Patrice, Carolyn, me, and Shadow in the front yard, sheep in the big field. He stayed with me and we played Frisbee. I wasn't really sure what I wanted to do—didn't have anything in particular in mind, so Carolyn brought Dave (the dog) out and she fed him to keep him occupied, while Shadow and I circled him. We moved in different directions all around Dave. In the beginning Shadow looked at Dave with quick nervous glances, so we moved and he settled in within seconds. To end the session, I had him go visit Patrice once and then put him away. Could I have done more? Sure, but I felt that was enough. I am SO proud of myself!

Came home, took a nap, hung out for the afternoon and then took the boys to Chase Class. Five people plus Carolyn were in the big field while Shadow and I played Frisbee. I wanted Shadow to keep his focus on me while they jogged around us flailing their arms. I pointed toward the group to get Shadow to move among them to catch the Frisbee. He did not want to run into the group. I pointed in the opposite direction and he seemed to feel more comfortable doing that.

Then I called him to come to me and did TTouch on him. With the group standing still now, I had Shadow "go visit" and everyone tossed him food. One person actually bent over him to drop the food and I breathed! We all walked out of the field en masse and he was completely calm and relaxed.

Shadow, What Did You Do At Summer Camp?

JULY 22 – DAY 421

First vacation in four years! Did I go to the Bahamas? Hawaii? Some other exotic and exciting place? No, of course not! I went to Doggie Camp!

Session one. I wanted Shadow to jump into my lap while I sat on an ATV. For no particular reason other than "because it's there." He compromised by scratching the heck out of my legs (his feet were clenched) and then jumped up behind me. His mouth was very tight but his face was okay. Carolyn told me to turn the motor on. I did, he got scared and jumped off. I fed him at the base of the ATV and turned the engine off once his body was more relaxed.

When I turned it on again, he jumped off and it took him longer to come to me. After that it took another few minutes for him to jump back up onto the ATV again. I fed him some more and ended the session.

What I should have done was turn the engine on while he was on the ground, not while he was sitting on it. No harm done. We walked around and I practiced recalls a few times. Then I let him get ahead of me and started chasing him ("Mommy's gonna get you!"), touching his butt and feeding him at the same time. No bad reaction at all.

Session two. Jubilation! We went to my friend's house during an agility match. He was very focused on me and we did directionals and TTouch. My friend could not believe that Shadow was so calm—she thought it was Beau! She hadn't seen Shadow in quite awhile and was impressed with his progress. About 15 people and dogs were there, some dogs barking—no big deal for my normal dog! Carolyn started walking up to us and he dragged me to her. ("Wow, I actually know someone at this party!") She did TTouch on him and petted his entire body. He even put himself into heel position for Carolyn! At one point a man walked right by us and I instantly started singing. Shadow didn't care at all that there was someone there. I did more TTouch—he likes it so much now that I use it as a way to reinforce him—and ended the session.

JULY 23 – DAY 422

Session one. Had Shadow on the picnic table bench grooming him and I taught him to stay standing and "face forward." Brushed his body and his hind end and held each foot up, gradually using less and less food.

Session two. Had a play session after dinner. Let Cody, Beau, and Shadow play together.

Then we took a short nap. When I let them out of the room, Jen, Bob, and Sue were just getting out of their van. Shadow raced toward them barking. I said softly, "Shadow, here," and he whirled around, came to me, and then ignored them.

JULY 24 – DAY 423

Session one. "Doggie calisthenics." We all spread out in the front yard and practiced eye contact, directionals, heeling out into the middle of the yard and back. Then we rotated dogs and Sue asked me if she could pet Shadow. I said, "Ummm…" Sue is only 16 years old and basically has no clue about dogs but Carolyn said, "Sure, he'll be fine." So I went back to working with the dog I was working with. Bob also ended up petting him all over his body AND they both were leaning over him and then got down on the ground with him!!! And pet him in totally inappropriate ways! He was SENSATIONAL, TER-RIFIC, STUPENDOUS, AMAZING! I was breathing!!!!

JULY 25 – DAY 424

Session one. Group class with eye contact, directionals, sits, downs, and heel-ing—even when one of the other aggressive dogs popped off, Shadow was fine.

Session two. Swimming in the lake and Shadow almost swam a few times. He plants his front legs, kicks his back legs, but of course moves nowhere….very funny to see. He was trying VERY hard, one day he will get it. Only I could have a dog that truly doesn't know how to swim!

Session three. Did some agility with him. He gets overly excited doing this, so I had him lie down before and after each jump and it really calmed him down. Did a small series of things—tire, jumps, and tunnel. VERY focused and com-posed.

He has been very nonchalant around the farm with all of the people. I am no longer looking around to see who might be there—I just take him out of the van! **Brave Pam!**

Red Letter Days!

JULY 26 – DAY 425

Shadow—well, what can I say? TOTALLY normal doggie! Took him for a walk on the trail with Jen and Sara (a dog), Bob and Mattie (a dog), and Carolyn. WE DID NOT LEAVE THE TRAIL WHEN PEOPLE CAME BY AND WE BOTH WERE WONDERFUL!!!!!! I was breathing, he was unruffled. We passed people three times.

He had no reaction other than a slightly tight mouth and he was good with the other dogs. He stayed right next to me most of the time—very little forging ahead or pulling.

Later that day, I did a few sessions with him jumping in my lap and we just cuddled. There were sheep in the pen a few yards away from us, Carolyn approached and petted him. He was fine! He did not displace on her in any way despite the nearness of the sheep, which tells me he was truly calm! Later on, I did some agility with him—same stuff as before. Oh! And when we went to the trail, Carolyn RODE IN THE CAR WITH US—NOT ONE PEEP FROM MY NORMAL DOG!

JULY 27 – DAY 426

We started out with a bonding/follow the leader walk. At one point he alerted to a donkey and ran toward her. When he stopped running, I called to him and he came back at top speed! Then we went to a different field. I was very brave and took him off leash, he was perfectly at ease and very attentive. At one point I asked him "Hey lady, can I pet your dog?" and he looked around for Carolyn!!!!

It was so hot in the middle of the afternoon, we all took a "siesta" in one of the rooms. I had all three dogs with me and they were running around like banshees. I just lay down on the bed, completely ignoring them. After about 10 minutes, Beau was on my foot, Cody was on the floor, and Shadow was next to me. We all took a 15-minute nap.

Later on we practiced agility again—downs in front of and after each jump, then a small series—jump, tunnel, and A frame. He was very relaxed using this method—much more so than just taking him through a full course. In fact, his mouth was like velvet.

JULY 29 – DAY 428

We had a session at my building today. Gretchen (a dog) and Karen were in the building along with Jane and her puppy. I brought Shadow in and sat in a chair and fed him. This was the first time he has been in the building with a dog other than Cody or Beau. He was a bit tight and nervous, but when I started heeling him around he calmed down. I had him go visit Jane and she fed him. Ended the session after about 10 minutes. He did some nice work.

JULY 30 – DAY 429

Worked Shadow at my facility. Karen and Gretchen were there again. I stayed at one end, fed him, and then did some heeling. Then we all heeled around in a circle around the building. He was super dooper!!!!!!! Holy smokes!!!!

JULY 31 – DAY 430

Great Day! Private lesson today. We worked in the front yard, had Sue throw the toy for Shadow and she petted him in inappropriate ways. Shadow was incredibly nonchalant with the whole scenario—very calm, coming up to Sue without a problem, his face staying calm during the petting. A few times he moved away from her, but without any intent to then come back in and bite.

I Really Do Have A Completely Ordinary Dog!

AUGUST 2 – DAY 432

Breakfast Club class. Carolyn, Jen, Patrice, Cynthia, Sue, Shadow, and me were in the front yard. We repeated the same context we used a couple days ago— Sue petting in inappropriate ways. He was completely and utterly wonderful. Sue petted him all over his body, reaching for him, leaning over him, petting him on his head, butt and tail, throwing the toy for him. He actually brought the toy to her quite often! Then we all got down on our knees and Shadow went up to everyone gently and let them pet him. Jen was lying down on the ground, Shadow approached her and laid down next to her, kissed her face while she petted him all over, and then he just cuddled with her!!! He brought the ball to Cynthia and dropped IT IN HER HAND FOR HER THROW IT AGAIN! (Remember back on September 9, Shadow bit Cynthia for the same thing!)

Leaning over and inappropriate petting practice.

Second session. In the front yard with Dave (the dog). Shadow and I approached and heeled around Dave and Carolyn, and then approached head on. Carolyn and I shook hands, I fed Shadow as we were shaking hands, and we walked away. Repeated, we shook hands, and I fed him after we stopped shaking hands. Did this two more times. On the next trial, I didn't feed him until we had walked away. Repeated twice more and ended the session.

We practice greeting Carolyn and Dave.

At this point, I am past the "getting choked up with emotion" stage, and am now in the incredulous shocked stage, "I STILL can't believe that he is almost wholly normal!"

AUGUST 4 – DAY 434

Took the boys to the park today. Shadow still not swimming, still trying. I was very brave because there were many people and cyclists at the park; we walked between two groups of people. I fed Shadow and he was okay. I think he will be swimming within the next few tries.

I then gave a lesson in the park. My student came up to the van and looked in before I could stop her (sigh…). Shadow barked wildly. I told her that now she had to **stay there** until he stopped barking. Within a few minutes, I was able to reinforce him for looking at her calmly!!!

TRAINING CONCEPT

Stay there: If my student had moved away when Shadow aggressed we would have been reinforcing his aggression, "because it worked to drive the scary person away." She was safe because Shadow was in the crate, so there was no need for her to move. What I want him to learn is that quiet, calm behavior is what gets scary people to move away.

AUGUST 5 – DAY 435

Went to the park again, it has been entirely too hot to do anything else. He was a bit unfocused as we went to the river. Once there, he really tried to swim and just couldn't figure it out. I tried to rehearse in my mind what I would do if somebody just appeared out of nowhere—and did not rehearse enough. A man approached out of the blue. I asked him to stop for a second, Shadow heard me, saw him, ran toward him and barked. I called Shadow to me and he came—a little slowly—he just had to get in a few more barks. His mouth was VERY tight on the way back.

I should have called him sooner, but I froze and panicked for a second when I saw the man coming toward us. I guess I need more practice too… He has been super dooper today in the house. Very relaxed, calm, lying around sleeping.

AUGUST 6 – DAY 436

We met my friend Sevasty at the park. Shadow was fine with her. Once I had his focus on me for a few minutes, I had him go visit. He did not get nervous as she bent down to throw food. Then I tried to get him to do some directionals and some heeling so I could show off, and he couldn't do it. Isn't that always the way! Just when you have an audience, the kid or dog won't comply! It was brutally hot, so I didn't mind too much. He actually swam a few strokes and even learned how to turn while swimming! He didn't hesitate at all. I was so proud!!!! His mouth was very tight. There were some people (three small groups, spread out) in the park and we walked around them. He was fine all night. Mostly calm.

Red Letter Days!

AUGUST 7 – DAY 437

Swimming! Three sessions this week and both boys (Beau and Shadow) are SWIMMING—really swimming, not just a few strokes. They both even learned how to turn in the water. AND there was a mother and child on shore when I brought Shadow out. He looked at them, looked back at me as if to say, "To heck with them, LET'S GO SWIMMING!!! YAHOOIE!!!"

Later the boy and Mom and Shadow were all swimming together. I had him on harness and leash—no sense being stupid! At one point, Shadow just started swimming out into the middle of the lake. When I called him, he turned and came back to me instantly, "Oh sorry, I got caught up in the moment." I am so PROUD! I had despaired of ever teaching him to swim!

Holy Cow!

AUGUST 9 – DAY 439

Short but AMAZING session at Carolyn's today. Brought Shadow into the front yard and sat under the tree. Just petted and fed him. Jen called him to her and she petted him as well. Sue came over and I asked him to go visit.

Then Dale, a completely new person (with a huge moustache—did I mention Shadow really likes people with facial hair) came over. I had him go visit and

Dale fed him while leaning over him. Then Dale sat in a lounge chair, and Shadow JUMPED IN HIS LAP AND LICKED HIS FACE! AMAZING! We all continued to pet him and he was so normal, I was stunned beyond belief! We threw the ball for him a few times and to show off, I had him walk up to the ball, lie down in mid-chase, and then allowed him to get it.

Later today, I took the boys swimming at the lake. Shadow was on a 15-foot leash and harness and I had him heel the last few steps to the lake. There was a large group of adults and children playing on shore and in the water. He was only mildly interested in the kids and just wanted to swim. At times, we were only 17 feet from the kids but he wasn't bothered by their closeness. I really tried to keep his focus on me, but not in an "oh my God, DON'T LOOK AT THEM" kind of way. If he glanced at them calmly—fine. Then I would redirect him back to the toys and me. I was proud of myself too. I was mildly nervous but tried to keep my focus on Shadow, watching for any sign of stress. He even does directionals in the water. This dog is so incredible!!!

AUGUST 10 – DAY 440

Got together with three of my friends and their dogs. I took Shadow out and heeled him around everyone. He focused on playing with a ball he found. I was able to get his attention, but I could sense his heart wasn't in it and he was sluggish, so I ended the session. Maybe he was disappointed that we didn't go swimming…

Did some TTouch and boy is his tail soft now! He has been super tonight, although he did eat one of Jim's socks…His stealing of things has drastically reduced—now it is only one item per day.

AUGUST 15 – DAY 445

Have done nothing with Shadow other than swimming. It has been entirely too hot, and I have been too busy with teaching. He is now the Mark Spitz of the doggie world, a very strong swimmer, and he loves it!

I had Carolyn come over to my house because I haven't done enough work there with Shadow and people. We started outside. He was a tad nervous and instead of lying down for the go visit, he jumped all over her. After a few minutes we all went inside and Carolyn sat on the couch. Shadow jumped on the couch with her but wouldn't look at her. I had him come on the loveseat with me. His eyes finally started to relax and his breathing slowed down. Then he went back to Carolyn on the couch and he was much better. She was petting and doing TTouch. This was the first time since August 6th at a session with Lisa D. that I had someone come in the house with him loose.

We went swimming later with Carolyn, Sue, and two of their dogs. Two tiny tiffs with the dogs and then he was focused on me.

Lo and Behold!

AUGUST 16 – DAY 446

Breakfast Club. Shadow and me in the front yard with Carolyn, John, Patrice, Sue, and Jen. I heeled him over to the group (off leash) and asked him to go visit. I had everyone pet him and feed him, calling him to me between each "go visit." Then, to continue working on CGC behaviors, I had everyone rotate. They petted his ears, then lifted each front foot, and brushed him. He was simply perfect. He even saw the Boomer Ball, sniffed it, and came back when called!

Later that day I brought him to the grooming shop. While John was grooming another dog, I moved the steps over to the tub. Shadow instantly jumped up on them. It took a small amount of food to lure him into the tub but he would only put his front feet in. I stood there and passively waited. Within a few minutes he jumped in all the way with no food lure. Jackpot! He jumped out, I continued to just stand there passively and he started to get into the tub faster and faster. After he did this six times, I hooked him up and started bathing him. John helped by feeding and petting him. Shadow was super—John is very tall and so has to lean over, and we were both crowding him—the only way to feed and bathe him. Shadow was calm enough to eat! He stood when I put my hand under his belly, and he handled the blow dryer very well. Basically, he just had this very unhappy face, but no aggressing in any way, shape, or form.

On the way out of the shop, a man suddenly came out of a store and, instead of avoiding him, I decided in an instant to continue walking to the van. I shortened up on the leash (not tighter, just shorter) and fed Shadow while we walked past. He was fine—better than I was that's for sure!

When we got home, I had him on the deck to brush him out. I did not want to do it at the shop—I felt he had been so perfect I didn't want to do anything to ruin such a great session. He stood quietly while I brushed and combed his butt and tail, and trimmed the hair on all four paws!!!!!

Good Doggie! Shadow has finally turned the corner here about being groomed. He stands patiently while I brush his entire body. He doesn't move away in avoidance, or move as if to bite me. I showed Jim how well he handles it now and he was suitably impressed!

In the evening, we had a new group class. For our first session, if he gave me attention, he got to go see the sheep in the pen. We did walk-ups, theres, get back outs, lie-downs. I was able to build his eye contact to 12 seconds before he was allowed to go back to the sheep. He was off leash, so it wasn't as though I was "controlling" him by the use of a leash. I was able to get him to play my silly game by the use of our relationship! Just how cool is THAT!?

For our second session we went into the barn. I had him "go visit" each of the six people there. Shadow was great. After each visit, I called him back to me before allowing him to go to the next person.

AUGUST 21 – DAY 451

I had Shadow heeling around the supermarket parking lot, ignoring other people and cars. A woman approached and I moved back a few feet. She was smart enough to ask permission to approach further and I told her that Shadow is afraid of people. He handled it calmly and there was no reaction from him at all.

My goal is to eventually be able to sit on the bench at the front door of supermarket and have him be relaxed and calm. He has been great at home. Doing a lot of lying around calmly, and he is letting me pet the other dogs more and more without horning in.

AUGUST 22 – DAY 452

An e-mail from Ted—I had asked if these posts were getting boring…

> No, not at all. The reports are fascinating and insightful. I'm anxious to see Shadow in action. In fact, I'd like to video the exact same context that we filmed the first time, i.e., Shadow in the van, then move on from there. I have lots of questions for you but will save them for when I see you. Keep going!

I had Shadow meet Karen in the front yard. To start, I had her sit down on the steps by the road. He and I heeled around the yard until he was relaxed and focused on me, then I had him go visit. We tried three times before he could greet her properly and calmly. I called him away from Karen and heeled again around the yard while she stood up. We took turns feeding him. It was quite funny—he looked like he was watching a tennis match. His mouth softened up nicely.

To change the context slightly, we heeled around the yard while Karen walked up and down the sidewalk. Shadow was nervous with this, and would look at her with quick glances and then whip his head back to me. After doing this for about three minutes, I had her hand-feed him and lightly touch his chin. He was nervous—his body was tight and ears were back. I petted him for a minute, had her feed some more, and then ended the session.

AUGUST 23 – DAY 453

We went to the supermarket parking lot again. Shadow was super dooper! Great heeling around cars and people coming out of cars. I moved away from one person—and I willed myself not to move away from some others. I brought him closer to the building. He was only mildly nervous. It started to rain so I did not do anything else with him today. He has been mostly great around the house.

Rolling With The Punches

AUGUST 25 – DAY 455

Took Shadow to a music festival. We stayed VERY close to the van. He was nervous, eyes clear, but face and mouth tight. I worked on attention and he was fine but I had a hard time getting him to relax, even though people were very far away. He had done some barking in the car beforehand while I was taking Beau and Cody out for their turn. He loosened up somewhat when I did directionals. Then I just sat in the van, petted him, and let him watch the people go by. He was able to relax. I didn't take him out for a second session. Jim came over and we both sat with Shadow inside the side the van and petted him.

Once home, he has been super.

AUGUST 27 – DAY 457

We worked in the house with Carolyn. She came right in without greeting Shadow outside. I had her sit on the couch and just pet and feed him. Shadow was less nervous than last time Carolyn was here. She did directionals and get back outs with him. He was still nervous so she did a lot of head turning (a calming signal). Then he jumped on the couch with her and let her pet him. Session lasted about 15 minutes.

We went swimming in the lake—Carolyn brought Wolko (a dog) and Shadow did not react to him in any way. Shadow was doing some great work in the water—directionals, get back outs with him turning his head away and swimming straight out. He was not bothered by Wolko or Carolyn and was just having fun swimming.

AUGUST 30 – DAY 460

Breakfast Club class. Shadow was wonderful as usual. I worked on "supervised separation." Started at 15 seconds and ended with three repetitions of one minute each. Shadow was completely fine. I had John do roll overs with Shadow and we did a little bit of heeling. Only did one session with him today.

An unexpected wowie-zowie later that night in Chase Class. We were outside the sheep pen, off leash. We had a "recall" contest, where the one who gets the most recalls (dog must come to us, within arms length and we had to be able to pet the dog for three seconds before sending them back to the sheep) in five minutes is the winner. Shadow did 13 recalls. I was a bit tired and slow on the uptake—otherwise I think we could have gotten more. He was in fourth place. First place had 16 recalls—a non-herding breed of course!

I was damn proud—I thought he did wonderfully well. I took him out again and heeled him around the other students while they stood around talking with their dogs. Then we went for ice cream, and sat with two people and their dogs, all stayed within three feet of each other and the parking lot!

Shadow did a super job! At one point a car drove up and parked right in front of us. I DID NOT MOVE AWAY. SHADOW DID NOT REACT! He saw the man walk by, and then looked at me. The other two dogs had an argument over some ice cream and I just moved away about two feet and petted Shadow gently. He was fine and did not feel the need to get in and break it up. Then we just sat around, I gently petted him and he was calm. I was so very proud!!!

A Plethora of (Almost) Perfect Performances!

SEPTEMBER 1 – DAY 462

Took Shadow to a dog show today. Lisa P. was outside the van talking and Shadow did not react. I brought him out of the van, had him focus on me for a few seconds and then had him go visit Lisa. I had her toss food between his front legs and his body was soft and relaxed. To change the context slightly, I had her hand-feed him and his mouth was a little tight. I walked him around on the outskirts of the show and he was super focused on me.

SEPTEMBER 2 – DAY 463

AMAZING DAY!!!! Took the boys to another dog show today. I walked Shadow around and got close to the obedience rings. We were within 25-30 feet of several people and barking dogs and he was very focused on me. Ended session after about 15 minutes.

The vet on call was offering to do microchipping and she was nice enough to come to the van to do the boys. I explained about Shadow's issues ahead of time. The vet was sitting on the ground when I brought Shadow out. I made sure I had his attention coming out of the van. Then I had him go visit. He jumped on her in the beginning, looking for cookies, and then he lay down. She fed him and I also tossed him food.

I forgot to give her my whole litany of instructions (don't lean over him, don't pet him, yadayadayada), and before I could get one word out, she leaned over him, hand-fed him, pet him roughly all over his body and HE WAS FINE FOR ALL OF IT!!!!!!!!!!!!!! Then I asked him to lie down so she could insert the microchip. She grabbed the skin on his withers and he froze, looked at her very deliberately AND DID NOTHING ELSE!!! I had her stop because I couldn't redirect his attention back to me, not even with a cookie.

We tried again, this time he tightened up even more. I walked away with him and he was blowing and puffing. I tried one more time with him between my legs and her coming up from behind, and he scooted away. I went to the van to get the muzzle and he jumped in his crate. I got him out again and put the muzzle on. He did not want to take food once the muzzle was on, so I aborted the microchip idea for today and just let him go back to her. At first he was nervous but then she was able to feed him through the muzzle. I took the muzzle off and he was back to being good with her. At no point did he do anything that smacked of aggression. I was thrilled with the whole thing even if we couldn't do the chip—we'll get there. And although he had the muzzle on, I just did not think it was worth stressing him out and having him display fear or aggression—the chip can wait.

Thirty minutes later Laurie came over and I had Shadow go from the van right over to visit. She petted him all over, and then we both sat on the ground while we hugged and petted him. At one point Shadow was almost sitting in her lap! He was watching Lisa work her dog and was very interested but calm. At one point I grabbed the skin like the vet had done and he was nervous, so I stopped. I'll work on this so when we try again with the chip, he'll be able to handle it. I also did a stand for exam with Laurie touching him and Shadow was completely calm about it. Laurie finally admitted to me that the first time she met him (August 5th of last year) she was scared to death of him, but she did not feel any fear of him today whatsoever!

A few hours later (yes, this was truly a "dog day" for training all of the dogs) I met John and Cynthia at a park. They came out of nowhere to see Shadow and he was terrific. Not stressed, just excited to see them. I tried to do some heeling with him but he couldn't do it, so we played with a stick and then just sat around and gently petted him.

SEPTEMBER 3 – DAY 464

CHICKEN TRAINER DAY and SUPER DOG DAY! Dog show again today, and Shadow was his amazing self again! We were near the obedience rings and his attention on me was incredible.

Andrea came over, I had him focus on me and then had him go visit. She hand-fed him and petted him and when he got bored with her he sat next to me. We were able to get within 30 feet of dogs and people working in the rings. We were also next to a tennis court (TENNIS BALLS + Border Collie = !!!) and he stayed focused on me.

For our third context I stood by the van while many people and dogs walked by. John and Cynthia came up out of nowhere, I kept his focus and then let him go visit. He is getting really good at only going up to people on my cue. Two of my students came by and I whipped behind the van—me playing the CHICKEN! Cynthia asked why I did that and I had no answer—reflex action at this point. I came back around and the students were still there, Shadow could have cared less. The husband did start to approach him and I asked him not to—still chicken! But a safe chicken is one that can cross the road again tomorrow! He was completely fine with all of the pedestrian and canine traffic.

I put him away after a few minutes.

I brought Shadow out again and basically repeated the same context—just paying attention to me while people and dogs walked by. He was amazingly calm, cool and collected.

And there's more—boy, was this a busy day or what? We met John and Cynthia with two of their dogs. We all went into an empty field and I heeled Shadow around at the same time as they worked their dogs. He was super calm. We started out relatively far away and moved in closer and closer—about 30 feet. He was heeling beautifully! On our way back to the van I was so brave that I did not even bother to look both ways or shorten the leash up!

SEPTEMBER 4 – DAY 465

Carolyn came over to do the "familiar person in the house" game. She came in, I let him out of his crate, and he zoomed into the living room and dive-bombed her…(not in a bad way—just his normal way). I took him back to the crate and we started over—this time he laid down instead of jumping. Repeated the process a few times, in the crate and out again, and he calmed down after three tries. We sat and watched a movie while we fed him for get back outs all the way into the kitchen (15 feet). Continued to do this for about 20 minutes and then he was really tired. I had him on the loveseat with me and we cuddled. Carolyn left the room, and when she came back in Shadow was fine—wagged his tail at her but did not move off of the loveseat. Ended the session.

Did not do anything else with him the rest of the day. The past three days have been nothing but training and I wanted to give him a break. Plus he was still so tired this morning when Carolyn was here, that I did not want to push him at all. In four days we have had 13 training sessions! Yikes!

SEPTEMBER 5 – DAY 466

Marvelous training session at the building today. Karen was sitting in a chair and I brought Shadow in. I got his attention on me, and when he was calm, I took off his leash and allowed him to go visit. Karen fed him for a few minutes and then we all walked around for a few minutes. Shadow even did some heeling with Karen! We both sat on the floor and fed and petted him all over for 20 minutes. He was so relaxed he rolled over on his side so we could pet his belly! Holy smokes!!! He has only met Karen a small handful of times, so I don't know if he really remembered her.

HINDSIGHT

Stupendous, miraculous, amazing, awesome, incredible progress with Shadow these last two and a half months. He has truly turned the corner into normal ranges of good doggie-ness. I have done many context changes with him—grooming, handling, petting, strangers, new places, new contexts—and Shadow has handled them all wonderfully. So many meetings with new people that I can't even count them all. Each and every day has become such a huge leap forward in his "recovery," that I am just floored beyond belief. Each and every day should be labeled **"Good Doggie"** and **"Good Pam!"**

Each and every day IS truly a miracle.

7

It's the constant and determined effort that breaks down resistance, sweeps away obstacles.

—Claude M. Bristol

"I Can't Believe This is the Same Dog!"

SEPTEMBER 10 – DAY 471

TOO COOL! Ted Turner is here in person for a day of private lessons! Can you believe it? Jim and I took Ted out to dinner last night and they would not let me talk about dogs for more than two minutes…the big meanies!

Shadow's first session. I had Ted come outside just so Shadow could see him before we (several of Shadow's dog bait friends were here as well) all went inside. Once we were all inside, I made sure Shadow was focused on me and we did some heeling. He relaxed in about a minute so I took his leash off and we continued heeling. We did some dumbbell retrieves and he was incredible. I was so very glad that Shadow complied since I really wanted to show off Shadow's brilliance for Ted!

Shadow and I showing off for Ted Turner.

Then I had Shadow go visit Ted. He jumped up on Ted once and Ted petted him all over—even roughing him up a bit, and Shadow did not care! Ted said, with an incredulous look on his face, "I can't believe this is the same dog!" That look was the greatest compliment I have ever had! At dinner last night, when Jim and Ted finally let me get in a word edgewise, Ted said that he had held his breath a few times reading my e-mails, thinking that I was making some mistakes and rushing Shadow a bit. I don't think he feels that way anymore!!!

I Can't Believe This is the Same Dog!

I had Shadow go visit Cynthia. Cynthia and I did some **team training** with Shadow—Ted taught us how—we had never done it before. This session was mostly calm behaviors around some new or almost new people. I had him roll over, then Cynthia had him roll over and did some heeling with him. Session lasted about 20 minutes.

TRAINING CONCEPT

Team training: Involves two or more trainers and one animal. The dog goes from one trainer to the other with ease and will work for all trainers.

Shadow works on heeling with Cynthia.

For our second session we did a mock CGC test. When we first came in Shadow was jumping on everyone, so I took him out into "tomorrow" and we started again. I call these do-over sessions, "going into tomorrow." This time he was very focused on me and we went through the whole test and he was amazing! Even the "out of sight stay with a stranger" was perfect. He stayed in a down the entire time, watched everyone else walk around (I was outside), and actually relaxed even more. We used Gretchen (a dog) for the "being calm around a strange dog" exercise and while we did not go right up to her, we did come within 20 feet of her. I could have pushed it but did not want to. For the "reaction to distractions," I had someone knock on the door. He barked once. I ignored his barking.

Shadow looking relaxed during the "stay with a stranger" exercise.

Ted then jiggled the doorknob and there was no reaction from Shadow, so I reinforced him. I did a lot of heeling around everyone, following them as they walked, squishing in between people.

For our next session we tried to work the same context in which Ted met him last year (in the van). I wasn't really sure how Shadow would react since I haven't worked this very much at all. Suffice it to say, it did not go well. After we tried for a few minutes, we canned that idea. I brought Shadow out and had him re-greet Ted and Shadow was fine.

We tried one more time with the van context—no go again. Ted wants me to do some work with changing around crate pads, adding other scents in the crates, moving the dogs around to different crates. Ted feels that Shadow's

Ted Turner re-greeting Shadow.

reaction may be due to crate possessiveness and feels that this is the best way to get rid of this issue.

I asked Ted, "How long does it take to train a new animal at Sea World for a show?" He said, "Nine months to a year." I asked him if I was on track or behind schedule with Shadow's progress. He said, "You are right on schedule." "How can I be on track with Shadow," I asked, "if you can take a completely wild animal and put it in a show in nine months and I have been working with Shadow for one year and three months?" His reply, "Because the animals we deal with do not a have a prior bad history with people and Shadow did. You had to desensitize him first, then countercondition."

I also asked him if I would ever be able to forget who I had at the end of the leash and he said, "Yes, but it will take more time. It takes a good three years for an animal (any animal) to be totally reliable."

I asked him, "What is the first behavior(s) you teach a new animal?" Ted replied, "Be calm and eat from my hand, eye contact, name recognition, come, let me touch you." Those are the first things I teach my own dogs, and in my classes! Cool!

Looking back from a great distance of time, I now realize that his crate aggression is not about possessiveness or guarding—it is about him feeling vulnerable: stuck in a crate with nowhere to move away if he is afraid.

SEPTEMBER 12 – DAY 473

We did another session with Carolyn at my house. I let Shadow out of the crate and tried to keep him with me as we walked into the living room. Tried is the operative word. He dive-bombed her—we tried again—and this time I was able to keep him with me. Then I repeated the same thing—back in the crate, walk with me to the living room and go visit or go sit next to her while looking at me. I had him next to me while Carolyn approached and fed him. He was nervous the first two times she did this, then got better with it. He is more used to approaching people, rather than them approaching him. I put him in the crate inside the van and had Carolyn approach him. We kept these sessions short—two to four cookies delivered through the crate door. I ended the session, brought him into the house, rewarded him for calmness, and then back outside into the van. We repeated this five times. There was no aggression.

Then we just sat in the living room and watched TV. Shadow alternated between sitting near me and sitting near Carolyn. He almost fell asleep while Carolyn was petting him. At one point while he was sitting near me, he heard Cody barking outside, and he leaped at Carolyn. No noise, just a leap. I called him to me and he stopped being an idiot.

He doesn't normally displace anymore when Cody is barking so I don't know why he reacted. And this wasn't the first bark he had heard from Cody. Maybe he was still nervous about Carolyn being in the room, even though he seemed to be calm. This session lasted about 90 minutes. No other displacement behaviors after that incident or later that night.

SEPTEMBER 14 – DAY 475

Shadow has been doing major stealing for attention today and chewed up three of my socks plus various and sundry other items. Could be displacement. Could just be that he is still quite young and annoying—he is only two years and four months at this point—still within puppy range.

Took Shadow to another dog training facility today with the other boys. Put him in a strange crate and he did not make one peep. Good doggie! Brought him out, worked on attention around the instructor there (Julie), tried to put sniffing on my cue (some success, some not). Heeled him around a bit, and got loads of attention from him. Brought him closer and closer to Julie but always striving for complete attention to me. When I felt the time was right I gave her some food, and had him go visit, he did not jump on her.

She hand-fed him and petted his head. I asked her to tell him to "go see mommy," which he did instantly. Had him go visit again, he jumped on her and sniffed her face. She ignored him and I called him back. Repeated a few times and ended the session.

HOLY SMOKES! I am brave enough and Shadow is ready to enroll him in a NORMAL beginners obedience class!

SEPTEMBER 17 – DAY 478

Had Shadow meet Linda, one of my students. I am trying to lessen the amount of time from when he first meets someone to when they can pet him for the first time. I will need this for the real world and for the CGC test. I heeled him around and did some dumbbell retrieves. When I felt he was calm enough, I had Linda feed him and within a few minutes, she was able to pet him. Shadow was excellent. I then had her hold the leash while I went out to the car and he did not care!

Later, I took him over to the supermarket parking lot and, for the first time, I did NOT feel the need to scan the environment continually! I focused on him and he focused on me. When he did see someone walking by, he just looked at them and then back to me. No nervousness, no stress, just a calm doggie and a calm Pam!

He has still been stealing things, but tonight, as I was sitting on the couch, he brought me a piece of paper. I completely ignored him and he dropped it in my lap and left it there! It is hard for me to ignore him most of the time—he usually has dangerous items like razor blades, steak knives, and the like. The other day he was eating a wooden ruler, ran out of the bedroom, and did not judge the distance correctly. He rammed into the wall and jammed himself in the throat with it. I am so glad I have desensitized him to me looking in his mouth! He just sat there patiently while I checked his gums and the back of his throat. No damage done—thank goodness!

He had a tiff with Cody tonight. Cody is really a big pill—he pushes Shadow's buttons, gets attacked and then goes back in for more!

SEPTEMBER 18 – DAY 479

Received an e-mail from Ted today:

> Finally have a moment to sit down and write a few lines. Thanks for the excellent day! Really enjoyed it. Shadow is simply remarkable. What a testimony to you! Great work and a great animal.
>
> With Shadow, two problems remain: aggression in crate and aggression in car when someone approaches which is now stimulating your other dogs to get aroused. The solution is simple. The key... "Change, Change, Change." You are too predictable in your car transportation scheme with your pets and that allows them to establish spaces and territory. I would rearrange, change bedding, travel without crates for short distances, etc., and even take the crate out of the car and use as a reinforcer during your sessions. I would ask Shadow to get in the crate in areas where he isn't so comfortable and protective, and let others reinforce him. I could get into a long technical discussion here but I won't. I think you'll see progress very quickly if you do this. Your goal? All dogs in car, relaxed, without crates. You can set crates up at your destination for holding when you get there. Sometimes you should have people already in the car when you send Shadow in, let him play in the car with people etc. These should mix things up nicely.

Pushing the Envelope Yet Again!

SEPTEMBER 20 – DAY 481

Breakfast Club. Tried twice to get Shadow's full attention from the instant he got out of the van. Second time was the charm. We heeled around five people (Ali is a new person) and he kept his attention on me.

I stood right next to each person, reinforcing Shadow for eye contact with me and did not let him go visit. I had everyone approach him rather then him approaching them and they pet him without feeding first. He was super. Even with Ali!

Then they all converged on him and everyone was bending over and petting him and crowding him and generally being obnoxious—petting his face, butt, tail, sides, feet, ears, all at the same time. A proverbial orgy!

Shadow calmly handling part of the petting orgy.

For the second session I repeated the same context as the first. Shadow was really enjoying himself! At no point did he show any signs of fear or aggression. Too cool for words! I still can't get over that my boy is in a "REAL" obedience class!

Class tonight. Two sessions, both incredible! Scads of attention, ignored the other dogs completely. I had the assistant come over and stand so I could heel Shadow around her.

He was a bit nervous at first—would look at me and glance at her in a nervous kind of way. We repeated this six times. If he looked away and then looked back at me, I was careful not to reinforce him too soon. I **waited for three seconds** of solid eye contact before reinforcing. Then I had the assistant pet Shadow while I fed him. I ended this session. For the second session I went in toward her much faster, did less heeling, and had her pet him. I petted him too. Then she left and we just sat together and cuddled.

His mouth was a bit tight, but that may have been because he was really hungry—he is on a diet due to my past liberal use of treats! He was super dooper. Each session lasted about 10 minutes.

I am continuing to work on shortening the time frame from when he first meets someone to them being able to pet him.

TRAINING CONCEPT

Waiting for three seconds: It is imperative to wait a minimum of three seconds before reinforcing a dog after a "bad" or unwanted behavior. If you don't, you are actually reinforcing the dog for the wrong behavior. For instance, your dog jumps on you, and then sits. You immediately reinforce for the sit. Well, the reinforcement came too soon and you may just see an increase of "jump up, and sit" behavior. The dog isn't doing this to drive you crazy, it is just a behavior chain of "jump up, and sit" that you inadvertently reinforced.

My new rule of thumb—if the dog is doing something you like, reinforce it as fast as possible—within one-half to three seconds. If the dog is doing something you don't like, redirect him into a more desirable behavior, wait passively for three seconds, ask for three simple behaviors, then reinforce. You should see a decrease in the unwanted behavior.

Nice Job, Sweet Pea!

SEPTEMBER 22 – DAY 483

I brought Shadow to Becky's house today. Becky, Jared, (Jim's daughter and four-year-old grandson) Jim, and three cats were in the fenced-in portion of the yard. Shadow, on leash, and I were outside the fence. We walked around a bit and then Shadow saw Becky. He was very nervous and his face was pushed forward, his cheeks were puffing slightly. I moved him around a bit (staying the same distance away—about 25 feet) and he relaxed.

I asked her to say "hi" to Shadow. The look of amazement on his face was priceless. His ears went up and he ran back to me, "Mommy, that lady knows my name! Wow!" After that he was calmer. I started to move closer to the fence and we all started talking.

Shadow did not alert to our voices and just sniffed the ground. Then he saw the cats and alerted slightly, but his tail was down— more like a Border Collie crouch rather than an aggressive stance. Jared was walking around, and Shadow was fine. Jim came up to the fence so he could pet Shadow and brought Jared with him. I tossed wads and wads of food as Jared came closer and continued feeding until I saw his body completely relax.

Jared has an uncanny natural sense of what to do and what not to do. He crouched down and remained motionless while I fed Shadow. We all moved around a little. At one point Jared came running toward the fence (heck he is only 4 years old) and Shadow ran up to meet him. I couldn't see what Shadow's face looked like and Jim isn't versed enough to recognize what he saw. But I called Shadow back to me and he complied. Then I had Jared stand still while I tossed more wads of food on the ground and Shadow lay down in a relaxed posture of his own accord. We moved around more and then ended the session.

I was very impressed with him. We had spent most of the time right next to the fence. Sure, he was nervous, but this session had completely new contexts—new location, two new people, one of them a little boy (I think little kids teased him in his old home, throwing things at him and generally being cruel to him), and three cats. I don't have any cats and I don't know how he is with them. Other than the initial crouch, he seemed curious rather than murderous. And he showed no aggressive tendencies toward Jared. Yahoo!

SEPTEMBER 23 – DAY 484

I worked a pet fair today. I wasn't sure how Shadow would be—we were right next to the sound system and it succeeded in freaking Cody out for his Freestyle demo. Shadow handled it so well that I brought him out twice.

The first time, I brought Shadow out and walked around the van to my table. Cathy and Lisa P. were there. He had never met Cathy before. He glanced at them two or three times, then sat between them and stared at me. He was nicely calm and Lisa was able to pet him after feeding only a few cookies. I had Cathy hand-feed him just a few cookies and then pet him. He was really super. At one point he was squished between the two of them and he seemed to feel quite comfortable. All body parts soft and relaxed. I tried heeling with him and he was too distracted—doing a lot of sniffing, but not pulling on the leash.

Our second session was a few minutes later and we did the same things except I did not have Cathy or Lisa feed him—they just petted him. Again, every body part was COMPLETELY relaxed and serene and soft. I was tickled beyond belief and was tempted to do his CGC test right then and there (there was a group doing CGC tests at the fair), but I didn't. I really want to make absolutely sure that he is ready for the test. (I actually know he is ready—it is ME who isn't quite ready. I need more practice being calm.) He was a bit more attentive to me in terms of doing obedience exercises. We did some directionals and a few steps of heeling before his nose went down for sniffing.

SEPTEMBER 24 – DAY 485

I asked Karen to come to my house and brought Shadow outside to see her. Eventually I want Karen to be able to massage Shadow, so we are working on her really petting him for longer periods of time and doing gentle massages. He is very tight in his groin area, and I am not trained for massage work like Karen is. I had no food. I got his attention after a few minutes—he was staring at Karen—in an interested way, not an aggressive way. I had given her a small bag of food and she fed and petted him while she was standing. Then we all sat on the stoop and fed and petted him, and then just petted him. He was so relaxed his eyes were closing! Ended session after about 10 minutes.

SEPTEMBER 25 – DAY 486

Took the boys to the park with Cynthia. Took Boomer and Shadow out together. After a few minutes of them both being on leash, we let the leashes drop. Boomer went after Shadow and we kept walking. It broke up within seconds and then we all just walked along on our merry way WITH SHADOW IN A PUBLIC PLACE (I knew no one was around) ON A TRAIL WITH THE LEASH DRAGGING ALONG WITH A STRANGE DOG!!! He was super focused on me and I might as well have been holding the leash. He was right next to me 99 percent of the time anyway. The other one percent of the time, he was off sniffing and came back to me within seconds—with me calling him or on his own. Walk lasted about 15 minutes.

No displacement stuff later at home. His stealing is gradually reducing again. Yippee! I have decided that I will not be taking him to private lessons anymore—he really doesn't need it—I certainly work enough on my own now, and he has enough calm behaviors under his belt to make them obsolete.

More Than You Can Shake a Stick At!

SEPTEMBER 27 – DAY 488

Breakfast Club. Tons of new contexts. First I got his focus on me, and then I sent him over the few jumps that were lying around. Carolyn approached him and fed and petted him. Jon K. (new person) was there with his dog. Shadow approached them and although he completely ignored Jon he had a tiff with his dog. It was over within seconds. I became more proactive and fed both dogs at the same time so they wouldn't aggress…a "duh" moment!

I put him in the van and we did the "people approaching the van" context. He was fine with Carolyn and Cynthia feeding him, but not okay with Jon feeding him. He did one growl and bark, we just stood still. Once he was calm and quiet—he lay down on his own without my having to ask (!), I had Jon move away. I am rethinking the car thing—it isn't really necessary to have someone feed him in his crate, so I may change it to just having people approach him. I am not sure—just thinking. We repeated the van thing a few more times with Carolyn and Cynthia and he was very calm.

Basic obedience class this evening. SUPER again! I was able to keep his attention for a full 30 minutes. Last week I did not push it and only did two 10 minute sessions. Today he was able to focus completely on me. We did heeling, stays (while the other people were cheering and talking loudly to their own dogs), directionals, and TTouch. We went up to a new person who was observing and I got great attention while we stood next to her. I did not have him go up and visit. Then I let the assistant come over and pet him—no food at all. He was a tad nervous, so I fed him and petted him and he relaxed. As she was leaning into him, he jumped on her. She instantly turned her head away and he stopped. It wasn't a "bad" jump, but he wasn't calm. His pupils were big, and his face was a little tight.

She did not feed him first and that was a context change. One of the other dogs was barking incessantly with a very high-pitched obnoxious bark, so that may also have contributed to his nervousness. Even so, it was a super dooper day!

OCTOBER 1 – DAY 492

I haven't done much with him for the past few days. Took him to the park a few times. Yesterday I did something a little different and brought him out with Cody instead of by himself. I dropped the leash and we walked on the trail for about 15 minutes. On our way back, I looked up and saw a person with a dog. Shadow didn't care at all! He came instantly when I called and we went off the trail. I had both dogs in a down as I fed them and Shadow remained completely and utterly calm. I probably had a more stressful reaction than he did!

He has been very lovey-dovey the last three nights, coming over to sit with me and then laying on top of me with his belly up and eyes closed. I have also been leaving him out of his crate when we are gone and he is actually calmer. The other dogs seem to be calmer about him as well.

Yikes!

OCTOBER 2 – DAY 493

Had a simply thrilling morning—Jim left the wooden front door open. Cody was outside barking—Shadow was inside with me. Shadow started barking along with Cody and ran to the front door. The screen door wasn't closed properly and he rammed through it. I ran outside, barefoot and in my jammies, yelling "Shadow HERE!" No Shadow in sight! My heart was beating a mile a minute: I am clapping, calling, no dog. Finally, I saw him come from my neighbor's yard. I called him; he started toward the house and went right past me! I called him again and again and again. He ran off to another neighbor's house! I saw the Boomer Balls and started bouncing them. (GOOD THINKING PAM!) He came flying to me, and I put him and the balls in the back yard. Phew! Took ten minutes for my heart to start beating at a normal rate. Even thinking about it now sets my adrenalin racing. Do I know why he didn't come? He comes instantly 99 percent of the time, so this was a shock to me. I don't think he was doing this to drive me crazy. I think he was just out for a "jaunt around the block." He looked very pleased with himself.

Took him to the park again—THIS time I had him on a long line and held it! Practiced recalls—he was super again. Maybe this morning was just a freak, but I am going to continue to practice recalls with even more fervor than I was (if that is possible!).

He has been very lovey in a really obnoxious way tonight. Jim said Shadow wasn't content to sit next to him—he HAD to sit ON him. Well, I guess I did encourage him to sit calmly on my lap. Better be careful what you train for, you just might get it!

A Little of This and a Little of That

OCTOBER 4 – DAY 495

Breakfast Club. Shadow was a bit distracted and I had a hard time keeping his attention in the beginning. I wanted to do a mock CGC test with Ali as the tester and not use any food at all. He was too distracted for me to not use food, so I kept it to a bare minimum. Shadow had only met Ali once before, a few weeks ago. When "accepting a friendly stranger" he jumped on her instead of sitting by my side. We did it again and he was fine. Then during the "walking through pedestrian traffic" he jumped on Patrice, but I was able to get him to focus. Other than those two things, he was fine for the rest; petting, brushing, examining both ears and front feet, supervised separation, greeting another person with a dog, sit, down, stay, come—all wonderful. For his second session, we practiced having everyone come up while he sat next to me. I did not give him permission to go visit. He was a tiny bit nervous at first but then relaxed. John was actually stepping over Shadow and Shadow didn't care!

Learning to greet a friendly stranger.

Beginners class. I made a firm decision to use a minimum amount of food. Ted Turner has been bugging me about using too much food and I have been cracking down on myself. Shadow again had a hard time focusing. I did not give in and use more food.

Good Pam! I did become more animated as a reward for good behavior—NOT as a **cheerleader**—and crammed in all sorts of unexpected behaviors including touch while heeling, getting ready to heel and then having him lie down instead, tons of praise when he was heeling, silence if I lost him, back-ups, sits, downs, finishes, tennis ball retrievals—anything I could think of.

At one point one of the other dogs was looking at him and coming closer. Shadow growled at the dog and I ignored him (NCR'd) and kept going. We went over to Carolyn and I practiced standing next to her with Shadow giving me attention. He jumped on her once and then was fine. We heeled around her. I went over to one of the other students (Scott) and did the same thing. Shadow was completely calm and focused on me until he smelled the peanut butter Scott was using for his dog...We walked away and returned to Scott and had Shadow go visit. Scott was able to pet him, lean over him, and generally treat him like a normal dog, all without the use of any preliminary food!!!!!

TRAINING CONCEPT

Cheerleading actually reinforces behaviors you don't want. For instance, let's say you want your dog to heel in perfect heel position and he is lagging behind. If you cheerlead, you are actually reinforcing the dog for lagging. If your dog is "blowing you off" and you cheerlead him to get his attention, you are reinforcing his inattention. If your dog is reacting with fear to an object (like a drain pipe or person) and you cheerlead and continuously encourage him to approach that object, you are reinforcing the fear he is feeling. I am very careful to cheer Shadow on ONLY when he is deserving of it, not as a way to get him to do something.

Huge Oops Pam!!

OCTOBER 10 – DAY 501

I have been working Shadow as diligently as before. Walks in woods and on trails (and I am not nervous!), formal training sessions in my building. He has been super in all respects—focus, calmness, quick in learning new things.

Today I was in my training facility, with Lisa and Karen sitting on the window seat. I brought Shadow in on leash and he was focused on me. I walked all around and he was giving me great eye contact. I approached the girls and he jumped on them. I called him to me and we started again—walking around, getting closer, all the while keeping focus on me.

Once he was calm, I sat on the floor and had Karen come over. She got down on the floor while I was feeding him. Shadow was a bit nervous at first. I started to pet him and Karen was feeding him. His mouth got softer and softer, as did his face. We were talking and laughing, petting him gently as Karen was feeding him. In the meantime, the bowl of food was right in front of him. I asked Karen to slow the food delivery down somewhat. She slowed it down a tad too much—just as I was about to tell her to feed him again he looked at the bowl, looked at Karen, looked at the bowl and growled, bared his teeth and lunged at her face simultaneously. Luckily he did not bite her, he just gave her a **warning**. Thank God she has super reflexes and leaned backwards and froze. There was no second attack and no contact. I called him to me and we moved away.

TRAINING CONCEPT

If Shadow really wanted to bite Karen, he would have. What he did was a **warning**. I have been bitten once in my career by a huge Malamute. He bit my hand HARD six times in the span of two seconds and did not break the skin. He did not break skin on purpose. If he were truly serious, I wouldn't have a right hand.

After the lunge, we all froze, and then talked calmly about what we should do. We didn't know what to do. I put him away for about two minutes, brought him back in the building for about one minute, fed him for eye contact, and put him away for one hour. Brought him out again for one minute, did some heeling (Karen and Lisa were sitting in chairs) and eye contact, and ended the session.

Later on I had time to ponder what had gone wrong: (1) the session lasted too long, it was about 20 minutes and should have been only three to four minutes. This wasn't our first session with Shadow and Karen, but it was the longest; (2) the food bowl should NOT have been used—in the past we have given him some food, then just petted him and he was fine; (3) our body positions were such that Shadow was between us, rather than me off to the side—this may or may not have been a factor.

Another thing that may, or may not, have had a bearing: I have been leaving Shadow out of his crate at home when we are gone. This has been making him calmer around the house, but less focused on me when we are training. I am going back to crating him when we leave for more than half an hour. This truly has been the only change in our lives, everything else is still the same—training sessions three to five times per week—different contexts. I am wondering if I should rethink having his CGC test November 17, one month away.

HINDSIGHT

I now believe that this reaction was probably due to food guarding. The bowl was next to Karen and he was definitely focused on it. Cynthia also mentioned that her dogs wouldn't be able to handle continual petting from a stranger for 20 minutes either…so…this was a truly STUPID human moment. Damn! But, unlike last year, I now know what to do. First of all, I will not put him in any situation for the next few days that may stress him out. Secondly, I will be crating him more when we are not home. Thirdly, I will build up his threshold for petting by seconds at a time, NOT huge chunks of minutes at a time.

OCTOBER 11 – DAY 502

Breakfast Club. Played Frisbee for 10 minutes while everyone stood around. After playing, I told Shadow to go visit. He lay down instead of jumping—many times!!! Everyone petted him and fed him just a tiny bit—they had all been apprised of what happened yesterday—and he was fine. His eyes were a bit wild when we were playing Frisbee, but I don't think that was because of playing. We did two more sessions—the second one identical to the first, and for the third one, I heeled him around and then ended the session. I was also working on food guarding—I think that was the main problem yesterday. I tossed a cookie and at the same time called him to me and he came! I gave him wads and wads of food, petting, and praise.

Evening obedience class. First session was a bomb. He couldn't give me attention once in the door, so I put him away while I worked another dog. Brought him out again and this time he was more attentive to me. Tried some go-outs, he was mildly successful but he seemed to be a bit out of it (so was I actually, so perhaps he was picking up on my mood). We both rallied and I got some good heeling from him. Ended the session after about five minutes. Brought him out a third time and he was super. I just sat on the floor and petted him and fed him for looking away from a dog that was barking. He was calmer this session and more focused on me. Came home and he put himself in the crate! He was pooped.

OCTOBER 14 – DAY 505

I have been crating him again during the day and I have already seen more focus as a result. I am going to play around with it to get a nice balance between focus on me when we are out, and calm behaviors at home. Went to a new location yesterday where I had the opportunity to bring him among a group of 35 people. He was too nervous outside, so I didn't bring him inside the building.

I am having nightmares about his CGC test (scheduled for November 17). I'm actually jolting awake in the middle of the night, worried about it. I know this is silly—I can always sign up and then, once I assess his mood the day of the test, bow out if needed.

Later that day I received a long e-mail from Ted:

> Let's talk about the food bowl incident. I'll try to make this short. As you have seen, food is a wonderful tool to begin the training process with, however, as I have stated many times, reliance on food to motivate will eventually get you into trouble. Many trainers don't advance past it simply because they are reinforced for using it with excellent progress.
>
> An interested animal is excellent. A hungry animal can be dangerous. Increased hunger (i.e., Deprivation to use the correct term), exacerbates the emotional response when food is no longer available, is in danger of being taken away, or the environment seems competitive (for food). That is why there is so much aggression response around a wolf pack, lion pride, orca pod, when a kill is made. Watch how cranky Jim gets when you eat off his plate at the beginning of a meal vs. at the end of a meal when he's full.
>
> Now, the food bowl itself. The presence of a food bowl is usually associated with an expectation of heavy feeding. This did not appear

to have happened. Schedule-induced aggression was a predictable response. Again, the reliance on food as the main motivator is erroneous and causative in my opinion.

Another opinion of mine is more controversial but important. One should be able to walk up and take a food bowl away without having any aggressive reaction. In fact, with domestic animals (and some zoological species), this becomes a necessity where even strangers must remove food from large animals. Most people, however, allow this behavior to occur because they believe it to be normal. It is normal to want to punch a jerk in the nose. However, it's illegal and therefore controlled through punishment. We wish to train appropriate responses differently. Food bowl possession comes from animals that are too food motivated, i.e., hungry, and get positively reinforced for aggressive responses, displacement, or attack of others near their food source. The pattern, once acquired, requires work that most people don't want to put forth, but the animal is still dangerous, especially to others that may have to care for it at some point in its life. You can train Shadow to see this as a fun game eventually. We can talk more about this later.

Finally, given Shadow's history, I expect a little regression. Frankly, you've done a remarkable job with him...no B.S.! Start weaning him away from frequent food reinforcers and watch his hunger level. He should be interested in a snack, but not too hungry for a meal. The real reward comes from interacting with you. Let's keep our eye on this but don't over correct! Some regression is normal during the long-term process.

OCTOBER 15 – DAY 506

A day of e-mail exchanges, the first from Ted:

A few thoughts that probably don't apply, but here is some information for future reference. Begging for cookies can indicate too much focus on food. This is not appropriate. Work to diminish that by avoiding a strong hunger drive, supplement his diet with extra volume, spilt his meals up, watch his weight, etc. A healthy and well-balanced animal is in good shape, with very little fat, but not thin. Animals that get too thin become frantic for food and metabolize muscle. This is dangerous. Sometimes trainers will use a little extra hunger drive as "insurance" for better behavior, but it catches up to them if they don't shift over to a true, variable schedule.

I would use crating sometimes and sometimes not. Regardless of any regression you feel might be related. A reduced focus on you is the natural by-product of more environmental freedom. Also, if too hungry, he may be foraging for food. Either way, you'll want to increase the reinforcement history of staying with you while out of the crate and this can only be done with more opportunity, not less. The choice should be based on convenience and not on behavioral criterion. Again, get your confidence level up. Remember, every time you fly, there's a chance of going down but it is a very SMALL chance and one that needs to be taken if you are to have a normal life.

Same thing goes with Shadow! He won't ever be perfect (like every other dog) and you shouldn't try to make him perfect. But he will be terrific...looks to me like he's there already!

My response:

Okay! Thanks! Comments(C)/Questions(Q):

C—He is glued to me when out of the crate (which is sometimes annoying)and I reinforce him a lot for chilling out—otherwise he is frantic. He is like this whether I crate him more or less, hence the name Shadow. It is outside in the real world that he had been losing focus once I let him stay out of the crate when we aren't home. I also had an issue with him "guarding" me and chasing the other dogs away, which is definitely causing a problem with Beau, so again, I reinforce him for chilling out—sometimes next to me, sometimes in another room.

Q—So how do I allow him more freedom (again, when we are NOT here) and yet retain his focus? I have been using much less food—I had to because all of a sudden he got really fat (really fat to me is gaining two to three pounds and not being able to feel ribs).

C—Here is my list of reinforcers. I taught him "tag, you're it" a chase game involving me, we play with the Frisbee, ball, petting, roughing up (gently), clapping, praise (not a boring goodboy goodboy goodboy kind of thing) a new game I developed called "Oh my God what's that!?," a gentle touch on the head, food, the ability to work (he loves to work), targeting my hand (he really likes that), walks in the woods/trails (I am brave enough now to walk on certain very wide trails—all by myself!), car rides.

C—When we were first desensitizing and counterconditioning him to people, we used lots of food to change the meaning of people from something scary to something good.

Q—So now, how do I counteract the idea he now has that people are Pez™ dispensers? I have been working on him not greeting people, and also for them to not always feed him—to pet him as well or even just say "hi."

OCTOBER 16 – DAY 507

Took Shadow for a long walk on the trail. I am looking for a nice balance between focus on me and letting him "just be a dog." Practiced recalls with Shadow on a 33-foot leash and he came very quickly to me. Tried to practice tiny bits of heeling with attention and had a modicum of success with that. Only used a few pieces of food—mostly petting. I may be weaning off of the food too fast.

OCTOBER 18 – DAY 509

Breakfast Club. I have been noticing a one percent reduction in attention from Shadow. I thought it was because of reduced crating. I had him back to being crated if we aren't home and it hasn't made any difference.

So, I put my thinking cap on. It may be because he is doing so well that I am constantly doing new contexts with him, letting slide the very foundations I have worked so hard on building up. Kind of like when the pavement on a bridge has potholes and you are constantly working on filling them up and smoothing them out, but the support beams need repair. (GOOD ANALOGY PAM!) I decided that I needed to add some basic, easy stuff for him to do in between the more difficult things.

Good Pam! For not letting this slight reduction of attention slide. Ignoring that would be the first step on the road to disaster.

I started with just focusing on me the instant we got out of the car, and heeling around the group—some of them standing still, some moving. Had a smidgen of success with this—not as much focus as I am used to. I had him "go visit" and he didn't jump on anyone. We went back to the "tie-out," where I tied him up on a long line. I asked him to sit and everyone in class approached him and fed and/or petted him if he remained seated. If he broke the stay, they stood still and waited for him to reposition himself. He did really well with that and actually gave me better attention.

On the way home I had to stop and get gas. Since Shadow is still reacting to people coming up to the van I drove in at top speed and jammed on the brakes. Leaping out of the door, I ran to the other side of the van, whipped open the side door and started to throw food in his crate, in probably 2 seconds flat—all before the attendant could even register that I was there! Whew! There was no reaction from Shadow at all, not one little peep.

Group class in the evening. I had to bring Shadow in twice before I could get his attention. I am really cracking down on myself. If he loses attention for five seconds, back in the car he goes for a few minutes. Like they say, the third time is the charmer. Nice attention, mostly calm, a new person there observing the class, reactive young dog barking continuously, and my boy did very well. Ended the session after about 10 minutes.

Brought him out again 15 minutes later and had great attention from him. As I was packing up to leave I was going to take a group picture. (Shadow's first obedience class—proud mommy!) I put him on a tie-out with a shortened leash. As I was getting the camera out of the case, a young dog rushed the bowl of food. Shadow aggressed at the dog—not terribly—just one growl and then a tiny bit of lip curling. I decided that would be a bad time to line the dogs up after having a "bad" reaction and I left the class. I should have stayed a few minutes longer and fed him until I was sure he was calm.

Give Yourself a Break Pam! Shadow is just a dog and you are just a human. Both of you are flawed sometimes and perfect other times.

What I am noticing here is that if he has a tiff with a dog, there are no displacement behaviors at home—like when he and Boomer had that tiff a few weeks ago. He only seems to displace when humans are involved. Now that we are home, he is just lying around and relaxing.

Shadow is also really good now with giving things up to Jim or me. I sometimes think he is still stealing once in awhile from habit—not even for attention anymore. I am definitely going to work more on this food guarding issue. I don't see it here at home because I stand next to him while he is eating and once he is done, I put him outside. When I first got him he would wolf down his food, and then go and steal everyone else's food.

OCTOBER 20 – DAY 511

Took Shadow to a seminar that Ted gave. On day one, I did not bring him into the building. I did eight small sessions with him, trying to get his attention in the parking lot with people and other dogs around. Each session lasted about one to four minutes. The first five sessions I had a real problem getting his attention. Sessions six, seven and eight were super amazing! Scads of attention and we were able to do all sorts of behaviors—heeling, hand targeting, weaving between my legs, directionals, sits, downs, grooming, brushing, feet trimming, and tail brushing. I have been continuing to train him to stand straight while I brush him and he let me work all over his body. I used dramatically less food—about three quarters of a cup the whole day! I really practiced the No Change Response—if I lost his attention and then got it back, I did not reinforce him for three seconds. Then I asked him to do three behaviors (easy) and only then reinforced him. I used myself as a reinforcer and I practiced NOT having food in my hands—that is so hard for me! For reinforcers we played "Tag, you're it," petting roughly, and the chance to do more work. I was really careful to reinforce what I wanted. Sounds like it should be pretty easy, right? We often reinforce much less than we want—not on purpose of course.

At the end of the seminar today, Ted asked me if I wanted him to work with Shadow. I really, really wanted to but felt it would not be a good idea. His last three sessions were so good, I did not want to push it. Plus it was late in the day and he may have been tired. Tomorrow I will see if I can get him in the building calmly. If I can do that, perhaps I may join the group.

Home again, and he has been a whirling dervish! I just put him in his crate to chill out for a few minutes. Once out, he was calm.

OCTOBER 21 – DAY 512

Second day of Ted's seminar. I did three sessions with Shadow and was brave enough—and had enough attention from him—to bring him into the hotel hallway! He was super amazing. Nothing like the early sessions of yesterday— he gave me scads of attention from the get-go. I even had him do a sit-stay 10 feet from the door so I could peek in to make sure no one was coming. I had him lie down and petted him as a reward for eye contact. After lunch, I brought Shadow in the seminar room—with 40+ people and dogs there. **Brave Pam!** Worked him for about 15 minutes while Ted talked. I had solid attention from him. I was VERY nervous at first and was practically hyperventilating.

During our approach into the room, I would walk one step and have him lie down, walk one step and then lie down. I was shaking like a leaf! After about five minutes of working on the low stage, I was brave enough and relaxed enough to go into the middle of the group. I worked on so many behaviors to keep him (and me busy) that I almost don't remember them all—eye contact, lie- downs, sit, directionals (towards the crowd—VERY VERY BRAVE PAM!), retrieving the dumbbell, scent discrimination, recalls, rollover, shake paw, heeling, weaving between my legs, hand targeting, walking on the "scary" dance floor, back up on the stage, and petting as a reward for eye contact. Whew! I was exhausted when I was done! Shadow had a blast though, and his

On stage with Shadow at the seminar.

OCTOBER 23 – DAY 514

Took the boys to the park. I had to take Shadow out of the van two times before he could focus on me, but then he was fine. Heeling, hand targeting, attention were great. We went to the supermarket parking lot. We got to within 100 feet of the front door! He was calm, cool, collected, and completely focused on me. Did not have to put him away for any inattention!!!

OCTOBER 24 – DAY 515

Left him out of the crate while I was gone for eight hours. Later that night I took him to the building and worked on a few new behaviors. I want him to "settle," to lie down on his side and let me "examine" him all over his belly and underside. Sometimes he lets me and sometimes he doesn't. Once I had to cut out some pubic knots and he did not like it at all. After three short sessions, I was able to say, "settle" and he laid down, head resting on the ground while I gently touched his side.

I also wanted to work on the food aggression thing, so I tossed a cookie and as I tossed it, I moved away from it and called him to come. In about six trials of doing this he came to me four times. Then I changed it slightly and had him in a down-stay, put a piece of food on the floor, moved away and called him to me. Out of five tries, he was successful in coming to me three times.

OCTOBER 25 – DAY 516

Breakfast Club. Did tie-outs again on a different part of the farm. Shadow was mostly calm with everyone except Ali. She seems to make him a tiny bit nervous, so I reinforced him for looking at me when Ali was petting him. I worked on having him look at me in between looking at the people approaching. He has this tendency of looking straight up at people, head raised as if he is going to sniff or lick their face and most of the time he doesn't move, BUT the possibility is there for him to get nervous in a split-second and then lunge and snap. Of course, I don't want that, so I am reinforcing him more for focusing on me while people pet him.

Our second session was in the backyard. People were milling about and there were sheep in both pens. It took me a while to get his attention as I only had a dumbbell with me, but I DID IT! I thought it was going to be "Hmmm, dumbbell—sheep, dumbbell—sheep. No contest, Mom. I want sheep!" He ended up ignoring the sheep and the people and I got some good stuff out of him. I also practiced our new trick, the "settle." He was super!

Afterwards, I brought Shadow to the grooming shop (he was VERY stinky) and had John help me groom him. It was so funny. I had pulled the steps over to the tub and was trying to get him to jump in by himself. He was nervous and did not want to do it. He would get his front end in the tub but his back end was firmly planted on the steps. Tried for ten minutes—every small movement forward got a "YES!" and backward movements got complete silence. I softly said to him, "Shadow, I really want you to go into the tub on your own, but no matter what, even if I have to pick you up, you are going into the tub." And, don't you know, he looked at me, swallowed, and took the plunge! (I really do know that dogs do not speak English!)

Shadow was wonderful in the tub. I soaped him up, John soaped him up, we took turns rinsing him, blowing him dry and he was super calm. You could tell he wasn't happy, but it was more of a "sad puppy dog, oh poor me, I am sopping wet" look rather than a stressed look. He even saw some people outside and did not react at all. Shadow has been great all night—very relaxed and sleepy.

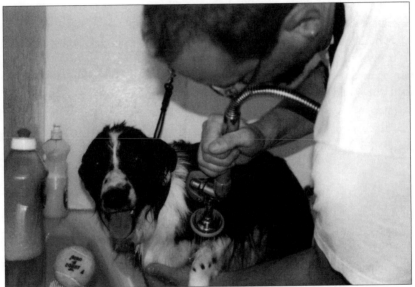

Learning to handle the tub with reinforcements at the ready!

I have enrolled Shadow in a new obedience class starting in two weeks—new place entirely. I realized that Shadow is getting calmer and calmer, but I still need practice being calm in new situations and I haven't yet generalized "calmness in all new locations." This will be a small class, the instructor knows Shadow and what we will require in terms of space and "emergency exits." I realized this when I took Shadow to the seminar last weekend. While walking into the hotel, I was so nervous, I was chanting literally every step, "Shadow, here, lie down, heel, here, lie down, heel, here, lie down!"

OCTOBER 28 – DAY 519

Took Shadow to a match show today. Did not enter him. For the most part he was great. I walked him around and he was focused very nicely on me. Looked around a tiny bit, but nothing terrible. Brought him close to the rings and he was calm. There was one little thing however: we were on top of a hill, just hangin' out, I was petting him and we were surveying the land. A woman was by her van, about 200 feet away, smiling at us, saying "What a pretty dog." Shadow was looking at her and I said, "Wow, that nice lady is talking to you." His face pushed forward and he growled a very low, tiny growl, but he did not move. I instantly moved him and then he promptly forgot about her. I need to work on people staring at him and talking to him.

Other than that, he was quite calm, mouth soft, body soft, very attentive. Once we got home, he began displacing on the other dogs (specifically Cody, who was barking incessantly). I don't know why because today was such a great training day. I was going to train tonight with some friends of mine, but decided that would be a baaaad idea. He is spending most of the evening in the crate because he is also stealing things for attention again.

"Regression is a normal part of learning." "Behavior is not static." Where have I heard these things before???

OCTOBER 30 – DAY 521

I wrote a letter to Ted today:

> I just wanted you to know how much I truly value your help, your ears, and your humor. I have been reinforcing the dogs for even the slightest "play-like" behaviors.

> What I don't know how to do is to make Shadow less possessive about food/toys. He stole my pork loin roast, right out of the pan on the stove and there was no way I was going to try to get it from him. I know how to do object exchanges when they are pups, but how do I do this with Shadow at this age? I can trade toys with him, but how do I trade food? I tried trading with food for the roast and he ignored my attempts. I am trying to throw one piece of food and then running away and calling him. Sometimes he comes to me, leaving the other food and I jackpot him. Is that the right way to start? What would be the next step? You don't have to give me the whole enchilada—just step two.

Ted's response to my last e-mail:

> Your progress should tell you that once a behavior is learned through consistency, it is important to provide UNPREDICTABILITY. That is the final training stage and it means, unpredictability in:

> 1. Use of food (when where how much etc.)

2. Toys

3. Behaviors requested

4. Timing of sessions

5. Unpredictable daily, weekly schedule of events

6. Unpredictability in feeding order, bedding placement, crating

This will be critical for advanced animals.

Possessive Behavior. The key with food? Don't work it when hungry. The primary philosophy: Taking something from the animal yields a far greater return if no reaction is exhibited. Start by sitting down beside him, giving one piece on the ground, ask Shadow to "stay," then give him a small amount in his bowl. Take the food bowl when done and give him another food bowl with a little in it. Do this a few times then begin to take the bowl when not quite empty and replace with a fuller bowl. Over time, taking the food bowl will elicit no response. So...take food bowl and give another, put food in mouth and take back out, take toy and give two back etc. etc. Eventually, the concept of "giving" becomes ingrained and no longer evokes an emotional or aggressive response.

Your exercise of throwing a piece and calling away is good. Eventually you will want the animal to move away from his food bowl whenever you require. Remember, a hungry dog is very possessive, so kick up Shadow's intake when possible.

Keep going!

OCTOBER 31 – DAY 522

Two sessions today at the training facility. In the first session, we were by ourselves and worked on go-outs, heeling, settle, dumbbell retrieves on the flat and over the jump, and recalls. He did well with all but the go-outs.

Second session. I had a friend in. She sat in a chair and I worked him on heeling, weaving between my legs, settle, dumbbell retrieves. He was very nervous at first, but relaxed toward the end of the session. I don't work enough in my building with other people around and even though he sometimes does well, today wasn't perfect, so I kept him on leash and did not have him "go visit."

I am seeing a tiny bit of regression here in terms of Shadow being nervous around new people. Nothing terrible, but I am continuing to work on bringing him back to where he was a few weeks ago.

HINDSIGHT

This past month and a half has had a lot of highs and a few lows. The highs have been higher than high, with Shadow letting me show off for Ted and not eating him (always a plus!) and being a very normal dog at the seminar, while Mommy almost fell to pieces. The lows, while truly not terrible (like when he reacted to Karen and the food bowl, and his slightly decreased attention to me) were unexpected and really not pleasant. I was getting just a tad complacent, something I really can't afford to do with Shadow at this point in his "recovery." I was really floored by his reaction to Karen and it has made me somewhat more cautious and nervous, which in turn is not helping Shadow at all.

Shadow is still continuing to make great strides into normalcy. There are still a few things we both need to work on—food guarding, more attention in new situations, actually going to more new locations while practicing calm behaviors (that's my issue as well!). Shadow has almost completely stopped stealing for attention (Yippee!), has gone back to playing nicely with Beau, and he's learned to chill out in the house about 99 percent of the time. (My students don't believe that a Border Collie can learn to just lie around!) Shadow's competition behaviors are steadily improving and my "being more variable in how I reinforce behaviors" is improving. Every time I feed a cookie, I think of Ted and feel guilty. When I pet, play, tell him to "go sniff," or just clap and cheer as reinforcers, I feel virtuous. When Ted was here and I was heeling with Shadow, he asked me, "Pam, do you have a cookie in your hand?" and I, quick as a wink, put the cookie back in my fanny pack and said, "No."

This dog training stuff is HARD! Especially because we have to THINK! Ouch!

8

I may not have gone where I intended to go, but I think I have ended up where I intended to be.

—Douglas Adams

And the Countdown Begins!

NOVEMBER 1 – DAY 523

Breakfast Club. We did two sessions. For the first one, we did "pop-outs" where people just pop out of nowhere and STARE HARD at Shadow. I haven't done this in a while and felt it would be a good thing to review for him. Cynthia made Shadow a bit nervous, but he got over it quickly. Everyone milled around him and he remained focused on me. I played ball with him and then he really wanted to heel.

I came up with an important thought—I had been working Shadow on leash a lot lately because we had been doing a lot of off leash work. I got a bit lax in keeping him focused because I was relying on the leash to keep him out of trouble rather than relying on our relationship. So, NO MORE LEASHES, within reason of course! Amazing how one can fall into bad habits. I think this is one of the reasons his focus on me has lessened slightly over the past few weeks. I thought it was because I had been crating him less; but the more I think about it, the more this makes sense.

Our second session was super. I brought Shadow in the backyard and tried, with varying degrees of success, to keep his attention on me while the sheep were in a pen. He almost got into the pen but I asked him to lie down and stay, and he did. When I asked him to come, he did! I let him go back to the sheep. I called him to me and then released him back to see sheep a few times. I made sure I didn't call him to me until he actually looked back at me.

Trained Shadow tonight at my facility. One of my friends came over with her three dogs and we trained together. Shadow was amazingly calm. I even dropped the leash! I kept baby gates between us—I am no fool. We did scent articles, directed retrieves, heeling, "settle" and then I ended it. Shadow did not react to any of the other dogs at all. His mouth was relaxed from the minute I took him out of the van.

He is lying down now, sleeping. Only 16 days until Shadow's CGC test! "I have a normal dog, Shadow will be fine, breathe, I have a normal dog, Shadow will be fine, breathe…" I have to keep reminding myself that this isn't competition obedience, AND I wouldn't have set this up if I didn't truly feel he was ready to pass. Am I quaking in my boots anyway? Yeah…

Two Shakes of Lamb's Tail

NOVEMBER 6 – DAY 528

Brought him to the farm to do "tending." Cynthia brought the flock of sheep out in the big field and I worked Shadow on a long line far away from the sheep. My goal was to walk all around the flock so that the sheep wouldn't move at all. Periodically I allowed him to walk up slowly on a loose leash, lie down, and then I called him to me. My reinforcers were food, petting, praise, cuddles, the Frisbee, and the chance to go see sheep again. Shadow was very calm, focused on me when I wanted him to be and focused on the sheep when I wanted him to be. His recalls were terrific, and he was one happy boy! He ignored Cynthia and Boomer, even when Boomer was barking. Session lasted an hour.

NOVEMBER 7 – DAY 529

Two quick sessions with Karen at my facility, each one lasted 10 minutes. She was sitting on the window seat and I heeled him around the building. We also did recalls, directionals, the two-toy game, drop on recalls, settle. Amazing how much I can cram into 10 minutes isn't it? I held his leash for the first few minutes of each session, but since he was so attentive to me and non-reactive to Karen, I let the leash drop. Shadow was aware of Karen but I just had this feeling that I wanted him to focus on me rather than have him go visit. I was still a bit nervous because of Shadow's last reaction to Karen when I made the mistake with the food and he lunged at her. Ten more days until his CGC test! "I have a normal dog, Shadow will be fine, breathe, I have a normal dog, Shadow will be fine, breathe…" I am very nervous today and am practicing breathing exercises and positive mental imagery.

NOVEMBER 8 – DAY 530

Breakfast Club class. For the first session we did "pop-outs" again. He was incredibly focused on me, so everyone really stepped up their obnoxious behaviors. Walking right up to him, bending over and STARING HARD at him. We had a new student there and she was suitably impressed!

Second session. We did another mock CGC test. He still does this initial jumping on the first exercise and then he stops jumping. Ali gave the test again and Shadow is still a bit nervous about her. At one point when she was leaning over him in an aggressive stance, examining his ears, he had a very worried look on his face. I had her stop for a second, moved him away, regained his focus, and had her proceed. He was then fine with her.

I am feeling a tiny bit less nervous now because of the success of today's mock test. Cynthia and I took the sheep out again for tending. Shadow was stupendous! He has so much sheep sense—much more than I have. (Of course he does! Shadow is a Border Collie and Pam is a primate!) He worked sheep and was relaxed around the flock for about an hour, coming back to me when I called him and working sheep when I asked him to. At one point, Cynthia left me ALONE WITH THE FLOCK OF SHEEP! VERY SCARY! In a quaking voice, I asked her, "What if they go out in the road?" She replied, "They never go into the road, there is no grass there." So, don't you know—the instant she left, they started to go for the road! Yikes! Here I am, huffing and puffing, running to bring Shadow to the far side of the flock to drive them back into the field. SUCCESS! Good doggie! Whew! Anyone want some fresh road kill lamb???

Shadow herding sheep.

Although I am a total novice as a stock dog handler, even I could tell that he truly has some great moves and knows what he is doing. At one point we had to move the flock away from someone's lawn and some of the sheep wouldn't move, so Shadow rushed them. They moved, and Shadow held himself in check and came back to me without me even calling him!!! AND he ignored a new person that was standing near me—he didn't care one bit about her. This is one of the few moments since November 1 that I have felt really confident about the CGC test. "I DO have a normal dog!"

Shadow returns to me despite the allure of the sheep.

NOVEMBER 12 – DAY 534

Took the boys to the park and met Cynthia there. She had Mia (the dog) with her and we walked all around the lake. Shadow was incredibly calm, didn't care much about Mia or Cynthia. His recalls and attention were superb (I had him on a 33-foot long line.) We all enjoyed ourselves immensely! Five more days until the CGC test! We are getting down to the wire now and although I know in my head we are doing well, I am having, not doubts, but some fear that I will be so nervous that I will make Shadow nervous. "I have a normal dog, Shadow will be fine, breathe, I have a normal dog, Shadow will be fine, breathe…"

NOVEMBER 13 – DAY 535

Took him to a friend's house today with Marsha and her dogs. We were in different parts of the yard with a fence in between, and I took Shadow off leash. His attention on me was wonderful! We did heeling, finishes, directionals, and played with the Frisbee. I encouraged him to approach Marsha's dog and they sniffed each other through the fence and then went about their business.

For our second session I had Shadow visit Marsha a few times. She was able to hand-feed him and pet him. I haven't been working on this context lately and need to get back into it. A few weeks ago, I went back to basics—just attention on me, and had been letting the direct contact with strangers slide a bit. Now that I have his focus back, it is time to go back to petting from people. Especially since his CGC test is only three days away! "I have a normal dog, Shadow will be fine, breathe, I have a normal dog, Shadow will be fine, breathe…"

Third session. Shadow was in the van with the side door open, I had Cody out next to the van, and Marsha was with one of her other dogs. We were all walking around, heeling, playing and talking, and Shadow did not react in any way!!!

NOVEMBER 15 – DAY 537

Took the boys to a new group obedience class. New location, new dogs, new people and Shadow was completely calm! I did not join in the group exercises (chicken!), but stayed off in a corner. I know I will be able to join in soon—I just need to feel comfortable. I did two sessions with Shadow of about 10 minutes each and his focus on me was stellar! Two more days until the CGC test! "I have a normal dog, Shadow will be fine, breathe, I have a normal dog, Shadow will be fine, breathe…"

TRAINING CONCEPT

So, what is this **Canine Good Citizen (CGC)** test I have been talking about? Below are the particulars and some of my editorial comments about each exercise. The dog must pass all 10 skills to earn their CGC title.

1. Accepting a friendly stranger
Evaluator approaches dog, shakes hands with handler. Does not touch dog. Dog may not eat the evaluator.

2. Sitting politely for petting
Evaluator pets dog, dog must show no shyness or resentment. Dog may not eat the evaluator.

3. Appearance and grooming
Evaluator inspects dog, combs or brushes lightly, examines ears and each front foot. Dog may not eat the evaluator.

4. Out for a walk
Handler takes dog for a short walk including right turn, left turn, about turn and stop.

5. Walking through a crowd
Dog and handler walk close to several people, dog may show casual interest but not jump up. Dog may not eat anyone in the crowd.

6. Sit and down on command/Staying in place
Handler shows dog can do sit and down, then chooses a position, leaves dog and goes to the end of a 20-foot line and returns immediately.

7. Coming when called
With dog still on a 20-foot line, handler walks out 10 feet and calls the dog.

8. Reaction to another dog
Two handlers and dogs approach, shake hands, exchange pleasantries, move on. Dog may not eat the other handler or dog.

9. Reaction to distractions
Distractions are presented; dog may not panic or show aggression.

10. Supervised separation
Handler goes out of sight for 3 minutes. Dog is held on leash by an evaluator. Dog may not eat evaluator.

The Big Day! Did we do it? Did we pass the test?

NOVEMBER 17 – DAY 539

Shadow is two and a half years old today! I had been trying for days to be calm about this momentous occasion. Surprisingly enough, I was able to sleep last night. I woke up two hours before the test, ate some dry toast to settle my stomach, took some St. John's Wort. Chanted to myself, "I have a normal dog, Shadow will be fine, breathe, I have a normal dog, Shadow will be fine, breathe…"

Jim woke up and my first words to him were, "Good morning. I have a normal dog, Shadow will be fine, I have a normal dog, Shadow will be fine."

I got to the test site an hour ahead of time to get Shadow used to the location. I also wanted to play with him to get his excess energy out. Cynthia was there and I had Shadow go up to her a few times and she petted him for a few minutes. I was trying to be calm, but felt very disconnected (not with Shadow, but with myself), weird and nervous. We practiced heeling and recalls and stays in between Frisbee throwing. He was hot! Super attentive, focused, accurate and sweet. I put him away after half an hour to rest.

By 9:00 a.m. eleven people had showed up to be "the crowd" and to help out. This was a group of people who knew about Shadow but had never met him before. I was still nervous, but trying really hard to look confident and calm. I felt I had a great deal to "prove" which only made me more nervous. Not only am I an instructor, but I also wanted (needed) to demonstrate that you can take an aggressive dog and retrain him to like people using positive methods.

I brought Shadow out of the van, trying to breathe and to focus myself so he didn't pick up on my vibes. Shadow was very calm. I tried to be nonchalant about the whole deal, but…

During the "accepting a friendly stranger" exercise Shadow was a bit excited and jumped on Jane, the tester, searching her pockets for food. I had forgotten that you could talk to your dog during this test. All I had to do was say, "stay." He got off of her instantly and then sat like the gentleman he is while Jane and I shook hands. (Phew! One down, nine more to go!) When we repeated this exercise later on he didn't jump on her at all. He also sat wonderfully for the photo she took and ignored her later on while we were standing close together looking at the rule book.

Accepting a friendly stranger.

For the "sitting politely for petting and appearance and grooming" exercises Shadow was outstanding! When Jane was inspecting his feet, he was so funny—he kept giving her the one she had already touched. I told him he had to give her his other paw and then he said "oh," and let her pick up his other paw. Shadow had no problem whatsoever with her leaning over, petting him on his head, examining his ears or brushing him.

Sitting politely for petting.

"Out for a walk" was excellent—almost perfect competition-style heeling. "Walking through a crowd" was a tad less than perfect…he decided that sniffing the ground was more fun than walking with Mom. I found out later that Jane thinks there was a bear in her yard the day before…talk about distracting smells! But he still did well and was mostly ignoring the people standing around.

Walking through a crowd.

"Sit," "down," and "stay" were perfect—even though the neighbor dog was barking incessantly, and the neighbors were yelling at the dog to come. Shadow was alert to the dog and people but he responded to me instantly. (Whew again! Only four more tests to go! Hang in there, Pam!)

"Coming when called" was perfect again and, although he was still looking at the neighbor dog, he came instantly with no side trips to the fence. Breathe!

"Reaction to another dog." This was actually funny—well it wasn't funny at the time, but it is now. Jane brought her dog out with a big fuzzy coat on (it was cold and her dog has short hair) and Shadow did a double take and said "What the heck is THAT!?? He was straining, but not frantically, at the leash and his nose was all aquiver. I asked Jane to take the coat off, which she graciously did. He was just really interested in the dog—not in a bad way at all, in an "I have never seen a dog with a coat on" way. It is allowed in the test that they sniff, but me, being the "anal, must have it PERFECT" person that I am, wanted his complete attention on me. So I heeled away, did a small competition pattern and voila! Shadow did the exercise PERFECTLY. Good doggie!

Reacting to another dog.

"Reactions to distractions"—perfect again! I found out right before we took the test that the AKC changed the rules and now instead of just a noise distraction, there was to be a visual distraction as well. Talk about PRESSURE! Oh ye of little faith! Shadow handled it like a pro and ignored the bulky wheelbarrow and the two metal bowls that were clanging together. Breathe! Only one test left!

"Supervised separation." Shadow was great. Surprisingly, I wasn't nervous about this test. I just counted down on my own timer for when I could go back. By this time I was kind of numb from nerves anyway and probably starting oxygen deprivation symptoms…

Supervised separation.

Thank God it's over. But did we pass?????
Yes!! Houston, we have landed safely!
Behold the Power of Positive Training!

YES! YIPPEE! WAHOO! HOLY SMOKES! I wasn't really sure if we had passed because of his slight inattention to me during the crowd walk, and the initial inattention to me for greeting the dog. I was feeling a bit depressed. I had to remember that the CGC test is NOT competition obedience and Shadow did a very, very credible—HECK—INCREDIBLE job overall. I was also nervous because I had never practiced the entire test without some food and there is no food allowed during the CGC. I really had to rely on our relationship! Talk about hard!

He didn't aggress or even think about aggressing. Cynthia was there on the sidelines as my "anchor," and told me afterwards that she was trying to will me to breathe! She taped the test and I watched it when I got home. Funny how when it was happening, I was so nervous that I thought he did terribly and yet, when I watched the tape, I saw that Shadow truly did a great job. His focus was on me for most of the test, and even in between exercises. And he wasn't nervous. During the supervised separation, I saw on the tape that there were nine people standing on the deck (about 10 feet away) watching him, plus the person holding the leash, and Jane the tester. Everyone was talking and he did not care at all! He sniffed a bit, laid down, stood, but wasn't obnoxious or aggressive in any way.

He can now officially be called, "Ewe Are Beyond a Shadow of a Doubt, CGC!"

And if that isn't enough, my cup runneth over when I entered Beau at the last minute and HE passed the CGC too! I hadn't been training him for this at all, so I had no idea how he would be. Beau was so good he was even the "friendly dog" for the next dog taking the test! So he can now be called "Surely Ewe Beau Jest, CGC!"

We passed with flying colors!

The CGC test is not just about whether the dog can perform the above exercises but also about the dog/handler relationship in the real world. For a dog like Shadow, the relationship, intense training, counterconditioning and desensitization that we have developed, is essential.

The support from everyone was great! Lots of hugs and kisses. I thought I would jump up and cheer when it happened, but I was in shock at the time and ended up having a delayed reaction—I cried for joy later. For the next few days, I was deluged with phone calls and e-mails of congratulations.

NOVEMBER 18 – DAY 540

A day of congratulatory e-mails!

From Ted:

> HA! What a testimony to positive training. People seriously won't believe it. GREAT JOB PAM AND SHADOW!!

From Lisa Pattison:

> FANTASTIC, SUPER-DOOPER, GREAT JOB!!! I am very proud of you for sticking with that dog and helping him. I think this is a badge of honor that few professional trainers have really earned. I think you have gone out on a ledge and pushed yourself (not your dog) to learn more and try harder. Reading behavior is the hardest to apply in the context you were working with. You are proving yourself by picking the behavior you want and not picking the dog you want to train.

From Ali Brown:

> Kudos to you! You can now say that you have achieved the impossible AND have used positive training to do so. Did I mention that IT IS SUPER FANTASTICALLY PHENOMENAL!!!! I have to tell you—I still don't believe it happened—the idea that an extremely aggressive dog can get a CGC is unbelievable—I saw it and I couldn't believe it. It is truly miraculous.

From Jane Killion, tester for the CGC test:

> Shadow is a darling boy and I would have loved to pet him forever. He is just a marvelous success story!

From Marsha Dominguez:

> Congratulations to Shadow on achieving his CGC! What an accomplishment and tribute to totally positive training. You have done what most people would consider impossible!!

Only a mere eighteen months ago, Shadow was a fear-aggressive dog, slated for, at best, living in a crate for the rest of his life or at worst, being euthanized. And now he has passed his Canine Good Citizen test! HOLY SMOKES!

It is astounding to me how much Shadow and I have achieved this last year and a half. Shadow was sensitive about touch, space, noises, people, and some dogs. Our first few months together were simply horrible and I regretted keeping him many, many times. I was afraid of him for a while, and depressed about what I had gotten myself into. ("This is a fine mess you've gotten us into Ollie!") I can now groom Shadow by myself and he enjoys it. I can pet him whenever and wherever I want to, not pet him when I don't want to, kiss his face, bring him to new locations and he can be calm about it. Shadow no longer steals things for attention and Wal-Mart stock should go down because I don't have to buy seven new pairs of underwear each week! He rarely scuffles with Beau and Cody and in fact, they all play quite nicely.

Not only is this a substantial triumph for me and Shadow, but also for anyone the world over who has an aggressive dog they want to help. They may be running into the old school of punishment training, "Gotta show them who's boss, can't let the dog get away with anything, prong collars, choke collars, alpha rolls, scruff shakes, ad nauseum, etc.," until, in the end, the dog is so aggressive and reactive that he needs to be put down before or after he really does some major damage. These old style methods are cruel, inhumane, abusive, and do nothing to fix the problem. Punishment only suppresses behavior, it does not eliminate it. Answer aggression with aggression and what will you get? More aggression! Had Shadow fallen into the hands of a punishment-oriented trainer, there is no doubt in my mind that he would have been pushed over the edge into seriously hurting someone and would have been killed long ago. He is damn lucky to have found me! And I am damn lucky to have found him!

When I first started with Shadow, I did not think he would get this far, this fast. I truly believed it would take three years to get his CGC title. At times I felt frustrated, disillusioned, that I was beating my head against the wall and the nay-sayers were right. Now I know in my heart that I am right—you can take a fear-aggressive dog and turn him around with positive training if you really want to (and have a huge well of patience, determination, consistency, helpful friends and mentors, and loads of time…). It won't be an overnight change—nothing worthwhile ever is, but the lessons learned (by both human and dog) make it well worth the effort.

I am grateful to this forty-pound Border Collie for the most remarkable experience of my life.

Epilogue

Was it the end of Shadow's training now that he had his CGC? No way! It was just the end of the beginning. Passing the AKC Canine Good Citizen test was a milepost along the way, an indicator of Shadow's progress at that time compared to where he was (or wasn't!) when I first rescued him. This was a major breakthrough in Shadow's life—and mine as well—but it was not the end of the journey! Passing the test was VITAL to his future, for without it, all else would have failed or at least be put on hold.

Although he had made a lot of progress, I was well aware that we still had a long road to travel. If I just wanted him to be a good pet dog, I probably could have stopped training him so intensely at that point. But, I fully intend that Shadow reach his ultimate potential as a successful competition dog and for that I still need at least two more years.

My immediate goal after passing the CGC was to be able to sit with him on the bench outside of the supermarket while people walked by, and to decrease the time between meeting new people and having them pet him, without the use of food. In addition, I continued to work on the "being in the van while people approach" context, food guarding issues, and having friendly people come to the house while he is out and about. I also entered him in a match show or two. And of course, I continued to work on all of the behaviors I had taught him so far, plus I hoped to teach him to be a water rescue dog!

Now when I train him he is not in a wild, out-of-control mode—he is calm and focused. Remember, this was a dog that could not be around ANYONE without aggressing. Now, 99 percent of the time, Shadow can ignore them and not react. His space issues have mostly disappeared; when he sees new people now his first reaction is NOT to growl, snap and lunge. Instead he either looks to see if they have cookies for him or looks to me—"What now, Mommy?" He is very "elastic" in most instances, and if he does get stressed, he is back to calm in no time. Shadow truly is a normal dog

It has certainly been a busy time since Shadow's CGC test. Since then I have had him in regular obedience classes and have had John groom him a few times without me staying to watch. I no longer move off of the trail when people approach, although I do cry each and every time because Shadow is so calm about it all now.

As Ted Turner told me again recently, "He won't ever be perfect (like every other dog!) and you shouldn't try to make him perfect. But he will be terrific... looks to me like he's there already!"

A few accomplishments since the "big day":

(!) Milestone! Shadow and I walked to the front of the supermarket!

We can now go to the supermarket together!

(!) Shadow thinks door etiquette while people are crowding us is great fun.

(!) Shadow is now happy when friends visit.

(!) Competing in APDT Rally Obedience—First place with a 198, third place with a 197, and a 191 to finish up his Rally 1 title with a R1MCL title. Finished his Rally 2 title with fifth place and a 197, fifth place with a 196, and a fourth place with a 188. To date, his name is Ewe Are Beyond a Shadow of a Doubt, CGC, R1MCL, R2CL.

(!) We are going for our ARCH (APDT Rally O Championship.)

(!) We have gone on vacation many times to various locations—he gets calmer and calmer and no longer barks in hotel rooms.

(!) We have been doing search and rescue style tracking—the boy is brilliant and is completely fine with finding the "lost" person!

(!) Shadow acted like a completely normal dog when ten guests came to visit the first time out and about when I had company over!

Shadow at home with my friend Jane Berger.

(!) Shadow went to his first ever competition obedience match show where he did every exercise—INCLUDING THE STAND FOR EXAM! HE WAS BRILLIANT! And we were both calm!

(!) Shadow got wicketed (measured) at an agility trial! After a week and a half of desensitizing him to being on the table with familiar and new people measuring him, he handled it like a pro. I was a basket case as the judge (even though I told her that Shadow is afraid of people) PETTED

HIM ON THE HEAD AND LOWERED HER FACE TO HIS! Shadow on the other hand was completely and utterly calm!

(!) I rarely use a lot of food at this point and have developed a large list of reinforcers.

(!) Shadow still has some minor issues—like being brushed when the other dogs are around, so I just manage it better. I also feed him in his crate rather than try to continually block him from the other dogs' food bowls. I am learning to pick my battles and these just aren't important.

(!) He is letting me taking empty or even half-empty food bowls away.

(!) First time in a pet shop—he was incredibly calm.

(!) We walked around Easton PA, our first walk on a real city street. He was fine!

Visiting Easton.

(!) First time ever approaching the judge for our ribbons! When I take him places, like trials, I don't need anyone to "ride shotgun" for me any more—even indoor trials.

Approaching a judge for ribbons!

(!) I now use him as a demo dog in my classes and at my seminars.

(!) I continue to practice our foundation behaviors, as well as training in new contexts a few times per week, and am always teaching him all kinds of new behaviors. He knows over 125 behaviors to date.

(!) Once in a great while I make a stupid mistake—about once a year—but we both bounce back quickly—Shadow faster than I because I kick myself in the head, whereas he doesn't…

(!) Earned his first Novice Standard leg in Agility with a First Place and 27 seconds under time!

(!) Earned his first JWW (Jumpers With Weaves) leg with a First Place and 16 seconds under time!

Competing at Agility.

(!) I am starting sheep herding lessons with him again.

(!) Every night before bedtime, I tell Shadow how much I love him and thank him for coming into my life. We are damn lucky to have found each other!

My award-winning dog!

APPENDIX

Positive Training Philosophy

I tend to believe that some of the myths surrounding positive training are seated in the word "positive." Those who don't understand the psychology behind the training may feel that people who choose to train this way are unable to control their dog's behavior and are not tough enough to issue corrections in an attempt to show the dog the error of his ways. They may mistakenly believe that positive trainers coddle their dogs and bribe them with treats. In actuality, positive training has deep roots in behavioral psychology and requires the handler to gain at least some knowledge of this very complex science. Positive training is precise manipulation of consequences, thereby influencing the dog to offer the desired behavior. In addition, positive trainers set the dog up to earn reinforcement, directly influencing the odds of the behavior being repeated in the future because behavior is reward-driven.

Positive training is not just throwing cookies around hoping for the correct behavior to happen, nor is it mindless permissiveness. It can however, be something as simple as requiring the dog to sit calmly before being allowed to go outside, or walking on a loose leash. These same principles can be applied to more complex behaviors, such as precision heeling, scent work, or directed retrieving for competition.

It has been conclusively proven by behavioral researchers over 80 years ago that using punitive measures as methods for controlling or teaching behaviors not only takes longer, but ends up creating a whole host of adverse behavioral side effects. When dealing with aggression, if you punish in ANY way, be it verbal or physical, you run a VERY high risk of creating an even more aggressive animal.

Being a positive trainer means setting the dog up for success as much as possible, learning how to read the dog, breaking down each behavior into the smallest of approximations or steps, and reinforcing each step. If the dog "fails" it is up to us, the handlers, to decide: Did we push the dog beyond his limits and understanding or should we let him fail—giving him the opportunity to THINK? Positive training is all about building a relationship with the dog based on trust, not fear.

Behavior is reward-driven. Dogs will do all sorts of amazing behaviors for a reward. Will they also do amazing behaviors to avoid punishment? Yes, but you risk having a dog that may be fearful or neurotic. Done correctly, positive training never causes aggression. Associative learning is always happening, whether you want it to or not. It is my goal as a positive trainer to make sure that those associations are good, strong ones that help create reliable behaviors. Behavior that is positively reinforced will increase. Behavior that is ignored will decrease.

Calming Signals

There are many observable behaviors or signals that dogs perform that let us know that they are nervous. Some indicate that they are trying to avoid conflict and some indicate that they are afraid, stressed, in avoidance of a situation or object (person or dog). These signals can be seen in most any dog, any breed, from any country. Some dogs, through lack of proper socialization with their own species or punishment from humans, may lose these signals. Turid Rugaas, a Norwegian dog trainer, is the leading expert on this subject. Her book, *On Talking Terms With Dogs: Calming Signals*, is invaluable to trainers working with aggressive dogs. Also available as a video or DVD.

Health and Physiological Factors

Having your dog checked out by a veterinarian to make sure its aggression is not being triggered by physiological factors is a must. Low-normal thyroid has conclusively been linked to aggression. Dr. Jean Dodds, DVM, is an expert on thyroid function. According to Dr. Dodds, a complete thyroid panel should be run, including total thyroxine (TT4), total TT3, free T4, free T3, T4 autoantibody, T3 autoantibody, thyroid stimulating hormone (TSH) and thyroglobulin autoantibody (TgAA).

There are two labs that I highly recommend for this test: Michigan State University (now the Endocrine Diagnostic Section, Diagnostic Center for Population & Animal Health in Lansing Michigan) or Dr. Dodds' lab in California. For info on sending blood to her lab, go to: www.itsfortheanimals.com/HEMOPET.HTM. They have the most experience in properly reading the results.

I have seen increased aggression due to the pain of Lyme disease, as well as arthritis, the onset of blindness or deafness, malformed joints, and hip problems. Many other health issues may exacerbate aggression. A poor-quality diet can also have an affect on behavior. Again, a visit to a vet can tell you whether any of these factors are impacting your dog in terms of aggressive behavior.

Books/Videos

On Talking Terms With Dogs: Calming Signals, Turid Rugaas. Calming Signals is available in book, video and DVD format. I recommend watching the video a few times per week for a month.

The Complete Idiot's Guide to Positive Dog Training, Pamela Dennison. My overview of positive dog training methods and philosophy written for all dog owners.

Culture Clash, Jean Donaldson. Teaches you that dogs are dogs, not little humans! A must-read for those interested in dog behavior. The first book I read about positive training. A real eye-opener!

Excel-erated Learning, Pamela Reid. How to teach and how dogs learn.

The Other End of the Leash, Patricia McConnell, Ph.D. Another excellent behavioral study by a top animal behaviorist.

Bones Would Rain From the Sky, Suzanne Clothier. Explores the dog-human relationship. Get out the Kleenex!

Purely Positive Training, Sheila Booth. Positive training methods for a variety of activities.

How Dogs Learn, Mary Burch and Bob Bailey. Explores the history of dog training and how methods have evolved over time.

Clicker Training for Obedience, Morgan Spector. Using clickers and operant conditioning to train competition obedience dogs.

Additional reading for those who want to get into more of the science of behavioral psychology.

Coercion and Its Fallout, Murray Sidman. This book is out of print but if you find it BUY IT!

On Aggression, Konrad Lorenz. An eye-opener for me to learn about aggression.

Learning and Behavior, Paul Chance. It takes you to new heights of understanding about behavior. Very readable.

These titles and hundreds of others on dogs are available from Dogwise at www.dogwise.com, 1-800-776-2665.

Training Tools

I am a believer in as few "tools" as possible. Comfortable harnesses and long lines are about my limit in training equipment.

Black Ice Dog Sledding X Back Sledding Harness. Go to www.blackicedog-sledding.com and order item #HS52. Phone: 320-485-4825. On their website look for the instructions on how to measure for a harness and order by phone because they don't take orders online. Measure TWICE, order once.

Harnesses from **Lawsonk9.com** are another pick for harnesses for loose-leash walking. Use this if your dog tends to back out of collars. They are beautifully made, comfortable, fully adjustable, and they ship quickly. Item # LTS 250 Phone: 877-767-0844 or 336-782-1784.

BridgePortEquipment.com has the best leashes. For the 33-foot long lines (leather and nylon) go to the tracking section. I use the 3/8" or the 1/2" wide. When buying a long line, don't get cotton--they rot and break at the worst possible moment! View their equipment at www.bridgeportequipment.com but they must be purchased by calling them at 1-800-678-7353.

E-mail lists

E-mail lists I participate in to keep up with positive training methods:
Pos-4-ReactiveDogs@yahoogroups.com
CIGPositiveDogTraining@yahoogroups.com

Websites

TTouch. For all the information you need on using TTouch.
www.lindatellingtonjones.com/TTouch.shtml

Clicker Solutions. A great resource for articles on clicker and positive
method training.
www.clickersolutions.com/index.html

Stacy Braslau-Schneck. Another great source for articles on
training techniques.
www.wagntrain.com/OC/

Competing at Your Peak. For handler performance anxiety.
www.competingatyourpeak.com

Dogwise. Best source for books, videos and specialized training tools in
the universe.
www.dogwise.com

My Website
www.positivedogs.com

Organizations

Association of Pet Dog Trainers. The leading dog trainer's organization. Find
a dog trainer in your area at their website. Be careful though—not all members
are positive trainers or have the same expertise. Go and watch a class before
signing up and check references.
www.apdt.com

Author Biography

Pam Dennison's first love is dogs and competition obedience. She started her dog training life like many trainers, using punishment-based methods. However, when problems occurred and her dogs refused to perform, she turned to positive training. Pam learned that virtually any behavioral problem could be fixed, even those that were supposedly insurmountable by applying the same techniques used by large mammal trainers like those at Sea World where there is no place for force. Ever since then, her passion has been finding creative, positive, and humane ways to solve both common and uncommon training challenges.

Pam started her own business, **Positive Motivation Dog Training** in 1996 in Blairstown, New Jersey. Since then she has helped over 1,000 dogs and handlers build their relationships and solve problems. Pam teaches puppy kindergarten, basic obedience, Canine Good Citizen, competition obedience, Rally-O as well as classes and seminars for aggressive dogs. Her camp for aggressive dogs is known as Camp R.E.W.A.R.D. Pam lives with her three rescued dogs: a Shetland Sheepdog and two Border Collies—Cody, Beau and Shadow and trains them all for competition including obedience, agility, Rally-O, herding, tracking and carting.

A member of APDT (Association of Pet Dog Trainers), NADOI (National Association of Dog Obedience Instructors), and DWAA (Dog Writers Association of America), Pam has written for local and national publications. She is the author of *The Complete Idiot's Guide to Positive Dog Training* and her next book *How to Right a Dog Gone Wrong* will be out early 2005. Her website is www. positivedogs.com, and she can be reached via e-mail at dennison@goes.com.

More GREAT books from Dogwise Publishing
www.dogwise.com or 1-800-776-2665

BEHAVIOR & TRAINING

Positive Perspectives: Love Your Dog, Train Your Dog, Miller, 2004, pbk, 258 pgs.
Transform bad behavior into good behavior with management, consistency, exercise and fun. For the new puppy or second hand dog owner, a complete resource for living with your dog.

Dog Friendly Gardens, Garden Friendly Dogs, Smith, 2004, pbk, 188 pgs.
Combine your love of dogs and love of gardens with the first book ever written that shows you exactly how to design your garden with your dog in mind and train your dog with your garden in mind.

Aggression In Dogs: Practical Management, Prevention & Behaviour Modification, Aloff, 2002, pbk, 425 pgs.
Learn how to solve dog to dog and dog to human aggression problems. Includes detailed protocols for retraining and a complete basic training course.

Behavior Problems in Dogs, 3rd ed., Campbell, 1999, pbk, 328 pgs.
The reference book your veterinarian has used for years to help solve problem behavior is now available to trainers and pet owners.

Dog Behavior Problems: The Counselor's Handbook, Campbell, 1999, pbk, 115 pgs.
Learn the people as well as the business side of being a professional dog trainer. How to set rates, manage time and handle sessions.

Dog Language, An Encyclopedia of Canine Behavior, Abrantes, 1997, pbk, 265 pgs.
Using research with wolves in the wild, this ethologist helps you learn what your dog's body language is telling you. Dozens of illustrations. A-Z format.

Therapy Dogs: Training Your Dog To Reach Others, Diamond-Davis, 2002, pbk, 264 pgs.
Become a therapy team by training your dog to work with elders, children, and the public in nursing homes, schools and other settings.

Evolution of Canine Social Behavior, 2nd ed, Abrantes, due 2005, pbk, 96 pgs.
Learn the scientific basis of domestic dogs' biological relationship to wolves. Understand how it is that we can understand dog behavior by observing wolves.

Mastering Variable Surface Tracking, The Component Tracking, Book & Workbook Set, Presnall, 2004, pbk & spiral, 226 pgs and 130 pgs.
A detailed program to train your dog for the newest AKC tracking sport. Consists of a training guide and workbook with training maps.

Training Dogs, A Manual, Most, 1954 (reprint), pbk, 204 pgs.
The book that educated the modern dog trainer. Methods were revolutionary for the time and the foundation for today's training.

New Knowledge of Dog Behavior, Pfaffenberger, 1963 (reprint), pbk, 208 pgs.
The landmark work that established the science of puppy temperament testing and critical periods of socialization and development. For breeders, trainers and owners.

HEALTH & ANATOMY

Raw Dog Food. Make It Easy for You and Your Dog, MacDonald, 2004, pbk, 86 pgs.
> Learn how to prepare a healthy raw food diet for your dog. Easy to follow instructions to produce and store this new but old way of feeding dogs.

Raw Meaty Bones, Lonsdale, 2002, pbk, 369 pgs.
> Why commercial dog food may be making your dog sick. How to feed your dog like his wolf ancestors by feeding uncooked meat with bones that contain a goldmine of nutrition for your dog.

An Eye for a Dog, Cole, 2004, pbk, 176 pgs.
> Develop your ability to assess dogs with these illustrated judging scenarios. For judges, breeders, conformation competitors and fanciers. Fun and challenging.

Canine Massage: A Complete Reference Manual, Hourdebaigt, 2004, pbk, 220 pgs.
> Use massage to help your dog relax, to condition the canine athlete and to help recover from injuries.

Canine Cineradiography Video, Rachel Page Elliott, 45 min.
> Moving x-ray footage of the structure of the dog. Helps in understanding orthopedic problems and injuries.

Dogsteps Video, Rachel Page Elliott, 65 min.
> Companion video to the classic work on canine gait and movement. A rare look at what is happening inside the dog as the he moves using x-rays. See both correct and incorrect structure in action.

Canine Terminology, Spira, 1982 (reprint), hbk, 147 pgs.
> A-Z dictionary of canine terms with detailed illustrations. Every judge, breeder and show person needs this resource.

The Dog In Action, Lyon, 1950 (reprint), pbk, 204 pgs.
> A classic book on structure and movement of the dog that opened up minds and eyes when it was first published. Still useful today!

The History and Management of the Mastiff, Baxter and Hoffman, 2004, pbk, 282 pgs.
> Learn about the challenges and tragedies that almost made this noble breed extinct. Pedigrees, info on the breed around the world, rare photographs.